ORKS

THE GREEN TIDE

CONTENTS

PRODUCED BY GAMES WORKSHOP IN NOTTINGHAM

With thanks to the Mournival, the Infinity Circuit and Adam Fasoldt for their additional playtesting services

British Cataloguing-in-Publication Data. A catalogue record for this book is available from the British Library. Pictures used for illustrative purposes only.

Games Workshop Ltd, Willow Rd, Lenton, Nottingham, NG7 2WS

games-workshop.com

INTRODUCTION

Welcome, Warboss, to *Codex: Orks*! Every greenskin worth his teef knows that books are best used for bashing people over the head. That fact notwithstanding, you will find that this squig-gnawed tome contains all the information you need to learn about the anarchic Ork race and gather your miniatures into a fearsome warband.

The Orks are the most savage and warlike species in the galaxy, and – also being one of the most numerous – can be found infesting its every corner. Far removed from the enigmatic and scheming nature of many other races, greenskins are simple beings who live for battle. They thrive on violence, and rarely think beyond their next punch-up, breakneck race or deafening gunfight. Yet when massed in sufficient numbers and led by a suitably mighty Warlord, Ork warbands sweep across the stars in frenzied crusades known as Waaaghs!, which can crush entire systems and turn whole regions of the galaxy green.

Ork armies are immensely varied, from hordes of brutal infantry and columns of ramshackle yet deadly vehicles, to 'skwadrons' of high-velocity attack craft, batteries of madcap artillery and mobs of clanking combat-walkers. Hailing from a number of different clans, such as the speed-crazed Evil Sunz, the brutish Goffs or the super-flashy Bad Moons – each of which have their own weird predilections and ways of war – Ork forces are very easy to personalise, both in terms of their look and their playing style on the tabletop. Every Ork Citadel Miniature is lavishly detailed and, in many cases, they have interchangeable components that allow greenskin collectors to 'kustomise' and convert their army in almost limitless ways. Coupled with the vivid colour schemes of the clans, and the flourishes of gallows humour that can be found throughout the Orks' background and rules, it is easy to see why these thuggish aliens are a popular and extremely enjoyable army to collect, paint and play with.

Within this book you will find all the information you need to collect an Ork army and field it upon the tabletop.

THE BARBAROUS HORDES: This section details the biology, society and history of the greenskins. It also explains how Ork tribes assemble for war, and the ways in which clan kulturs permeate their warbands.

THE ART OF WAAAGH!: Here you will find a showcase of beautifully painted Citadel Miniatures to inspire your own collection, displaying the colours of the Ork clans and the crude iconography with which they cover their wargear and vehicles.

WARRIORS OF GORK AND MORK: This section includes datasheets, wargear lists and weapon rules for every Ork unit for use in your games of Warhammer 40,000.

WAYS OF THE WARBANDS: This section provides additional rules – including Warlord Traits, Stratagems, relics, psychic powers and matched play points – that allow you to transform your collection of Citadel Miniatures into a conquering Ork horde.

To play games with your army, you will need a copy of the Warhammer 40,000 rules. To find out more about Warhammer 40,000 or download the free core rules, visit warhammer40000.com.

When Warlord Nazdreg of the Bad Moons Clan led a Waaagh! into the Tarvosa System, the Imperium's greatest defenders stood arrayed against him. Yet Nazdreg was huge and powerful, filled with low cunning and – above all – possessed of astronomical wealth. Armed and armoured by the finest Mekaniaks teef could buy, his endless hordes smashed Mankind's battle lines on every front.

THE BARBAROUS HORDES

Greenskins are one of the most dangerous and pervasive species to plague the stars. Numerous beyond belief and driven always to fight and conquer, the Orks and their ilk threaten to overwhelm every single galactic empire, stronghold and race.

Amid constant, seething tides of war and bloodshed, burgeoning greenskin empires rise and fall. Most are mercifully short-lived, soon destroying themselves in a maelstrom of violence, but should the Orks ever truly unify, they would crush all opposition. Their race's unquenchable thirst for battle has always proved their downfall: historically, the greenskin tribes have spent much of their time fighting amongst themselves, waging brutal wars in which only the strongest survive.

On occasion, an Ork leader will emerge who is mighty enough to defeat his rivals and unite the warring tribes. His success draws other tribes to him, and soon a great Waaagh! is underway – partly a migration, partly a holy war that can exterminate the populations of entire star systems. When the Orks are on the rampage, the galaxy trembles, and in these dark days there are more Waaaghs! rising than ever before.

THE ORK

Orks have but one philosophy: might makes right. Over the countless millennia in which the greenskins have waged their wars, not one of their number has doubted this for a single moment. This unshakeable self-belief is perhaps the most dangerous quality of the Orks, for they will never cease in their efforts to plunge the entire galaxy into eternal war.

The Orks rule their barbaric civilisation with an iron fist. Ugly and violent creatures, they are the dominant life forms of a race that includes the smaller Gretchin and Snotling sub-species. Orks see themselves as the toughest inhabitants of the galaxy, stronger by far than humans, Aeldari or T'au. To prove their point, the Orks are more than willing to fight and kill everything that crosses their path.

Orkoid physique itself is so robust that it can withstand tremendous punishment. They feel remarkably little pain, enabling them to fight on whilst horrifically injured – and even for a short time after being technically dead. It is believed by some who study these brutes, albeit from afar, that this goes some way to explaining the greenskins' ultra-violent sense of humour. As pain and fear mean little to them, they are highly curious and amused by the reactions of their weaker foes as they hack them apart, the screams of terror contrasting with the deep, throaty rumbling of the Orks and the cruel snickering of their smaller brethren.

The greenskin regenerative process itself is so powerful that an Ork who has been hacked to bits can simply be stitched back together, bewildered but ready to fight once more. Nothing but the most grievous of wounds will put them down for long, and burning them to ash is reputed to be the only way to make absolutely sure that they are gone for good.

A typical Ork stands around the same height as a man – though he would be much taller were he to stand up straight instead of being hunched over, as is his normal stance – and his frame is extremely muscular and solid. An Ork's arms are long and heavily thewed, knuckles almost scraping the floor as he lopes around, and his gnarled hands end in taloned fingers capable of tearing an enemy's throat out with ease.

The skin of an Ork is green and as tough as leather, and his body is dotted with scars, scabs, pockmarks and parasites. His skull is extremely thick, able to absorb impacts that would cave in a human head. His heavy brow protrudes over blood-red eyes that are afire with the need to kill. Jagged fangs jut from a rugged jaw that would not look out of place upon a far larger predator, and when an Ork speaks, it is in a slow, gruff tone thick with saliva and guttural curses. His words are sparse, brutal and straight to the point.

THE SIMPLE LIFE

One of the greatest strengths of the Orks is the simplicity with which they approach

'THE ORKS ARE THE PINNACLE OF CREATION. FOR THEM, THE GREAT STRUGGLE IS WON. THEY HAVE EVOLVED A SOCIETY WHICH KNOWS NO STRESS OR ANGST. WHO ARE WE TO JUDGE THEM? WE AELDARI WHO HAVE FAILED, OR THE HUMANS, ON THE ROAD TO RUIN IN THEIR TURN? AND WHY? BECAUSE WE SOUGHT ANSWERS TO QUESTIONS THAT AN ORK WOULDN'T EVEN BOTHER TO ASK! WE SEE A CULTURE THAT IS STRONG AND DESPISE IT AS CRUDE.'

- Uthan the Perverse, Aeldari Philosopher

their existence. For them, the universe is an incredibly straightforward place, free of the angst and worry that plagues most other races. Orks typically do not try to influence their own destiny, only to get frustrated when their plans do not work out as expected. They do not look for something to blame – except perhaps the nearest Gretchin or a hated rival tribe – and certainly do not reflect on weaknesses in their own way of doing things. They just try again a different way (usually because they have forgotten how they did it the last time). Thus the Orks make remarkable progress by trial and error, without counting the cost. Meanwhile, other races steeped in high-flown philosophy and cleaving to their millennia-old practices fall into the same traps time and again, doomed to stagnate and decline – unless, of course, they are first conquered by the Orks.

So long as the average Ork has someone to fight, someone bigger than him to tell him who to kill next, and someone smaller than him to beat up, he knows contentment. Orks do not tend to go hungry, as they can eat virtually anything, even Gretchin, Snotlings or one another at a pinch. Indeed, Greenskins feel none of the moral outrage towards cannibalism that the practice inspires amongst many other races, as it is only natural that the bigger Orks should live at the cost of those weaker than themselves. With war and killing as their only real motivators, most Orks have little interest in gathering material wealth or luxuries. The one exception to this is a desire to possess increasingly more ostentatious and deadly weapons and vehicles. An Ork will go to almost any lengths to get his hands on a louder, quicker-firing shoota or faster buggy, obsessing over its acquisition until the exact moment he has it – at which point his eye will stray to something even bigger and showier.

In greenskin society, teeth are used as currency and form the entire basis of the economy. The teeth, or 'teef', must be big, sharp, ivory-like fangs to have any value – those of races such as humans or Aeldari are just too fiddly and pathetic to have any real worth. Orks shed and replace their teeth every few years, meaning that the number of teef in circulation never diminishes enough to create a shortage, and that no individual Ork can be reduced to dire poverty for too long. This simple approach to an issue most civilisations agonise about has been in place since time immemorial, and is typical of the pragmatic attitude of the greenskin race.

Orks of the Evil Sunz Clan storm into battle upon the dust plains of Asmasoria II, their attack supported by a mountainous war effigy known as a Gargant.

GORK'S GRIN

In the closing years of the 41st Millennium, a monstrous cascade of warp storms tore its way across the galaxy and all but split the Imperium of Mankind in two. This catastrophe was the work of Abaddon the Despoiler, greatest of all mortal Chaos champions. Yet the vast majority of the greenskin race knew nothing of the events leading up to the Great Rift, or its true cause. All they saw was an almighty rent tearing across the vastness of space and consuming everything it touched.

The Orks have two gods: Gork, who is brutal but kunnin', and Mork, who is kunnin' but brutal. To the greenskins, it was obvious that the Great Rift was in fact the leering gob of Gork, opening wide to swallow the stars. Admittedly, a prodigious number of renegades, Daemons and other creatures of Chaos were issuing forth from this sprawling astronomical phenomenon, but as the smartest Orks of each tribe were quick to point out, Gork obviously did not want to swallow that sort of unnatural filth. Instead, he was vomiting up the Chaos worshippers so that the Orks could fight them and win. Equally, those Ork tribes whose worlds were consumed by the spreading of the rift bore their god no ill will. Clearly, Gork had decided that those tribes were 'goin' a bit soft', and so had eaten their planets in order to propel them out into space and send them on the warpath.

Soon it dawned on many enterprising Warbosses that if Gork could swallow up and spit out Chaos armies, he would gladly do the same for his own ladz. So it was that dozens of greenskin armadas plunged headlong into the Great Rift, vanishing into raging warp storms in the hopes of being catapulted into fresh galactic conquests.

THE GREEN MENACE

From pirate enclaves to system-spanning empires, Ork holdings are as varied as they are steeped in violence. When the greenskins invade a planet or star system, they bring with them a belligerent ecosystem that overwhelms each conquered world as surely as the Orks themselves crush its defenders.

Greenskin society and ecology is so robust that it can exist almost anywhere. The Imperium has encountered Orks and their kind living – even prospering – in such extreme environments as toxic death worlds, newborn planets still heaving with volcanic activity, or the depressurised carcasses of abandoned orbital platforms. Ork tribes have been found inhabiting drifting ice floes, and infesting irradiated asteroid fields perilously close to active stars. They have been discovered amid corrosive chemical swamps, on lightless nightmare worlds seething with horrific predators, and in the bombed-out remains of planets subjected to Exterminatus. It is rumoured amongst the Imperium's Rogue Traders that there are even Ork enclaves hidden within the Eye of Terror.

No matter where they are encountered or in what numbers, the greenskins are a deadly threat who will multiply exponentially if left unchecked. In a matter of weeks, a small raiding party can swell – as if some by some arcane alchemy – into an anarchic horde bent upon war and destruction. The other races of the galaxy have many theories regarding how the Orks' numbers increase so quickly. These range from spontaneous physical division to the release of windblown spores after death. The notorious Vandermeist Theorem posits that the greenskins inhabit an alternative pocket of reality, and simply fall through, fully formed, wherever others of their kind are already at war.

'Oomans is pink and soft, not tough and green like da Boyz. They'z all the same size too, so they'z always arguing about who's in charge, 'cos no way of tellin' 'cept fer badges an' ooniforms and fings. When one of 'em wants to lord it over the uvvers, 'e says "I'm very speshul so'z you gotta worship me", or "I know summink wot you lot don't know so yer better lissen good". Da funny fing is, 'arf of 'em believe it and da uvva 'arf don't, so 'e 'as to hit 'em all anyway or run fer it. Wot a lot of mukkin' about if yer asks me. An' while they'z all arguin' wiv each uvva over who's da boss, da Orks can clobber da lot.'

- Anon, on Humanity and its weaknesses

While many of these wild suggestions are patently ridiculous, it is certainly the case that where one Ork is encountered, more will never be far away. Combined with their relentlessly warlike nature, and tendency to grow larger and more powerful with every battle they survive, it is easy to see how rampaging Orks can quickly overwhelm a planet's defences. A ragged band of greenskins who are allowed to escape the wreckage of their spacecraft and disappear into a city's underhive will return within weeks as a horde of murderous savages, sweeping all before them in their desire for conquest. Those they do not kill are enslaved, and that which they do not destroy is looted. Before long, another world is conquered by the Orks, its cities reduced to ruins and its populace toiling in chains for their brutal greenskin overlords.

Those who have studied Ork settlements first-hand – and somehow survived their ordeal – have detailed a civilisation that is hierarchical in the extreme. The life of a greenskin is determined not by rank or birth, but by size and savagery. The largest Orks push around their smaller brethren, who in turn bully the diminutive slave-race known as Gretchin into doing their bidding. Smaller still are Snotlings, tiny and simple-minded creatures with little use beyond fetching, carrying or fungus-tending. The greenskin sub-species have a symbiotic relationship of sorts, with the smaller creatures performing menial tasks for their Ork overseers in exchange for a measure of protection.

GRETCHIN

Commonly known as grots, Gretchin are even more numerous than Orks. Although they possess a similar physiology to their larger brethren, they are not as strong or tough. To compensate for this, the Gretchin possess an abundance of low

THE LOST RACE

Ork legends are passed down by the Runtherds, those who specialise in the breeding and training of Gretchin, Snotlings and squiggly beasts. One enduring myth speaks of a species of greenskin who created the modern Ork race as warriors and protectors, breeding them to be as strong and fierce as possible. Described as being much smaller and far more intelligent than their servants, these mysterious figures – commonly referred to as Brainboyz – are said to have developed amazing technologies and directed their peoples' expansion across the stars. If the Brainboyz ever existed, however, they do not do so now. Some Runtherds claim a great plague caused the Orks' creators to die out or devolve; others violently assert that the Brainboyz were even more warlike than their servants, and that they took the biggest and best Orks going and set off to find the ultimate war. Whatever the truth, almost all Runtherds agree that the Brainboyz took steps to preserve what they could of their culture before their disappearance by using strange sciences to engineer pure knowledge into the bodies and minds of their slaves. This aspect of the myth has been given surprising credence by many amongst the Magos Biologis of the Imperium, who theorise that the Orks retain such a relatively high level of technology because the skills and information needed to do so are hardwired into their genes.

Whether or not the legends told by the Runtherds or theories posited by the Imperium contain a kernel of truth is largely irrelevant in any case. The Orks – though ignorant and brutish – are born survivors. They are resourceful and resilient in the extreme, and the vast majority of them couldn't care less how they got that way.

cunning. They scurry around the larger greenskins on scrawny legs, their grasping fingers overtly snatching and covertly stealing from the unwary. Gretchin have large, bulbous heads and wide tattered ears that flatten against their bald pates when they are afraid (which is most of the time). Sharp fangs fill their jaws, ever ready to be sunk into the flesh of the weak or infirm, and malice gleams in their eyes whenever there is an opportunity for violence.

The grots' large and protuberant noses give them an excellent sense of smell, their ears afford them a similarly advanced sense of hearing, and their eyesight is acute even in the dark. These traits, combined with an innate talent for self-preservation, mean that Gretchin can not only survive, but thrive in a society dominated by vicious predators. Some grots have their survival instinct honed to such a degree that they may possess a rudimentary sixth sense, and most improve their chances of survival by exhibiting fawning behaviour to their Ork masters. Though braver Gretchin will pull faces and make rude gestures behind the backs of the bigger greenskins, few are stupid enough to risk doing so openly.

Grots are fast learners and quick to spot an opportunity, meaning that many wind up as assistants or servants to more important Orks like Mekboyz or Nobz. Others simply attempt to stay out of the Orks' way, whole groups of grots fashioning hideouts amidst scrap piles or warrens of tunnels too constricted for Orks to squeeze their bulk down. When the time comes to go to war, the grots are flushed out of these hidey-holes en masse by the gnashing squig hounds of the Runtherds, or a few enthusiastic Burna Boyz.

On his own, a single Gretchin poses little threat to a human-sized adversary. However, if there is one quality the grots have in abundance, it is quantity. On the field of battle, Gretchin advance in great mobs, firing volleys of scavenged ammunition from their poor-quality weapons before diving upon the fallen and tearing them apart in their scrabbling haste to loot the corpses. Even the most accomplished warriors have found their arrogance punctured when cornered by an entire mob of shrieking grots. Gretchin can prove especially dangerous during naval boarding actions, for while their Ork masters tie up a ship's defenders in furious point-blank battles, these wily creatures – avoiding such bloody fighting like the plague – contribute in less-direct ways. Knots of them squirm through air ducts, sabotage or loot vital machine components, and overwhelm triage stations full of helpless, wounded combatants. When grots wreck a ship's void-shield generatorum, or burst from the ducts to overrun a vital choke point mid-battle, the foe quickly learns to fear, if not respect, these nasty little greenskins.

SNOTLINGS

Snotlings, or 'snots', look like tiny, immature Gretchin. Their scrawny limbs are too small to bear weapons larger or more complicated than shards of broken glass or chunks of scrap. Lacking the violent tendencies of their larger kin, they are predominantly kept as little more than pets for their Ork masters, although they make excellent ammunition for the strange weapon the greenskins call the shokk attack gun.

Nonetheless, snots do perform a valuable function in Ork society. It is they who cultivate the great patches of fungi that spring up around Ork settlements. In this way, Snotlings provide food, drink and medicine for the rest of the greenskin race. Snots also inhabit cesspits, areas known in Ork society as 'the drops', where they look after all manner of ferocious squiggly beasts. Their natural affinity with these life forms is far greater than that of other greenskins. Helpfully, this means that on any given day only a few dozen Snotling attendants will be devoured alive by their ravenous charges.

The Snotling populations that spring up around Ork settlements are monitored and cultivated by the Runtherds. These grizzled and merciless slavers use a variety of methods to bully their charges into a state of anxious obedience, not least of which are the much feared grot-prod and the ferocious squig hound.

GREENSKIN KULTUR

The Ork way of life is as straightforward and brutal as the Orks themselves. Much like their approach to everything else, Orks do not waste time pondering why they do things, or how they might do them better. Instead they simply act, instinct and ability driving them on in a never-ending cycle of violence and conquest.

The origins of greenskin culture, or 'kultur', are lost in the dim and distant past. Though likely a corruption of whatever may have come before, by and large it functions very well. Perhaps this is because the fundamental tenet of their society – might makes right – is a simple one that even the most pea-brained snot can understand.

ORK HIERARCHY

Orks instinctively obey those larger than themselves, provided they are a healthy shade of green – most would rather die than bow to a non-greenskin's will. The rulers of the Ork tribes are known as Warbosses, and with the exception of the truly mighty inter-tribal leaders known as Warlords, are the most powerful Orks of all. These monstrous killing machines tower over their lackeys, and their sheer muscular bulk makes them wider at the shoulder than a fully armoured Space Marine. Though some Warbosses rise to prominence through shrewd scheming, most seize power through the application of brute force. A tribe's Warboss will hold dominion over all he surveys, and beat the living daylights out of anyone who says different. His decisions are enforced by a ruling caste of Orks known as Nobz, who are larger, richer and more aggressive than normal Orks, and never miss an opportunity to remind them of it.

When the Orks of a tribe go to battle, they do so in anarchic groups known as mobs. These in turn belong to larger hordes known as warbands, each of which is lead by a lesser Warboss and their Nob enforcers. Goff warbands in particular are famous for the sheer number of Boyz that they can field in a conflict, often outnumbering their foes several times over.

Orks tend to be lazy and forgetful, and only war and the preparations beforehand really bring out their innate talents. Though the bigger, meaner Boyz will lord it over the smaller, ganglier ones, even a subservient Ork is of limited use when it comes to practical tasks that do not involve fighting. Most of the day-to-day running of greenskin society is therefore left to the Gretchin, whose duties include preparing food, taking messages, hauling stuff about, general organisation and just being around the place when an Ork wants something to kick. This gives the Orks plenty of time to swagger about, getting into fights and coming up with new ways to kill things.

The Gretchin are happy enough in their role. They bear little resentment towards their superiors, for to them Orks are just a fact of life. Questioning this usually leads to a clip round the ear, and not much else. Individual grots can enjoy a relatively

During the Battle for Dasnoth Spaceport, the Orks of Zuglug's tribe brought every weapon at their disposal to bear. Weirdboyz, Mekboyz and Runtherds worked in concert to support the anarchic Ork assault, unleashing psychic blasts of force, searing beams of energy and hordes of manic grots to tear open ragged gaps in the Imperial defences and left the humans ripe for slaughter.

comfortable existence by providing valuable services to their Ork masters. In fact, the Gretchin have created an entire enterprise culture of their own within greenskin society, with many operating their own black-market businesses on the side; these range from selling fungus beer or roasted squigs on sticks, to coordinating bets when a fight breaks out and then looting the resulting corpses.

A LIFE OF CONFLICT

Orks excel in the field of warfare, on everything from a personal to a galactic level. Conflict governs their entire society, their technological advances, and even their individual growth.

Prolonged periods of fighting lead to a proportional increase in the size and strength of an Ork, and those who have fought in a war zone for a few years tower over those deprived of such stimulus; in short, longer wars produce ever-larger combatants. At the climax of Warlord Thogza's decades-long Waaagh! into the Duros Sector, many of the Ork veterans were reputed to have grown to almost twice the height of a man.

When there are no enemies to fight, the Orks will test their mettle against any native predators they can find, and if that fails they will fight amongst themselves simply for the joy of it. Disputes between Orks become almost hourly occurrences if they are not engaged against a common foe. It is during such times that a Warboss' authority may be challenged by his Nobz.

Such power struggles are resolved through methods ranging from low cunning to high explosives, but ritual pit-fighting remains a firm favourite. Pit fights are popular, as they entertain the ladz and establish the victor as Warboss beyond dispute. Either rivals are dispatched by the incumbent Warboss, or he is overthrown (and usually killed into the bargain). Every Ork settlement has a fighting pit for this purpose, which is also used to settle other grudges and disputes. Pit fighting thus serves the Orks as a rough and ready judicial system.

Other tests of mettle popular in greenskin kultur are squig-eating contests, in which rival Orks attempt to eat a face-biter squig before it eats them, and breakneck races around the settlement's perimeter in rickety vehicles. It is generally disapproved of to open fire upon a challenger in such a race, or at least during the first lap.

As an Ork matures into adulthood, he will become involved in larger and more violent conflicts, ranging from border skirmishes to all-out war. Orks fixate upon things they enjoy, and the heightened state of excitement they experience during battle can mean that over the course of a particularly epic conflict an Ork will become addicted to one facet of warfare above all others.

Like-minded tribe members who share the same obsessions will often seek each other out, forming loose groups of specialists. An Ork who has experienced the exultation of destroying an enemy tank or walker may join the ranks of the Tankbustas, whereas an Ork who just cannot stop setting things on fire will soon start hanging around with the local Burna Boyz. However, the largest and most popular of all of these subcultures is the Kult of Speed.

THE KULT OF SPEED

Orks love to go fast. There is something about speed that fulfils some deep need in the Orkish temperament, just like the thunder of guns, the clank of tracks or the din of battle. They like to feel the wind whipping into their faces and hear the throaty roar of supercharged engines. It is hardly surprising that bikes and buggies of all kinds are popular with the Orks.

From Shokkjump Dragstas and Boomdakka Snazzwagons, to burly Rukkatrukk Squigbuggies and swarms of hurtling Warbikes, many greenskins will happily leap aboard any vehicle with the capacity to move fast and blow things to bits. These up-gunned vehicles may not be as sturdy as those used by the Imperium, but they can be built easily from readily available battlefield scrap, can pack a massive amount of firepower and, most importantly of all, they can achieve truly suicidal velocities.

Those Orks who become addicted to the sensation of 'goin' fast' will most likely find their way into the Speed Freeks, a kult whose members rarely, if ever, leave the saddle. These grinning loons roar into battle on exhaust-belching jalopies and crude but effective flying machines, intent on getting into the thick of the fighting before their ground-pounding comrades. Due to the large number of vehicles in each warband, they often have several of the Oddboyz known as Meks amongst their number to keep their contraptions running.

ODDBOYZ

If Orks were just single-minded killing machines they would be dangerous enough, but they would be unable to sustain the level of technology required to ply the stars. Gretchin, though obedient if beaten with sufficient regularity, are not inventive enough to maintain the weaponry that the Orks possess, nor to patch up casualties when the going gets tough. These highly technical demands are met by a caste of Orks known as Oddboyz.

There are many types of Oddboy in greenskin society, but the most important are Mekboyz, Painboyz, Runtherds and Weirdboyz. Mekboyz are responsible for the creation and maintenance of Ork technology. Painboyz are medics, though their penchant for bizarre and inappropriate surgery can make their ministrations more hazardous than helpful. Runtherds breed the lesser forms of greenskin, and marshal them on the field of battle. Weirdboyz are potent psykers who can discharge great blasts of Waaagh! energy – the psychic power subconsciously generated by greenskins, particularly during conflict – into the ranks of the foe.

Although it may seem strange to humans, these Oddboyz all possess an innate understanding of their fields of expertise without having to be taught. A Mekboy knows how to create engines and generators even though he has never been taught to do so, and a Painboy instinctively knows which squirty tube connects to which wriggly bit when he is delving into some unfortunate patient's abdomen. If asked where this knowledge comes from, an Oddboy might reply that it was in his blood all along.

It has been suggested that the abilities of Orks to build machines, practise medicine or even use psychic powers are passed down through the generations on a primordial, biological level, perhaps a legacy left to them by their legendary Brainboyz. No studies of the greenskins have ever successfully determined how this process works, or indeed if it exists at all.

Whatever the source of this latent knowledge, as an Ork matures it will start to make itself apparent, leading him to assume the role in greenskin society for which he is best suited. Should he lack any specialist knowledge, the Ork will happily join the vast throng of Boyz at the heart of each tribe and content himself with a life of murder and mayhem.

THE NATURE OF THE BEAST

Orks are uncomplicated creatures, yet for them this is a strength, not a weakness. Greenskins have been underestimated time and again by the galaxy's more culturally advanced races, and this has nearly always proved a fatal error. What others see as stupidity is in fact a simplicity of focus, an uncomplicated drive to fight and to win, time and time again.

Theories abound that Orks harbour the genetic traits of both animal and fungal life forms, and that it is this unusual biology that gives an Ork his remarkable constitution. Orks' green colouration could be explained, scholars suggest, due to some form of algae that permeates their cellular makeup. Such a substance could break down and repair damaged tissue at an incredible rate, accounting in part for the Orks' extremely durable metabolism. Those observers who maintain this theory point to the fact that an Ork's head can live for some time after being severed from the body. Indeed, operations to reattach these are a staple of many a Painboy's repertoire (staple being the operative word!).

Yet for all the questions that hang over the greenskin race, what cannot be disputed is its relentlessly bloodthirsty nature. An invasion by Orks has been likened by the Imperium's scholars to an incurable disease. Once a world or system has faced attack by the greenskins once, it will be ravaged by them time and again until it finally withers and dies.

Even as a planet's defenders are celebrating their first victory over the Ork invaders, new tribes of greenskins multiply in the shadowed corners of their lands. At the same time, Ork survivors carry word with them through the void, spreading the tale of how good a fight a particular world put up. Keen to have a go themselves, fresh hordes of Orks soon descend upon the locale, often before the damage from the previous incursion has been repaired. These attacks increase in severity, wave after wave of greenskins from space soon supplemented by the feral tribes that have risen up from the world's wilderness. The planet's populace is overrun one stronghold at a time, drowning in a rising tide of roaring, battle-mad greenskins.

Upon Danik's World, renegade forces thought to escape the Imperial yoke. The resultant civil war against the 68th Vostroyan Firstborn benefited only the Ork invaders, who gleefully attacked both of the bitterly divided human factions.

The true tragedy is that the harder a planet's defenders fight back, the worse their predicament becomes. Each Ork slain makes way for two of its bellowing brethren, while every attack-wave bloodily repulsed just draws more enthusiastic greenskins. In this way, some worlds become the unintentional focus of a Waaagh!, the Orks' numbers and frenzy reaching critical mass as they fling themselves against the planet's defences time and again. Eventually the pressure from Ork invaders both within and without becomes unendurable, leaving the defenders only two choices: stand and fight, dying to the last in the process, or flee with whatever they can salvage, abandoning their stricken world to the greenskins.

The advent of the Great Rift has taken even this stark choice from many of those planets invaded by the Orks. The defenders of worlds isolated in the darkness of the Imperium Nihilus have nowhere to run, and precious little chance of reinforcement. Thus they can only stand their ground, trapped behind their own barricades and forced into a war of attrition that they cannot possibly win.

With fierce battle raging across the entire galaxy between the servants of Chaos and the forces of the disparate stellar races, a number of hotly contested war zones have been thrown into absolute anarchy by the sudden arrival of an Ork Waaagh!. In these cases, both sides of the conflict – already stretched to capacity by their efforts to annihilate and resist annihilation – are fallen upon with reckless abandon by the belligerent greenskins.

The results are horrific. Grand strategies collapse in a matter of hours as the Orks smash everything in their path. Hard-won supply lines are severed and long-defiant worlds overrun. Even should the warring parties take their hands from around one another's throats long enough to fight back against the Ork invaders, it is inevitably too late. Soon enough, all resistance from both parties is crushed, leaving the barbaric greenskins to loot the wreckage of their victims' shattered ambitions.

THE ORK GODS

The Orks do not worship their gods in the way that other races do. They do not have priests or raise grandiose temples, but instead honour their deities by hurling down the idols and shrines built by others. What effigies the Orks build are towering walkers, around whose metal feet the greenskins surge into battle, offering praise only of the most instinctive and gestalt kind.

The Orks are a powerful force in the galaxy, their character traits having a reflection in the warp just like the impulses and emotions of Humanity and the Aeldari. These attributes are made manifest in the belligerent Ork gods known as Gork and Mork.

The Orks say that Gork is brutal but kunnin', and Mork is kunnin' but brutal. Gork and Mork are divine powerhouses, deities so strong that they are never truly defeated. They simply shrug off the attacks of other gods with a raucous laugh. Gork grins, bares his long teeth, and lands a mighty blow on his adversary's head with a spiked club the size of a comet. Mork, always the sneaky one, waits until his foe is not looking before clobbering him with a low blow.

An idea of the appearance of the Ork gods can be gained from looking at Gargants and Stompas, towering machines constructed in the image of Gork (or possibly Mork). The Mekboyz create these titanic engines of war to capture the essence of Orkiness in mechanical form, and as such they serve as potent religious idols. To the greenskins, these clanking behemoths behave very much like their gods, lumbering about and leaving a trail of devastation in their wake. They go where they please, and never shun a fight.

The aspects of Gork and Mork are likewise evoked by the Gorkanaut and Morkanaut. These huge armoured war-suits are intended as a tribute to, and imitation of, their chosen god, and their pilots are frequently gripped by visions of Gork (or possibly Mork) urging them on during the heat of battle.

Now that Gork's Grin has split the stars, the war cries of the Ork gods ring out louder and clearer. Visions of battle and carnage flash through the mind of every greenskin. Weirdboyz gibber and bellow with the voices of Gork and Mork, commanding their fellows to surge forth upon Waaagh! after Waaagh! and plunge the entire galaxy into anarchy. In the warp, the Ork gods lumber ever onwards along their metaphysical warpath, sweeping away tides of Daemons with every gleeful blow. They know that soon the veil will split asunder altogether, and then at last they will burst forth from the immaterium to lead their entire race in an apocalyptic crusade known as the Great Waaagh!.

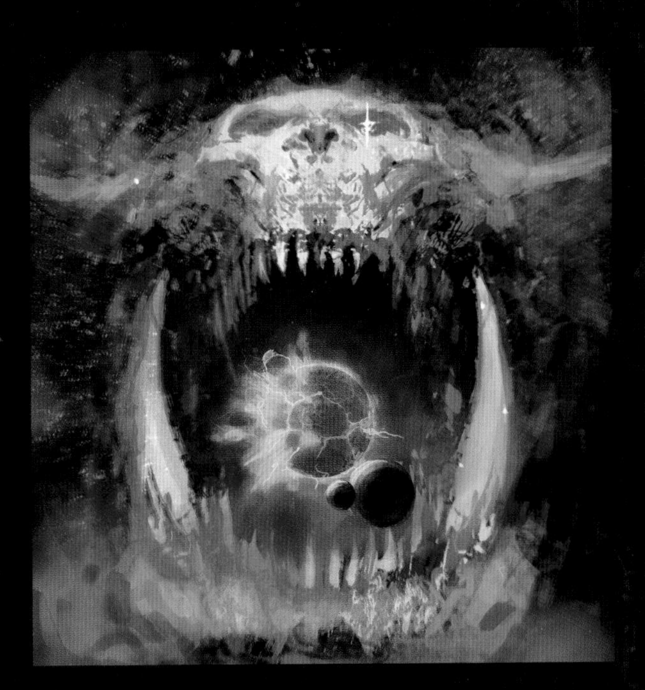

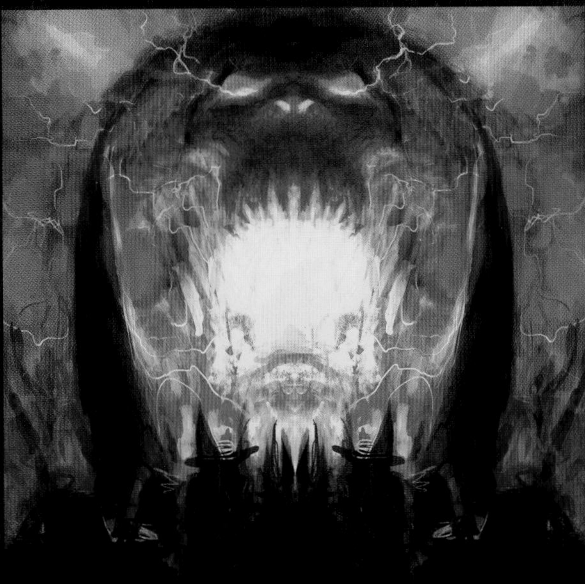

GORK (BRUTAL BUT KUNNIN')

It would be unfair to say that either of the Ork deities is anything other than a god of war, yet of the two, Gork more conventionally fits the title. He is the favoured patron of Warbosses and Nobz, Goffs and Snakebites, and really any Ork who has a particular hankering for stomping some enemies with a minimum of 'mukkin' about'. Gork is a landslide of brutality, a ferocious storm of hammering fists, kicking feet and tusks bared in a bestial and everlasting bellow. He is the summation of every greenskin's violent urges, and his cheerful belligerence drives them ever onwards.

MORK (KUNNIN' BUT BRUTAL)

When a Mekboy feels the inspiration to build a new contraption, or a Blood Axe gets a sudden strategic inkling, or a Deathskull spots an opportunity to stab an enemy in the back, this is the work of Mork. Although no stranger to brutal violence, Mork is a wily deity. He is the obsessive need in every Oddboy, the devious gleam in a grot's eye, and the fang-filled leer of a Kommando in the moment before he springs his ambush. Mork is the Orks' bestial cunning personified, and he delights in every instance of his race shocking, surprising and bewildering their luckless foes.

TRIBES AND CLANS

The Orks are an incredibly anarchic race, whose armies and settlements seem utterly disorganised to outside eyes. In truth, however, greenskin society is guided by a rugged set of tried and tested traditions. Central to these tenets is the system of tribes and clans.

Orks thrive on conflict. The strongest rise to the top while the weak become subservient and benefit from the superior leadership and head-kicking skills of their conquerors. To an Ork, this state of affairs is perfectly satisfactory; if a greenskin tribe is beaten by another, stronger tribe, the defeated Orks welcome the opportunity to be led into battle by a leader of even greater power.

A tribe is simply all of the greenskins in a given location, regardless of what clan they may belong to, because in the end an Ork is an Ork and they will always put aside their differences if there is an opportunity to attack a common foe. Each tribe is led by its biggest and most powerful Warboss, whose authority and power holds this loose confederation in check and prevents civil war between the rival elements of the tribe. Tribes can vary hugely in size, depending on the influence of the war leader at the top of the pile.

Because the ruling Warboss cannot be everywhere at once, the tribes contain multiple warbands, each led by its own Warboss, who is either one of the ruling Warboss' appointed cronies or else a local leader who has risen up to take command. Each Warboss leads a warband that can comprise all manner of mobs, armoured war-engines, aircraft, artillery and the like, forming a rough and ready army. Many warbands have a hard core of Ork infantry at their heart, but beyond this they vary enormously from one to the next; some may be entirely centred around skwadrons of ramshackle fighter jets, while others may consist solely of lumbering walkers and war effigies.

Like-minded Orks tend to cluster together, leading to warbands crammed with mechanised Speed Freeks or pyromaniac Burna Boyz. The Warboss' preferences can also dictate how their warband looks and fights; some favour masses of charging Boyz and hulking Nobz, while others prefer columns of ragged armoured vehicles or batteries of massive shootas and artillery.

Although all Orks belong to a tribe, most also belong to a clan such as the Goffs or Evil Sunz. Tribes are constantly breaking apart and reforming in the crucible of battle, but the clans are constant and enduring. A large tribe usually contains Orks from many different clans, and as each clan has its own distinct character and identity, its members tend to form warbands together whenever possible. This is not to say that they do not intermingle within a single army, but certainly Orks fight most effectively when not distracted by inter-clan rivalries. There are six clans in particular that have spread from one side of the galaxy to the other: the Goffs, the Snakebites, the Bad Moons, the Blood Axes, the Deathskulls and the Evil Sunz.

FERAL ORKS

Though the majority of Orks will never venture far from their tribe, there are those strange few who are driven to explore the remote locales of their world, compelled to do so even in preference to fighting. Such pioneers will seek out the deepest jungles or most arid deserts, where the majority of creatures would struggle to survive at all, and become the founders of new tribes of greenskins. In time, it is common for these tribes to degenerate into savages, sometimes known as Wildboyz. Should they endure and multiply, some of these groups will come into contact with their parent warband. There they learn about Ork kultur and take their place in the warrior society, exchanging spear and axe for slugga and choppa. However, should the new tribe emerge on a world where their Ork ancestors have been driven off or slain, the Wildboyz will instead develop into a tribe of Feral Orks.

At other times, Ork armies that suffer a sufficiently crushing defeat may be all but eradicated, and their survivors scattered in small pockets to the wildest and most inhospitable parts of a world. Such hidden greenskin enclaves retain little in the way of technology, and rapidly devolve into Feral Orks through force of circumstance. Greenskins have notoriously short memories, and before long the only record such tribes possess of their more technological origins lies within the oral traditions of the Runtherds. The Orks look with wondering eyes upon the crude glyph paintings of war engines that adorn their cave walls, but only until their attention wanders to catching a tasty squig or punching their mates in the face. What rusting wrecks remain of their Battlewagons and combat walkers are treated as sacred relics, squatted in as huts or smashed up and used to make clubs and arrowheads.

At first, Feral Ork tribes pose little threat to the planet they infest, and living in remote areas, often go undetected by the world's other occupants until it is too late. They are uncivilised, even by the low standards of their Ork brethren, and live by the old ways of hunting and exploring. As the tribe increases in size they breed ever-larger varieties of squig, riding around upon great tusked beasts that vary in size from that of a horse to that of a Baneblade. Exploring the stomping grounds of their predecessors, the Feral Orks soon learn to scavenge weapons and equipment, and rejoice in the noise and destruction their new tools allow them to cause. Shortly after this discovery the tribe will mobilise for war, whooping and howling as they pour out of the mountains, jungles or deserts, charging into the cities and fortifications of the unsuspecting enemy and starting the whole cycle of warfare afresh. As the war drags on and the mighty Squiggoths are slain one by one, they will be replaced by crudely constructed Battlewagons covered in beast fetishes that hark back to the squigs that came before. Should the Feral Orks survive the fighting long enough, they will inevitably mature into a fully fledged and technologically capable society akin to a typical Ork tribe, only to spawn wandering Wildboyz of their own.

THE GOFF CLAN

A Goff sees himself as very much 'an Ork's Ork'. Big, violent, brutally direct and utterly disinterested in anything they consider to be 'mukkin' about', the Goffs go to war in huge hordes and trample their enemies into the floor by dint of sheer aggression.

A Goff likes nothing more than hearing the hammering of guns and that satisfying wet crunch when his choppa finds its way deep into the throat or chest of an enemy. They seize upon any excuse to start a fight, even with each other. Often all it takes is a grunted insult or a misinterpreted glance in their general direction for the fists to begin flying, the Boyz quickly forgetting the reason for the bust-up and simply enjoying the resulting brawl. With the Goffs preferring to fight their enemies up close and personal, this tendency towards near-constant scrapping amongst themselves also serves a practical purpose by keeping their hand-to-hand skills honed between battles.

Goff warbands are notorious for the sheer number of infantry they muster in times of war. All it takes is the hint of a good conflict and the Goffs appear in droves, flocking to any Warboss who can promise them the chance of opening some skulls. Because of their preference for close combat, Goffs like to fight on foot, though they will happily hitch a lift on a passing Trukk so they can get stuck into the enemy as soon as possible.

Goff mobs are usually dozens strong, and a true Goff warband has multitudes of Boyz at its heart, so that when they go to war, the ground shakes to the stampeding thunder of steel-capped boots. Enemies often interpret these massed infantry assaults as a deliberate tactic by the greenskins to overwhelm set defences. More likely, though, is that each individual Goff is just following the rest of their mob without giving a thought to wider strategy, rightly reasoning that if an Ork is charging across the battlefield then there will be something to attack at the other end.

The Goffs use a bull's head as their clan emblem, as they feel a kinship with bad-tempered, violent and flatulent beasts. Horned helms are also seen as a symbol of the clan's aggression, and can even make handy weapons, making a headbutt or charge even more vicious. They dress predominantly in black, on the basis that dressing up in flashy colours 'is fer wimps and Madboyz'. Though they sometimes decorate their wargear with patterns, the majority of the clan's members – Kommandos aside – are disgusted by the concept of camouflage. They consider the idea of hiding from a fight cowardly, and cannot comprehend why an Ork might not want to 'have a go'.

Most Goffs see it as their Gork-given right to lord it over other greenskins, especially those of other clans, who they view as inferior. The longest-lived and most battle-hardened Goffs are known as Skarboyz, and form their own mobs of veteran killers within a Goff warband. Meanwhile, Goff Warbosses and Nobz are amongst the most fearsome examples of their kind, and are natural leaders with a talent for keeping unruly mobs of Boyz in line. Goffs also have a fearsome reputation in the fighting pits, although consider making teef off of these contests only a by-product of the fights themselves. As any self-respecting Goff will tell his Boyz, fighting for teef is all well and good, but a proper Goff should always be willing to break faces for free.

Goff glyphs typically feature an Orkoid bull's head with massive horns and tusks, stamped in black over bare metal or black and white checks.

Different Goff mobs may adapt their glyphs with blood-red tusk or horn designs, while chequerboard patterns are much in evidence.

Boss Nob Dregbadd, a hulking fighter of the Goff Clan. He rules over his Boyz with an iron fist, and is part of Warboss Urguk's warband.

THE EVIL SUNZ CLAN

Not every Speed Freek belongs to the Evil Sunz Clan, but the vast majority of the Evil Sunz are most definitely Speed Freeks. If it goes fast, kills people violently, and is painted a bright and garish red, then an Evil Sunz Ork probably already has three of it, and undoubtedly wants another.

The Orks belonging to the Evil Sunz Clan are irresistibly attracted to every conceivable kind of fast vehicle. Be it low-riding buggies, monstrous Warbikes or supersonic aircraft, Evil Sunz will spend every toof they possess in order to own them. The richest Evil Sunz can even afford to have a Mek kustomise their ride, bolting on more wheels, bigger engines and louder rockets. Anything that looks like it might make the vehicle go faster is fair game, so it is not unusual to see wings attached to Warbikes, jet engines mounted on the back of Trukks, or even more bizarre means of propulsion such as squig treadmills and massive propellers.

Should an Evil Sunz Ork live long enough, he will inevitably acquire his own vehicle, whether he buys it with carefully hoarded teef or takes the simpler route of just nicking it from another clan member. If he cannot drive into battle then he will ride, and if he cannot ride, at least he can content himself with being close to the throaty, growling engines of his warband, his nostrils filled with a satisfying promethium stink. Evil Sunz who therefore have to fight on foot usually race into battle crammed into Trukks or Battlewagons, or at least run as fast as they can towards the enemy, bellowing a throaty battle roar.

The Evil Sunz never stay in one place for long, always on the lookout for new victims to slaughter. Clan members have a tendency to leave a battle midway through if it looks like the main part of the fighting is over, or abandon a burning city or ruined world if there is nothing left worth killing. They especially like a good chase, as it gives them a chance to really open up the throttle on their vehicles. Enemy forces who turn tail on the Evil Sunz often learn this to their misfortune, the Orks running them down with frenzied glee – even after being given a sporting head start by the speed-addicted greenskins.

'Evil Sunz like two fings most: going fast and krumpin' stuff. Dat's why we'z so good at it.'

- Lugnut of the Bladed Wheels

The armies of the Imperium find it extremely difficult to engage the Evil Sunz on anything other than the Orks' terms, for the heavy vehicles of the Imperial Guard are outmanoeuvred with ease by the greenskins' super-charged speedsters. A favoured tactic of Evil Sunz warbands is to charge headlong into the enemy lines, but then keep charging out the other side so they can wheel around and charge again: long columns of Warbikes, buggies and Trukks snake in and out of the foe's formations while the Orks on board whoop, yell and fire their guns. This tactic is devastating against more static armies, who struggle to redress their firing lines or turn to engage the Orks before the greenskins are surging back through their outflanked defensive positions, and then back around and through again until all cohesion is lost. Even highly mobile forces like T'au Hunter Cadres or Drukhari raiding parties are threatened by the Speed Freeks of the Evil Sunz, who are capable of keeping apace and even revel in these so-called speed wars.

The totem of the Evil Sunz Clan is a blood-red Ork face grimacing from the heart of a jagged sunburst. They wear red armour and often paint their machines red too, firmly believing in the old greenskin adage that 'red ones go fasta'. Evil Sunz Warbosses will usually have their vehicles painted red from grille to exhaust. This Ork habit of painting vehicles red has its roots in the ritual covering of mounts with the blood of the foe, a tradition that is still observed with manic relish by some Evil Sunz to this day.

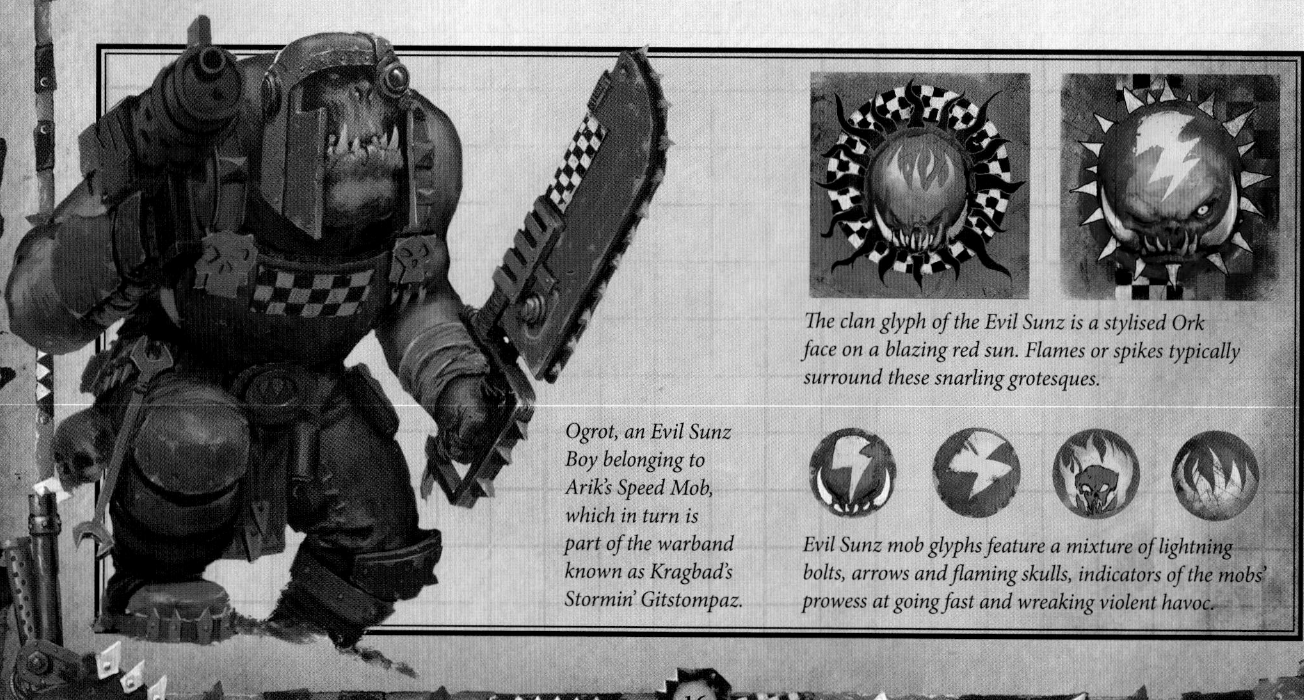

The clan glyph of the Evil Sunz is a stylised Ork face on a blazing red sun. Flames or spikes typically surround these snarling grotesques.

Ogrot, an Evil Sunz Boy belonging to Arik's Speed Mob, which in turn is part of the warband known as Kragbad's Stormin' Gitstompaz.

Evil Sunz mob glyphs feature a mixture of lightning bolts, arrows and flaming skulls, indicators of the mobs' prowess at going fast and wreaking violent havoc.

THE BLOOD AXE CLAN

Blood Axes are generally held to be 'a bit un-Orky' by most greenskins. This reputation comes from their tendency to use actual battlefield tactics, often to great effect; nothing surprises an enemy commander like Orks who actually think about how, where and when to fight.

The Blood Axes are viewed with distrust by the other clans, as they trade openly with the Imperium's more isolated worlds, plan their battles in advance, and even consider retreat to be something that can be done on purpose. These are qualities that would recommend the Blood Axes as natural leaders amongst most of the galaxy's other races, but instead see them labelled as treacherous scumbags by the vast majority of greenskins.

In fact, most of the Blood Axes' reputation is undeserved. True, they have made the most contact with the Imperium, occasionally even fighting for the humans as mercenaries, and making extensive use of Imperial war materiel. Then again, every Ork can see the funny side of extorting weapons from human planets only to use them against their former owners.

The Blood Axes' reputation amongst the clans is not helped by the fact that a lot of their young Orks end up in the Stormboyz. These odd formations are a place where a 'yoof' can rebel against the anarchy of greenskin society by following orders, conducting precise military drills and polishing their boots. Heckled and laughed at by most other Orks, the Stormboyz spend hours each day marching about and chanting, saluting each other and generally carrying on in very un-Orky ways. As they age, most Stormboyz leave for 'proper' mobs, but some – especially Blood Axes – gain a taste for it, and will rise to command whole formations of black-booted young Orks.

Blood Axes view the act of getting shot before they reach the enemy lines as a waste of a good fight, and so many have adopted the practice of wearing camouflage. For this reason the clan has a natural affinity for Kommando mobs, and makes extensive use of them in battle. Unlike other kinds of Orks, Kommandos like to sneak up on their foes, using all the dirty, underhanded tricks they can think of to get the drop on them.

'Us Blood Axes have learnt a lot from da humies. How best ta kill 'em, fer example.'

- Korporal Snagbrat of the Dreadblade Kommandos

Of course, Blood Axe warbands are made up of far more than just these specialist mobs. Blood Axe Warbosses have a better understanding of grand strategy than their equivalents from the other clans, knowing when to combine a Dakkajet strike with a ground attack, or send a mob of Kommandos on a covert mission. This grasp of diverse tactics means the warbands they lead are likely to comprise a strategically versatile mixture of infantry – either foot-slogging or riding aboard mechanised transports – supported by heavy armour, batteries of field guns, and wings of daring Flyboyz. Their Battlewagon Blitz Brigades are especially feared, while the Blood Axes' rather un-Orky ability to strike and fade with feral cunning has seen them erode, confound and eventually stomp flat many a surprised enemy army. This trait makes them especially dangerous to foes who assume the Blood Axes' grasp of actual tactics is as lacking as that of the rest of their race.

The Blood Axe Clan glyph features crossed choppas, usually boasting a stylised skull either in front of or behind them.

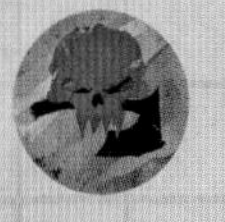

Blood Axe mob glyphs vary a great deal. Set upon a field of garish camo patterns, they can incorporate axes, fangs, scars, skulls and back-stabbing blades.

Murklug is a Kommando of Kommanda Nurk's Killkorpz, a formidable Blood Axe warband renowned for its ambushes.

THE DEATHSKULLS CLAN

Orks of the Deathskulls are cunning, light-fingered, untrustworthy and insular, with a mean streak a mile wide. That said, there are none more skilled when it comes to looting the battlefield and cobbling together weapons and tanks from the resultant junk.

The Deathskulls are plunderers without equal. They are tremendously adept at looting and scavenging on the battlefield, and are also especially talented at scrounging, stealing and borrowing things from their fellow Orks – and in the case of the latter, notoriously bad at giving the items back. Given their ingenuity and the higher than average density of Meks in their warbands, most Deathskulls would make capable scientists and excellent engineers if their fascination for new things lasted longer than the time it took to acquire them.

The Deathskulls see battle as a two-stage process, often hurrying the killing part in an effort to hasten the arrival of the scavenging spree that follows. After the battle, the Boyz really go to work, feverishly stripping corpses of everything from ammunition to bootlaces. Many Deathskulls will take grisly trophies from their victims in the bargain, such as scalps or skulls. Only when they return to their encampment with the loot does the inevitable infighting break out, as the Deathskulls trade their ill-gotten gains. Other Orks drawn to Deathskull camps in search of goods – perhaps looking for a specific bit of loot, or something of their own that was stolen during battle – usually leave with less than they came with, as the Deathskulls have the uncanny ability to knock another Ork around the head while going through his pockets at the same time.

'Wot, this? Naw, I've had this fer ages. Of course the paint's still wet, it's me favourite. Sell it to ya if you like. One careful owner.'

- 'Fingaz' Rutzeg, Deathskull Loota

Deathskulls do not limit their pillaging to corpses. Wrecked vehicles are especially popular, the burnt-out hulls of battle-tanks, armoured transports and aircraft all seen as fair game. Dragged off the battlefield, they can either be broken down for bits or taken to a Mek, who will beat some life back into them. Many foes have been horrified to see one of their own vehicles turned against them in this way, Deathskulls yelling insults from the turrets of their new acquisition as it delivers death to its former owners.

The clan uses a horned death's head as its totem, and this symbol is added onto anything its members have stolen, borrowed or looted so as to establish ownership. This process can also involve painting the item blue, which Orks believe is a lucky colour, with blue handprints and smears on vehicles common methods of staking a claim. The Deathskulls even use blue warpaint, daubing themselves from head-to-toe in it the night before a battle. Strangely enough, this practice seems to work, bullets missing the Deathskulls by hair's breadths while their own violent efforts are rewarded more often than not by disproportionate levels of success.

Given the Deathskulls' broad definition of what constitutes personal property, it is little wonder that so many of their clan are Lootas. This, in turn, means that most Deathskulls warbands produce an unrivalled amount of dakka on the battlefield, the better to break down the vehicles and wargear of the enemy into more easily lootable pieces.

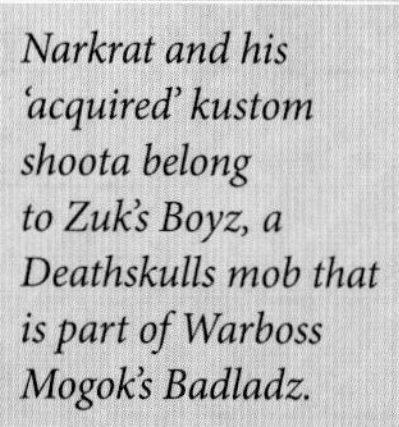

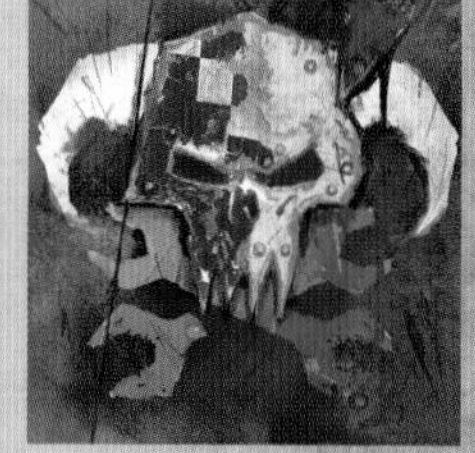

The Deathskulls glyph takes the form of a horned Ork skull picked out in white and lucky blue. Check designs and Mek spanners are also popular.

Narkrat and his 'acquired' kustom shoota belong to Zuk's Boyz, a Deathskulls mob that is part of Warboss Mogok's Badladz.

Deathskulls use distinctive mob glyphs, the better to avoid 'confusion' over who owns what. They feature blue and white skulls, spanners, fangs and the like.

THE BAD MOONS CLAN

Every Ork of the other clans knows that the Bad Moons are showy gits with too many teef for their own good. That said, they also know to dive for cover when the yellow-daubed loons open fire, for the sheer amount of dakka that a Bad Moons warband kicks out is amazing to behold.

The Orks of the Bad Moons tend to be richer than other greenskins. This is because their teeth grow faster than anyone else's, meaning that even the lowliest of them has a steady supply of wealth. This is not regarded as an unfair advantage, as any greenskin who is big and strong enough can simply smash the teeth out of a Bad Moons Ork's head. In fact, many Warbosses like to keep a mob of Bad Moons around for just this purpose, their toothy gobs a ready supply of extra teef. It is often not a terrible deal for the Bad Moons either, as any Ork tough enough to beat their teeth out of them is usually one worth following into a fight.

The Bad Moons fulfil the role of what passes for a merchant class within Ork society, and if something can be bought or sold, odds are the Bad Moons will have it. Some Runtherds reckon that it must have been the Bad Moons who came up with the whole concept of teef being used to buy things, when the clan figured out how quickly their teeth grow. Of course, many Runtherds say it is the other way around, and when teef became Ork currency, the Bad Moons made their teeth grow quicker so they would have the most. The subject is seldom dwelt upon for long, however, as knocking out teeth is far more interesting than talking about them.

All this wealth means that the Bad Moons have a reputation for ostentatiousness, and their vehicles are festooned with gaudy decorations and gold plating, as is the majority of their wargear. Bad Moons love gold more than any other metal, and will commonly have a couple of glinting teeth in their avaricious grins. As most Orks consider gold to be practically worthless, being too soft to make good weapons or vehicles with, they are more than happy to trade it away to Bad Moons for the more valuable teef.

'Nuffin' better than givin' da enemy some pricey dakka, and makin' sure everyone knows it!'

- Gorzbrag, Bad Moons Nob

Bad Moons mobs are always well equipped, at least by Ork standards. Their Nobz sport flashy banners and massive kustomised shootas, and are followed by entourages of scurrying grot servants and batteries of powerful Mek artillery. Indeed, grots find many way to prosper within Bad Moons warbands – the most capable amongst them inveigle their way into the good books of some boss or another and become their personal toady, lugging the extra shiny gubbinz the Ork can't be bothered to carry himself.

The Bad Moons favour golden yellow and black for their wargear, taking a snarling moon on a field of flames as their clan emblem. Their armour and weapons are painted with gaudy patterns in the clan colours, and they have more jewellery and piercings than the greenskins of any other clan. If something looks valuable, a Bad Moons Ork will find a way to wear it, stick it through his body or bolt it onto the side of his vehicle, preferably somewhere that every other Ork can clearly see it. However, only a fool would underestimate the raw strength of the Ork beneath the ostentation. The shiny bosspole of a Bad Moons Warboss is just as much a tool to smash skulls in as it is a symbol of vast wealth.

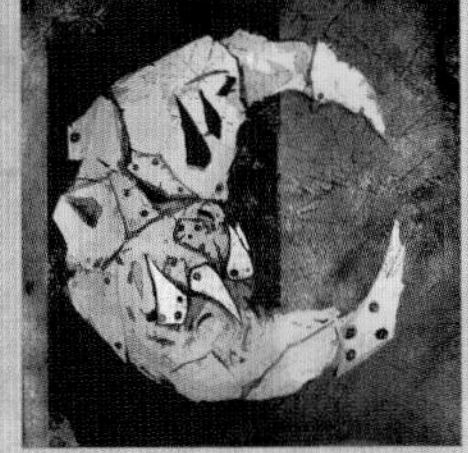

The glyph of the Bad Moons is, perhaps unsurprisingly, a large and surly looking moon with an Ork's face and a leering gob crammed full of teeth.

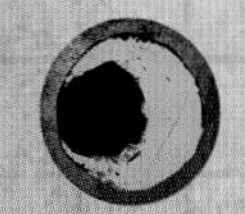

Bad Moons mob glyphs tend towards simple moon and fang designs. They are normally picked out in garish yellows and golds, to ensure they are nice and visible.

Bargrut is an Ork Boy from the Bad Moons Clan. He hails from Drug'z Killaz, a mob within Warboss Tragfang's conquering warband.

THE SNAKEBITE CLAN

Snakebites are traditionalists, and many of them are only one or two rusty rungs above Feral Orks on the ladder of civilisation. This has never held Snakebite warbands back, however, for when they unleash their tribal fury upon the enemy, there are few who can long withstand it.

Considered backward by the more technologically minded clans, Snakebites still follow the old ways. Scorning complicated technological gubbinz, they put their faith in things they can trust: a good bit of sharpened bone, a heavy stick or a nice keen-edged choppa. In battle they daub themselves with mud and warpaint, hanging the claws and teeth of beasts they have killed around their necks and wearing poorly cured skins.

As a result of their primitive lifestyle, the Snakebites appear weather-beaten and they are as tough as old boots. They are experts in the field of breeding stock, and their grots and squigs are the most genuinely vicious and dangerous in all of Orkdom. When a warband of Snakebites joins a battle, it brings with it a menagerie of these creatures, their camp a chaos of snarling squigs and running, screaming runts. When other Orks are looking for an aggressive attack squig or an unusually fierce or obedient grot, they come to the Snakebites.

The most fearsome beasts bred by the Snakebites are the mighty Squiggoths: huge, towering creatures capable of knocking over war machines and trampling entire platoons. A well-trained Squiggoth becomes almost completely loyal to its Snakebite master, recognising him by his distinct smell and serving him as both a living battle tank and an enormous beast of burden.

The Snakebites' name and emblem comes from a rite of passage that involves a yoof goading an extremely poisonous serpent into biting them to prove their toughness, then sucking out the majority of the venom. A Snakebite will repeat this process throughout their life, building up an immunity to venoms, and they usually bring poisonous serpents to each new world they invade in case the local wildlife proves disappointingly inoffensive. As far as a Snakebite is concerned, snakes make the best pets – obviously, the more aggressive the better.

The Snakebites' Runtherds cultivate hordes of Gretchin, who in times of war are given weapons and herded into battle, often to man artillery batteries. Ironically, the more sophisticated weapons that fall into the hands of the Snakebites usually find their way into the hands of their grots, as the runts of the tribe are left to figure out how they work. The Orks, meanwhile, gather into especially large and surly mobs who chant and bellow as they work themselves into a frenzy. When the Snakebites launch an assault, it is with such shocking ferocity that the enemy is buried under an avalanche of battle-crazed Orks, snapping squigs, gun-wielding grots and rusty, ramshackle wagons. Though they may be rather low-tech, the Snakebites are a deadly foe.

'Live off the land. Go to find war. Kill wot comes close. The old ways are best.'

- Grodd, Snakebite Runtherd

Snakebite Clan glyphs are crude and totemic in appearance, invariably featuring a fanged serpent rearing to strike.

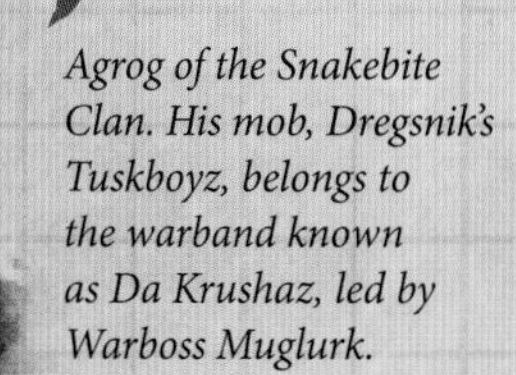

Agrog of the Snakebite Clan. His mob, Dregsnik's Tuskboyz, belongs to the warband known as Da Krushaz, led by Warboss Muglurk.

Snakebite mob glyphs usually depict either a snake or its fangs, fringed by tribal dag patterns or leaping flames.

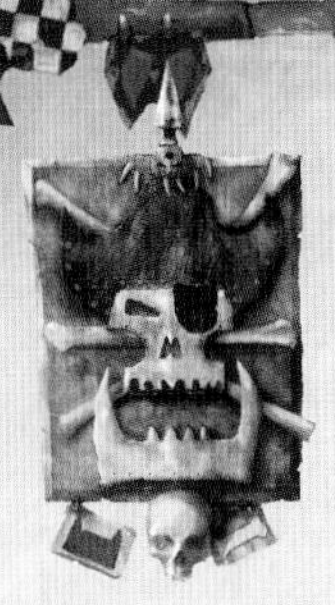

FREEBOOTERZ

Freebooterz are outcasts from Ork society, greenskins who by choice or through exile have left their tribe and clan behind. They rampage around the galaxy in piratical mercenary warbands, fighting together even as they compete viciously with each other to accrue the most loot.

Ork Freebooterz are notorious pirates and thieves. Many ply the void in smoking, sparking ships with the intent of causing as much mayhem and destruction as possible. They prey upon anyone foolish enough to stray into their hunting grounds, screaming out of the dark on plumes of fire to blast apart their foes. When an enemy vessel is crippled or foolishly tries to surrender, the Freebooterz will smash their way on board, killing anything that moves and stealing anything that doesn't. The Freebooterz then haul their booty back to their hidden bases and count their ill-gotten gains.

Freebooter warbands are typically made up of greenskins who have left – or, more often, been thrown out of – their clans. Some of these Orks have seen the majority of their tribe annihilated, either in a spectacularly destructive war or due to some apocalyptic disaster. In recent years, this has most often been the result of warp storms encroaching upon greenskin territories; while plenty of Orks have made it clear before their worlds or space-forts were destroyed, the encroaching energies of the Great Rift have sent many 'a bit perkooliar', skewing their rambunctious Ork nature and leaving them either viciously acquisitive loot-grabbers, or else straight up Madboyz.

Whatever their origins, Freebooterz are forever shorn from the greater masses of Orkdom, adopting their own unique kultur that many greenskins see as dubiously 'un-orky' in its outlook. Instead of trying to find a new tribe to join, or maintaining the traditions of their originating clan, they nominate a leader – invariably the biggest and meanest of them all – to be their Freebooter Warboss, before setting off to maraud around the galaxy and cause as much trouble as they can. While no Ork ever loses his love of a good punch-up, Freebooterz are notorious for being grasping and avaricious to a fault, motivated by the selfish desire to amass as great a personal fortune of teef as they can. Individualistic rogues, they garb themselves in garish colours and ostentatious trophies, festooning their wargear with precious metals, and displaying the glyph of the Jolly Ork wherever they can on back banners, vehicle hulls and the like. Freebooterz launch lightning raids against vulnerable worlds, bedevil space-lanes like opportunistic vultures, and fight for any Warboss willing to hire their services – at least until the teef run out.

Many Freebooter warbands are composed mainly of Flash Gitz, for the mercenary life tends to rapidly render an Ork one of two things: rich, or dead. However, beyond these ultra-competitive show offs, Freebooter warbands are every bit as varied as those of the Ork tribes, and often substantially more hotchpotch. Badmeks and Bad Doks are much in evidence, alongside ragtag mobs of Freebooter Boyz. Rebellious grots rub scrawny shoulders with Bad Ork Biker Boyz, dribbling Madboyz and wandering Gorkanaut and Morkanaut pilots. Lent support by low-orbiting Kill Kroozers, marauding Freebooter warbands hit hard, enjoy a chaotic brawl, and then steal whatever isn't nailed down before vanishing into the void as swiftly as they arrived.

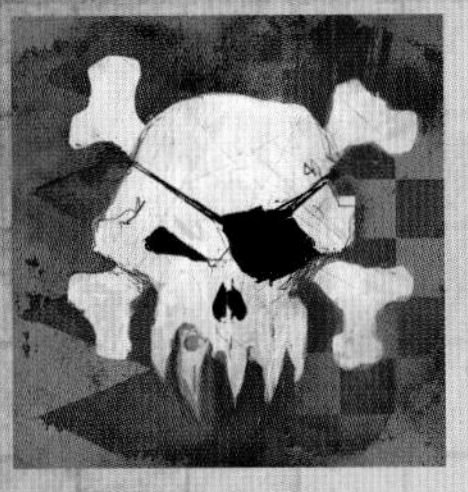

Freebooter warbands can be identified by their use of the Jolly Ork glyph, with each Warboss boasting his own variation of the Ork skull and crossed bones.

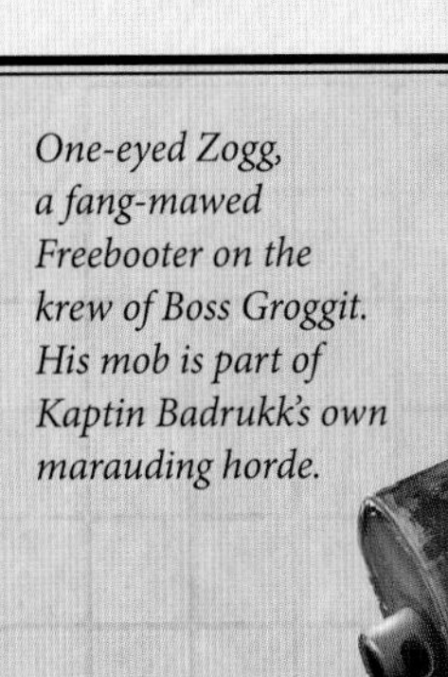

One-eyed Zogg, a fang-mawed Freebooter on the krew of Boss Groggit. His mob is part of Kaptin Badrukk's own marauding horde.

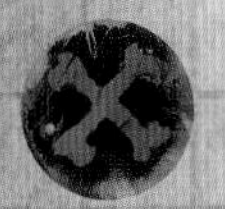

Freebooter mobs mark themselves out with skull-and-bones glyphs of various sorts, often adding teeth marks to show their talent for looting riches.

ORK GLYPHS

The Ork language is written in a form of glyphic script. The core of the script is composed of glyphs that indicate clan, tribe, common greenskin concepts and elements of Ork names. Orks typically daub these pictorial words onto things they own, things they want to claim, or even just things they want to deface. Or, more often, they get the grots to do it for them.

Bad'un *Renegade, outcast*

Bad *Evil, wicked, brave, strong, tough*

Bark *Voice, command, shout*

Beekee *Space Marine*

Blitz *Invasion, devastate*

Bog *Brown*

Bonk *'Eadbutt, duel*

Boss *Leader, officer, head Ork, Warlord*

Bugeye *Alien, Genestealer, Tyranid*

Dakka *Attack, noisy weapon, shoot, fight*

Dreg *Destroy, rip, cut, break up, take apart*

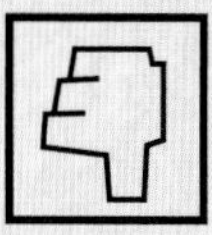
Duff *Vanquish, beat, chastise*

Dur *Fortress, stronghold, city, armour*

Duruk *Force field*

'Eadbanga *Weirdboy*

Fing *Mutant*

Flash *Banner, badge*

Fung *Drop, food*

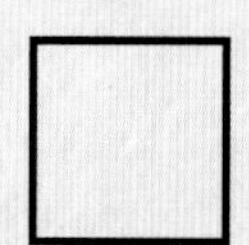
Garg *Huge, big, terrifying, powerful*

Gargant *Titan, large robot*

Git *Enemy, trouble-maker, nuisance*

Gob *Mouth, eat, drink, speak out of turn*

Gof *Warlike, spiky, metal, black, night*

Gog *God, power*

Gor *Blood, red, slaughter, wound*

Grim *Ruthless, prowess, face, dangerous*

Grod *Friend or favourite enemy*

Grot *Gretchin, servant, slave*

Grub *Cunning, find, dig, hide*

Grunta *Boar*

Gubbinz *Engine, workings*

Gul *Death, bones, skull, rocks, white*

Gutz *Flesh, workings, stamina*

Kan *Dreadnought*

Kannon *Big gun, artillery, cannon*

Kart *Vehicle*

Kop *Head, helmet, hill, catch, see*

Krump *Noise, amplify*

Lug *Hear, listen, earring, advisor*

Lurk *Danger, beware*

Manik *Insane*

Mek *Clever, technology, mechanical*

Miff *Mistake, wrong, bad plan*

Mob *Tactical, unit, formation*

Mor *Wild, feral, ancient*

Naa *No, negative prefix, not*

Naff *Rubbish, bad, boring*

Nar *Command, crew*

Naz *Moon, white, shine, light, wealth*

Nob *Nobility, authority, high rank*

Nosh *Feast, pickings, plunder*

Nurd *Unlucky*

Og *Owned by, property of, belonging to*

Ooman *Human*

Ordz *Many, loads*

'When I'z captured a buildin' or nicked a wagon or wotnot, I always stick a few glyphs on it. Uvverwise, how do the ladz know who did da fightin' and grabbed da prize? Plus, it annoys Rugblatz when I stick a few insults 'bout him on da end. Hur hur hur…'

- 'Grintoof' Gurblag (found with a choppa in his guts and 'Rugblatz woz 'ere' daubed in glyphs on his face)

Orky
Ork, Ork kultur, good, green

Pointy-earz
Aeldari

Rip-off
Buy, sell, merchant, auction

Rokk
Goffik rokk, loud, proper

Rukk
Attack, charge

Runt
Small, Snotling, Gretchin

Shak
Household, building

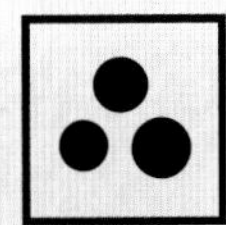
Shokka
Shokk attack gun, shokk rifle, shokk jump

Shuv
Build, construct, create

Skab
Traitor, unreliable, weak

Skar
Wound, trench, crater, cutting

Skraga
'Ardboy, Skarboy, veteran

Skul
End of battle, dead

Slag
Planet, settlement, stronghold

Slug
Ammo, bullet, shell

Smak
Stop, no further

Snaga
Sting, stab, wild beast, snake

Snik
Cut, kill, slay, execute, assassinate

Snot
Snotling, mischief, little

Spikee
Horn

Squig
Squig, food, eat, supplies, useful

Stash
Hide, conceal, secret

Stomp
Boot, Stormboy, drill, march

Stud
Bionik bit, cybernetics

Teef
Wealth, tribute

Thug
Guard, minder, henchman

Tin
Robot

Tuf
Old, ancient

Ug
By, with, from, to, of

Ulk
Space hulk, spaceship, cruiser

Unki
Big, muscle

Urd
Swarm, lots of, herd

Urty
Pain, medical attention

Uz
Sun, dry, yellow, hot, thirst, daytime

Villun
Freebooter, outlaw, mercenary

Vrum
Bike

Waaagh!
Warband, tribe of, watch out!

Warp
Space, the warp

Wazza
Speed, Kult of speed

Wizza
Fall, shell, bomb

Wort
Fungus

Wurr
Weird, strange

Zag
Lightning, movement, fast strike

Zod
Blue

Zog
Go away, get lost, no good

Zero

One

Two

Three

Four

Five

Lotz

GATHERING THE WAAAGH!

An Ork Waaagh! is war on an apocalyptic scale. Greenskins beyond counting swarm from one world to the next. Whole civilisations are exterminated and defending armies laid to waste as the Orks advance ever onwards, drawing more and more of their number with every fresh conflict and leaving behind a trail of anarchic destruction.

Orks need battle just as humans need food and drink. Due to their warlike nature, they constantly fight amongst themselves, or launch piratical raids upon nearby enemies. Such conflicts tend to be small-scale or localised. However, when a greenskin population reaches a critical mass, is displaced by a catastrophic event, or is galvanised by a prophetic or particularly powerful leader, a full-scale planetary migration will occur. This is known as a Waaagh!, a crusade of pure aggression that crashes through star systems in an orgy of violence.

Waaaghs! can be long in the making. An Ork Boy visited by dreams of carnage may rise up to lead his tribe, hammering his ambitions of conquest into his subordinates and leading them in attacks against the other tribes of his world. With each victory, the new Warboss' legend grows, and more greenskins are brought beneath his blood-soaked banner. As he fights to retain command of his ever-growing horde against a constant stream of challengers, news of his prowess spreads ever further, and the trickle of reinforcements becomes a green flood.

Meks from across the tribes under the Warboss' control will start to collaborate on more and more outlandish projects as the Waaagh! takes shape, building increasingly ambitious war machines and guns. Smoke-belching mobile fortresses and titanic engines of battle are cobbled together out of nothing more than scrap metal and heavy-handed enthusiasm. Gorkanauts and Morkanauts appear in growing numbers, their pilots seeking out the emergent Waaagh! with a feverish intensity. Whole mobs of Mekboyz raise towering scaffolds within which Stompas and even Gargants start to take shape, these mighty effigies igniting some primitive drive within the minds of the Orks who see them, causing the flow of Waaagh! energy they subconsciously generate to reach fever pitch.

Even though they are unified by a single leader, there is still much rivalry between the various clans and tribes participating in the Waaagh!, and each will strive to outdo all the others in terms of the sheer destruction that can be wrought by their war machines. Those Meks without the resources to construct Stompas and Gargants will instead create mobs of clanking Killa Kans and Deff Dreads, or Battlewagons from which the Warbosses can lead their armies to war.

Soon the Waaagh! begins to span worlds instead of just continents. By this point, the ruling Warboss, the Ork who started it all, will have been recognised by his subordinates as a Warlord, and is feared and respected accordingly. Entire native populations are forced into slavery merely to manufacture ammunition for his horde's guns. Crude factory-ships and war hulks are bashed into shape, the better to transport his armies into battle.

When the lure of bloodshed on a grand scale can be resisted no more, the deadly fervour washing through the horde overflows. Teeming Ork armies mass and swell with a roar like savage oceans, and the skies of a system's worlds fill with crude and bulky greenskin vessels.

As the Orks gather for battle, smoke from thousands of oily engines fills the sky. The ground trembles beneath great wheels, tracks and the thunderous strides of towering Gargants. Armies of greenskins stretch across the horizon, raising their banners high, their war cries audible for miles around. Looming Gorkanauts and Morkanauts, bizarre artillery pieces and force-field generators chug, clank and buzz. Armadas of rusty vehicles raise roiling thunderheads of dust into the atmosphere, while Dakkajets roar overhead. Speed Freeks rev their engines, and the Boyz fire their guns into the air as a carpet of Gretchin spreads out in front of the army.

Eventually, the battlefield is barely visible beneath the endless sea of green, each Ork warrior certain that the ground will soon be stained red. Here the power of the Waaagh! is palpable as a wave of raw aggression, and the Orks believe Gork and Mork are gazing eagerly down from the warp to see how their warriors will fare.

Then as one, with an almighty bellow, the Orks surge forwards, and another world is plunged into unending war.

THE SAVAGE STARS

The galaxy is a big place, its habitable systems separated by vast gulfs of cold and empty void. Yet the Orks have spread across it with unparalleled success, lurching from one world to the next and trampling everything in their path. The ways in which they achieve this are as varied and hazardous as one might expect, but no less effective because of it.

Orks live on innumerable worlds. On some they dominate completely, on others they live in a state of perpetual war, and on others still they act as slave-masters, bullying the local populations into doing their bidding. Hordes of greenskins roam the stars upon gigantic space hulks, establishing Ork empires across the galaxy. It has been tens of thousands of years since Humanity first encountered the Orks, and in that time Mankind has fought countless bloody wars against these savage creatures. There is no likelihood that this state of affairs will change.

Millennia ago, a probe was sent out from Terra, its mission to explore beyond the limits of the galaxy. The probe still sends back faint signals after fourteen thousand years adrift, and to the consternation of the Imperial Tech-Priests who monitor these signals, many are identified as Orkish. The depressing conclusion for Mankind can only be that wherever they travel in space, there is a good chance that the Orks will either have been there first or will not be long in arriving.

The Orks spread across the galaxy like a green stain. No system is entirely devoid of their touch. Some theorise that the Orks spread via fungal spores drifting through the void on cosmic winds, but the truth is that the greenskins have invented their own, typically crude and hazardous, methods of travelling through the blackness of space. Although these methods are generally inexact in their application, that is of no real concern to most Orks; they simply do not care where they are going, only that they get to kill something when they get there.

SPACE HULKS

The primary mode of interstellar travel for the Ork race is the space hulk. Space hulks are gigantic conglomerations of ancient wrecks, asteroids, ice and interstellar flotsam and jetsam, cast together after millennia of drifting in and out of warp space. Some are infested with alien life forms, Chaos renegades or even worse horrors, but most are simply ghost ships, plying the void for eternity. Tales of greedy scavengers meeting horrible fates aboard space hulks are told throughout the Imperium, but there are just as many tales of vast fortunes made from the ancient or xenos technologies they carry.

When a space hulk appears in an Ork-held system it is seized by any possible means, including colossal tractor beam arrays, and converted into a huge invasion craft. Cavernous launch bays are adapted for innumerable assault ships, and millions of Ork warriors and war machines honeycomb its irregular cavities. Once completed, the space hulk is sent back out into the stars with an attendant fleet of attack craft and kroozers as escorts. The space hulk is then guided into a warp storm or rift through the efforts of its Weirdboyz and Meks, where it is drawn into the immaterium and, if all goes well, spat out at a world ripe for conquest.

Being incredibly random in their trajectory, space hulks could appear in any place, at any time. This suits the Orks just fine, as their spirit of adventure and aggression owes nothing to organisation or direction. In this manner the Orks travel to the corners of the galaxy, spreading a plague of warfare across space and time.

ORK ROKS

Ork roks are asteroids hollowed out and fitted with drives, guns and crew quarters. Though roks are incapable of travelling through the warp, any system containing greenskins will quickly accumulate a growing number of roks. This is because the Orks 'build' them at a prodigious rate, often by breaking off large chunks of space hulk or welding space debris onto meteors. Orks can use Roks as a means of drifting from one world to another within a system, pulling them in and out of orbit with simple but powerful tractor beams. It has come as a fatal surprise to many an Imperial captain skirting an asteroid belt to find that some of the asteroids are drifting in his direction, guns blazing. Needless to say this is extremely entertaining for the Orks involved, quite making up for the lack of speed or manoeuvrability afforded by such a solid chunk of space detritus.

THE GREENSKIN EXPANSION

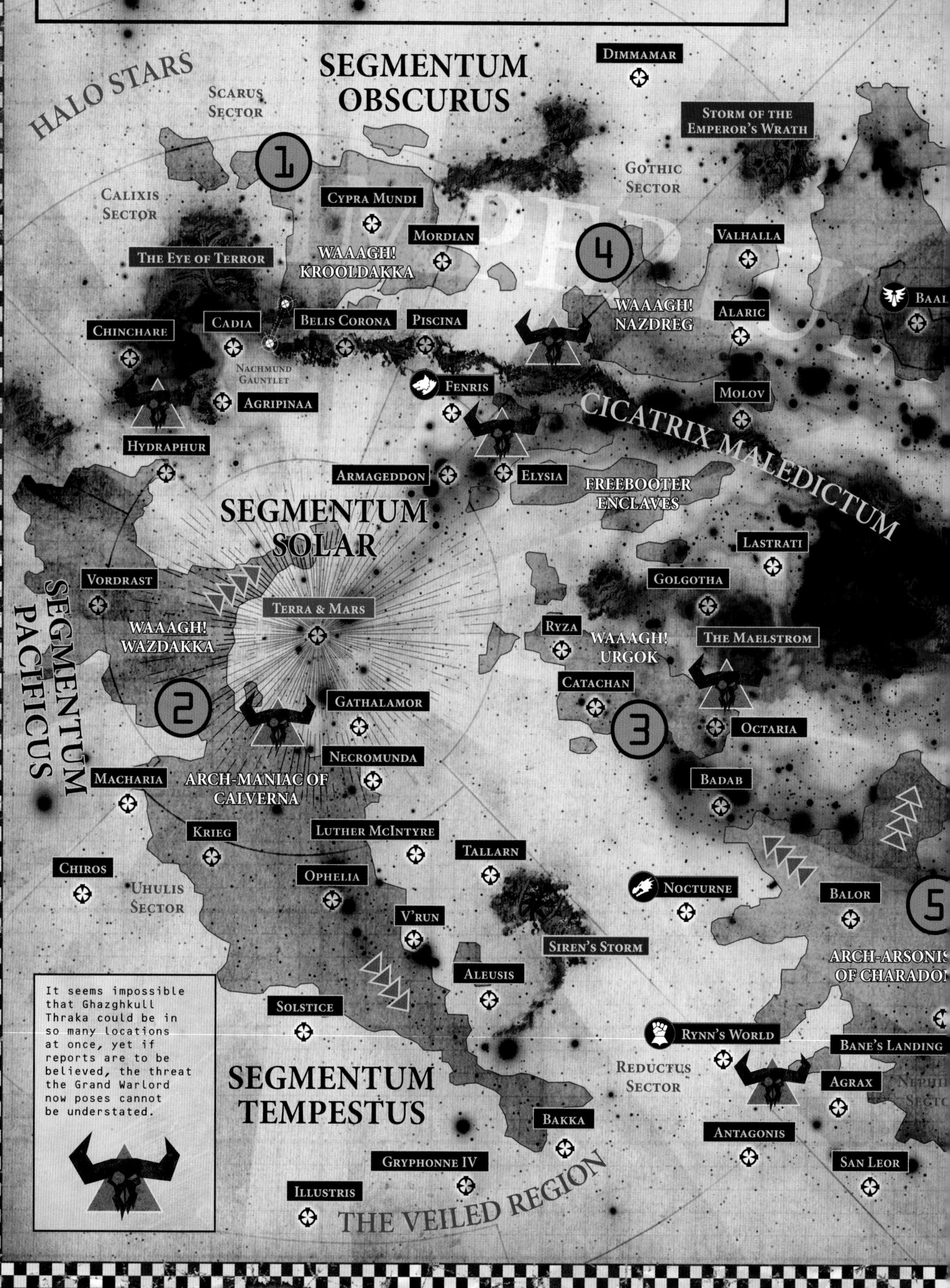

It seems impossible that Ghazghkull Thraka could be in so many locations at once, yet if reports are to be believed, the threat the Grand Warlord now poses cannot be understated.

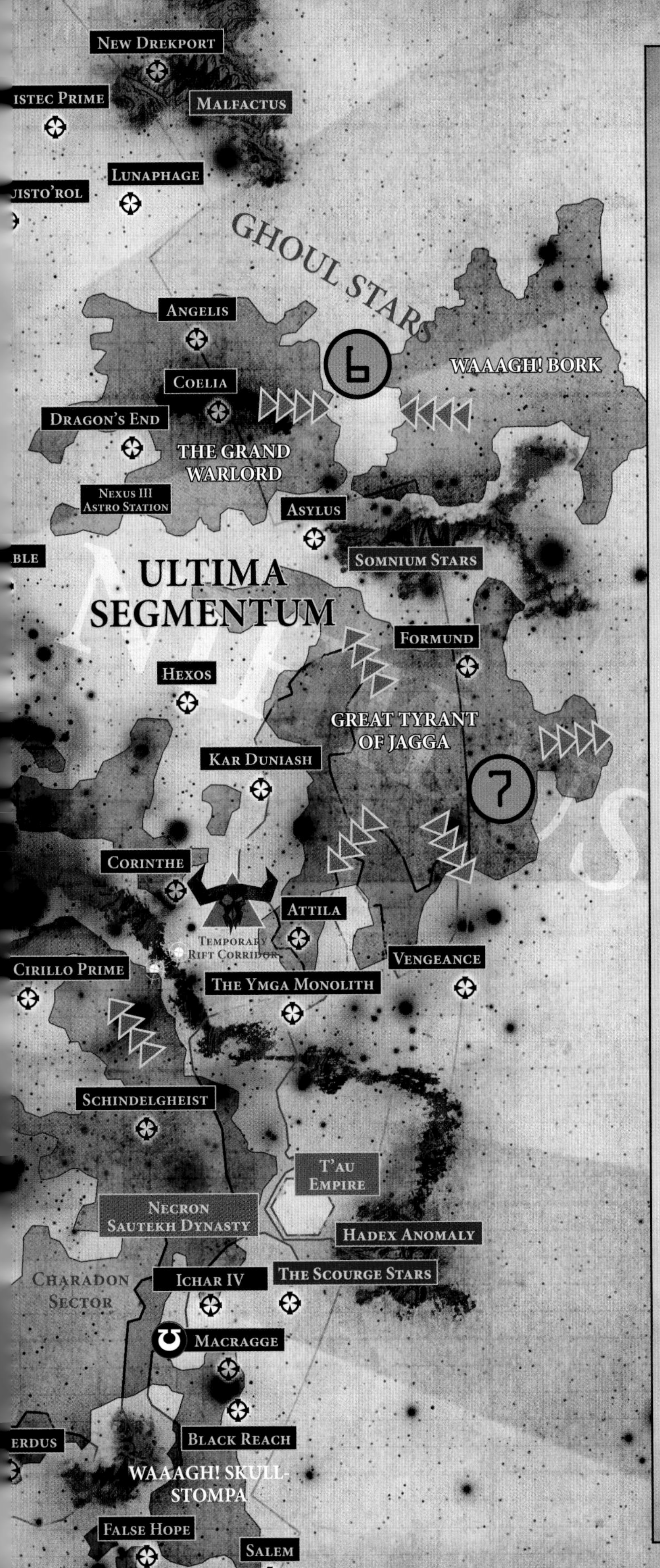

<<cf:// migrations/ invasions>>
<<dt:// expansionist trends>>

My Lady Inquisitor, as requested I have done my utmost to collate galactic data on greenskin movements. Even accepting potential inaccuracies due to warp dilation, bureaucratic error and a paucity of data from beyond the Cicatrix Maledictum, I think you will agree that the picture painted is a grim one. Let me say again, my lady, how wrong I was to doubt the scale of this threat...

1. As empyric anomalies spread through the Calixis and Scarus Sectors, the Great Despot of Dregruk has overthrown the Arch-Dictator of Gathrog. Unconfirmed reports suggest this ruler in turn has either joined forces with, or fallen to, Warlord Krooldakka, whose Speedwaaagh! has reached the crucial world of Vigilus.

2. Repeated rumours place Wazdakka Gutsmek at the head of a Waaagh! pushing alarmingly deep into the north of the Segmentum Solar. The Custodians of the Dread Host have been despatched to interdict this greenskin advance, which tells us much in and of itself.

3. The unbridled expansion of the Maelstrom will prove either the salvation or damnation of the forge world of Ryza. It has forced Waaagh! Urgok into an all-out attack as the worlds to the Orks' rear are swallowed up by ravening warp energies.

4. Bad Moons Warlord Nazdreg has been driven towards the galactic north by the opening of the Great Rift. Note the danger now posed to Valhalla, Goth and Alaric.

5. The Arch-Arsonist of Charadon has become one of the most dangerous Grand Warlords in the galaxy. His warbands maraud from Nocturne to Schindelgheist and beyond.

6. Vague tidings suggest that a self-proclaimed Grand Warlord has placed his greenskin hordes on a collision course with Waaagh! Bork. Perhaps this will give neighbouring Imperial worlds time to bolster their defences.

7. At least four separate Warlords now claim to be the Great Tyrant of Jagga. All are leading their Waaaghs! in different directions, to our great detriment.

Scrivener-penitentius Third Class
Allouicious Dunt +++

THE GREEN TIDE

The Orks have been a threat since before the earliest days of the Imperium, but the close of the 41st Millennium marks an unprecedented surge in greenskin activity. With Gork's Grin leering overhead to urge them on, and their enemies too deeply mired in their own wars to hold back the green tide, now is the hour of the Ork.

M15-M31 DA LOST AGE

A Time of Faded Mystery

The greenskins keep no histories save their oral traditions, and care nothing for questions of their origins save to say that Gork and Mork must have made the Brainboyz at some point so that the Brainboyz could, in turn, make the Ork race. Imperial scholars have gleaned little information about the greenskins' genesis, most of which comes from translated Aeldari texts that draw links between the Orks' creation and the fabled Old Ones.

Whatever the truth, it seems certain that some terrible catastrophe during this period deprives the greenskins of their leading caste and forces them into a crude and endlessly warlike cycle of existence. Certainly, those scattered records that survive from the Dark Age of Technology cite Orks as a tribal and rampaging xenos race, whose behaviours would be depressingly familiar to the Imperial commanders of the 41st Millennium.

Defeat on Ullanor

At the height of the Great Crusade, the Emperor of Mankind leads a vast army against the sector-spanning Ork empire of Ullanor, the largest concentration of greenskins yet encountered by Humanity. During the fighting, Primarch Horus Lupercal engages the fearsome Warlord Urlak Urruk, and successfully slays the enormous greenskin. With Urruk's death the coherency of the Ork defence collapses and their defeat is ensured.

M31-M32 DA AGE OF DA BEAST

A New Waaagh! Rising

An Ork Warlord known only as the Great Beast stirs greenskins into action across multiple Imperial sectors. Humanity is slow to react to this new threat, for they have enjoyed centuries of peace since the end of the Horus Heresy, and so the xenos press forwards on every front.

Destroyer Moons

As the Imperium struggles to hold back the Ork tide, the greenskins deploy vast attack moons. Planetoid-sized battle stations, these monstrous engines of void warfare wreak untold havoc amongst the human defenders, until at last one of them is seen hanging in the skies above Terra itself. When a crusade of faith is sent against it, the Imperial death toll is horrific, leaving the Orks in orbit above the cradle of Humanity.

Return to Ullanor

With Mankind on the verge of extinction, it seems that the Orks will surely claim dominion over the galaxy. Yet through the assemblage of the Imperium's greatest champions, the formation of the first ever Deathwatch Kill Teams, and the discovery that the greenskin invasions stem from the world of Ullanor Prime, the Imperium launches a last, desperate fight back. They meet the Great Beast and his monstrous lieutenants in a string of fierce battles that ultimately result in Imperial victory. The Orks are defeated again, their most formidable leaders in thousands of years slain and their strength scattered. Yet as always, they will return to bedevil the Imperium once more.

M33-M41 DA AGE OF WAR

Tuska the Daemon-killa

Great Boss Tuska acquires a taste for fighting Daemons and makes straight for the Eye of Terror, a Waaagh! of like-minded lunatics gathering around him as he goes. Waaagh! Tuska proceeds to rampage across Daemon worlds beyond counting, before finally the eye of Khorne, the Blood God, turns upon them. Though overrun and slain by never-ending hordes of Daemons, Tuska's followers are transported to Khorne's own realm, there to fight for all eternity, reborn with each blood-soaked dawn to make war against Khorne's greatest daemonic generals for the Lord of Battles' amusement.

Green Tide over Ultima

The Ultima Segmentum is punished by wave after wave of greenskin uprisings and invasions. Numerous outlying worlds are overrun, and only the tireless efforts of Marneus Calgar and his Ultramarines prevent far greater destruction from occurring.

Waaagh! Gazbag

Gazbag, a Speed Freek Warlord noted for his dogged determination if not his navigational skills, guides his Waaagh! towards a group of largely unprotected paradise worlds. The vengeful Asuryani of Craftworld Biel-Tan descend upon the invaders with destructive fury, yet find the Orks a numerous and deadly foe. Eventually the Aeldari are forced to withdraw, the flames of battle having reduced the paradise worlds' once verdant plains and jungles to smouldering ruins, providing Warlord Gazbag with a new empire to rule over.

The War of Dakka

Warlord Grog Ironteef leads a mighty Waaagh! against the burgeoning T'au Empire, gathering up all the dakka he can to counter the firepower of his more advanced foes.

Danger Overlooked

On the world of Hephastine, Rogue Trader Maximillian Trusk discovers archeotech weapons from the Dark Age of Technology. Staving off attacks by the world's greenskin tribes, Trusk prepares to transport his prize to his awaiting fleet. However, a strike force under Lord Inquisitor Shael appears in orbit, demanding Trusk surrender the proscribed archeotech. When the Rogue Trader – who by now is fighting off near constant attacks from an increasing number of Orks – refuses, Inquisitorial troops deploy to seize the weapons by force. As the fighting between the Rogue Trader's forces and Inquisitorial Storm Troopers escalates, Orks are increasingly drawn in, scavenging weapons and soon becoming a rampaging horde. Yet both human factions continue more or less to ignore the greenskins, more interested in pursuing their own vendetta. After more than three months of warfare, Shael launches an all-out offensive against Trusk's fortified dig site, and even as the bitter rivals lock blades, the jungle rings to the deafening battle cries of hundreds of thousands of Orks. From every direction, a tide of greenskins floods the compound, led by a vast Stompa that smashes its way through the defensive perimeter and charges headlong into the fight. Both Imperial forces are utterly annihilated, and the weapons over which they fought so hard are cannibalised for scrap.

Waaagh! Hruk
The noted Snakebite boss Hruk Teefsplinta enslaves the entire population of his old stomping grounds, the binary system Corva. He conquers the nine shrine worlds of Marlisanct and uses the Basilica Imperator Majoris as a breeding pen for his famously incontinent Squiggoths.

Hope's End
Earth caste engineers of the Ke'lshan Sept proudly reveal an immense new colony-seeding craft. This monolithic spacefaring vessel is named, in the T'au language, *Hope's Light*. On its maiden voyage, and with over three hundred thousand T'au colonists and warriors on board, *Hope's Light* is boarded by the Ork fleet of Megaboss Morkrog and lost with all hands. For the next decade, the Ke'lshan Sept faces brutal raids from Morkrog's vast new looted warship, *T'aukilla*.

Rise of the Weirdwaaagh!
Upon the backwater planet of Zurk, a Snakebite Weirdboy named Zogwort rises to prominence. Born amidst a nest of bloodvipers, Zogwort's blood seethes with their venom, just as his ragged clothes crawl with their hissing bodies. Yet it is Zogwort's peculiar ability to curse his enemies and transform them into puzzled-looking squigs that really inspires the ladz of his tribe to fall in line. After he 'squigs-up' his tribe's Warboss, Zogwort takes control and launches an unconventional Waaagh!. Replacing the ruling caste of Nobz with fellow Weirdboyz, and attracting Madboyz in their thousands to his banner, Zogwort's strange but undeniably potent horde conquers one planet after another, and shows no signs of slowing.

The Second War for Armageddon
The visionary Ork Warlord Ghazghkull Mag Uruk Thraka invades Armageddon at the head of a massive Waaagh!. Only the vast military experience and leadership of Commissar Yarrick prevents the world from falling to the greenskins within the first month of conflict. Space Marine reinforcements gradually turn the tide of the war, and Ghazghkull retreats to the Golgotha Sector to lick his wounds.

The Lost Waaagh!
The Ork Warlord Grizgutz, a noted kleptomaniac, launches his Waaagh! into the Morloq System. Whilst using warp travel in an attempt to reach the system, Grizgutz and his horde unwittingly move through time and emerge from the shifting chaos of the empyrean shortly before they set off. Grizgutz hunts down and kills his doppelganger, reasoning that this way he can have a spare of his favourite gun. The resultant confusion stops the Waaagh! in its tracks.

A New Weapon
Nazdreg, a Bad Moons Warlord noted for his wealth and flair, bullies his Meks into performing ever more progressive and bizarre experiments. Despite some nasty 'setbacks' ranging from spontaneous combustion to sporadic gravity reversal, Nazdreg's Meks perfect their tellyporta designs. The Warlord barters his new technology with Ghazghkull in exchange for an alliance.

Shyrrek's Folly
Archon Shyrrek of the Kabal of the Severed Hope seeks to turn the green hordes of Waaagh! Hammafist against the T'au Empire colony of Korvessa. Using hit and run attacks, Shyrrek's fleet lures the much larger Ork force towards the world, but in their arrogance they underestimate the greenskin forces completely. Using short-range tellyporta drives, a number of Warlord Hammafist's kroozers leapfrog the Drukhari, leaving them surrounded and cut off from escape into the webway dimension. Archon Shyrrek's forces fight with desperate fury to escape the tightening ring of ramshackle Ork vessels. However, their resistance comes to an inglorious end when Hammafist and his Meganob retinue tellyport on board Shyrrek's flagship and slice the outraged Archon to shreds with their roaring killsaws.

Waaagh! Snagrod
Snagrod, then Arch-Arsonist of Charadon, unites the Ork tribes of the Loki Sector. The nearby Imperial colony of Badlanding is destroyed despite a valiant defence at Krugerport. Intervention by the Crimson Fists Space Marines ensures that Snagrod's next target is the Adeptus Astartes planet of Rynn's World, where, after a titanic battle, the Crimson Fists' fortress monastery is atomised by a devastating explosion. The Orks are eventually driven off-world, but it is a hollow victory, for the once-proud Crimson Fists are reduced to a fragment of their former glory.

The March of Gork
A clanking horde of several hundred Gorkanauts sets out from the empire of Bork, beginning a destructive rampage that will become known as the March of Gork. From one world to the next, the lumbering machines smash everything in their path, the Meks building more Gorkanauts from every vehicle they destroy, until they are a nigh-unstoppable tide of rusting metal.

The Tide Rises Higher
Waaaghs! reach epidemic levels across the Imperium. The forces of the Adeptus Astartes and Imperial Guard, already under incredible pressure from a multitude of threats, find themselves stretched thinner still as they are forced to respond to one Ork invasion after another. Many cannot be stopped, and countless worlds are overrun by the swarming masses of belligerent greenskins.

The Third War for Armageddon
After five decades of planning and preparation, Ghazghkull returns to Armageddon at the head of an even greater Waaagh!, plunging the barely recovered Imperial world into another vast and bloody war. Yet after months of grinding conflict, the world has not fallen. As the Imperium commits reinforcements to War Zone Armageddon, countless waves of Orks flood to meet them and the war becomes a contest of grinding attrition with no end in sight.

M41 DA GREAT WAAAGH!

A Greater Purpose
Ghazghkull's visions become more frequent as his latest invasion of Armageddon drags on. They are now accompanied by blinding head pains and crackling green lights as Gork and Mork's roars of displeasure boom through Ghazghkull's mind. Leaving his

generals to direct the war, Ghazghkull retreats to his command ship, *Kill Wrecka*, to brood. The Warlord surrounds himself with a mob of Warpheads, hoping the deranged Ork mystics can help to interpret his visions. Yet it is Ghazghkull himself who is finally struck by inspiration. He realises that no other Ork has his ambition. For the rest of the greenskin race, a good fight like Armageddon is enough to satisfy their bloodlust, but Ghazghkull can see beyond this to something greater. Possessed by a sudden, manic energy, the Warlord orders *Kill Wrecka* to break orbit. Scraping together a ragtag flotilla from whatever Ork warships are nearby, Ghazghkull makes for the edge of the system. He has no idea what he is searching for, only that it is not on Armageddon.

A Deadly Pursuit

Ghazghkull's departure does not go unmarked. Deep space auger-stations identify *Kill Wrecka* moving out of the Armageddon System. High Command are notified, and both Commissar Yarrick and High Marshal Helbrecht of the Black Templars elect to give chase. These heroes of the Imperium depart Armageddon some days later, leading every warship that can be spared. The Imperium allowed Ghazghkull to escape once and it cost them dearly. Yarrick vows the same mistake will not be made again.

The Beast at Bay

Despite a sizeable head start, Ghazghkull is tracked unerringly by his pursuers. The faster, more efficient Imperial Navy warships catch the Ork fleet several weeks after leaving Armageddon. In a dead region of space known as the Haunted Gulf, Ghazghkull's ships turn at bay for a last, desperate charge into the teeth of the Imperial Navy's guns. The void comes alight with lance beams and blazing broadsides as the Ork ships thunder into the midst of their foes, yet they stand little chance. Though they cripple several Imperial cruisers, the greenskin vessels are torn apart one by one. Yarrick and Helbrecht prepare to board *Kill Wrecka* and ensure Ghazghkull's demise once and for all. Yet even as they ready their assault, the ship is engulfed in a blaze of green energy and disappears without a trace.

Ghazghkull's Great Task

Even as his fleet is torn apart, Ghazghkull stomps around his bridge bellowing orders. The Grand Warlord is incandescent with fury, possessed of a vision so powerful that green lightning arcs around him. Their brains overwhelmed by this sudden surge of energy, his entourage of Warpheads convulse as one and begin to howl and gibber madly. As the crackling energy that haloes Ghazghkull's skull lashes out to strike the Ork psykers, they are engulfed in green flames, their eyes bursting and skin sizzling. With ectoplasmic power gushing from their maws, the Warpheads speak as one, their combined voice the mighty roar of Gork and Mork that Ghazghkull has heard all these months. Every Ork within earshot falls to their knees in awe as the gods tell Ghazghkull that this is not his time to die. They tell him that the whole galaxy must echo to the battle cry of the Ork. They charge Ghazghkull with gathering a Waaagh! like no other, the Waaagh! of Gork and Mork themselves. To do this, he must defeat every other Warlord, bring every last greenskin under his sway, and unite them all in a crusade that will drown the stars in war. Ghazghkull must bring about this Great Waaagh!, and in so doing call forth Gork and Mork to lead the Boyz in a glorious battle that will last forever. Their message delivered, the Weirdboyz explode in ripe showers of wet viscera, and a tide of green energy rolls outwards from them, frying every system on Ghazghkull's ship and crippling his pursuers. *Kill Wrecka* is immediately hurled into warp space, emerging somewhere (and somewhen) else entirely.

Left in Ghazghkull's wake is a rapidly expanding spatial anomaly from which his pursuers are forced to flee in desperate haste. Within days it swells into a raging warp storm, which in turn joins with other cascading anomalies as the Great Rift tears its way across the galaxy.

Da Great Waaagh!

Kill Wrecka drops out of the warp into the sprawling territory controlled by the Warlord Urgok Da Slayer. Ghazghkull is revitalised, red eyes blazing with new purpose. *Kill Wrecka* makes straight for Urgok's mighty space fortress. Knowing his only advantage is surprise, Ghazghkull fires up his ship's tellyporta, transporting himself and a mob of his baddest Nobz in a roaring blast of light, directly into Urgok's throne room. Urgok looks on in horror as Ghazghkull tears through his bodyguards as though they were rowdy grots. Then, trampling over their mangled corpses with his shoota still smoking, Ghazghkull looms over his cowed rival and 'invites' him to join Da Great Waaagh!.

Most of Urgok's Boyz join the Waaagh! willingly. Those too slow to spot which way the wind is howling are quickly beaten into submission, or 'volunteer' to undergo the tender ministrations of Mad Dok Grotsnik. Within weeks, news of Ghazghkull's new Waaagh! spreads far and wide. The massive Warboss' legend reaches the ears of Orks hundreds of light years away, sparking the first stirring of a greenskin migration on a scale never seen before. With a whole new Waaagh! at his disposal and Urgok his personal toady, Ghazghkull turns his attention to the galactic southeast and the Ork empire of Octarius; If the whole galaxy is going to be engulfed in conflict, Gork and Mork will need a lot more greenskins for their Great Waaagh!. Besides, Ghazghkull has decided to show the Ork ruler of Octarius what a real Overfiend looks like…

M41 AGE OF DA ORK

Gork's Grin Widens

The Great Rift tears the Imperium in two. Renegade fleets, traitor warbands and ravening daemonic invasions bedevil worlds from one end of the galaxy to the other. War abounds like never before, and the greenskins are right in the thick of it. Weirdboyz are gripped by visions of the Ork gods. Gork's Grin chews up entire greenskin empires, spurring immense Waaaghs! that drive countless worlds to their knees. The remnants of shattered tribes form warp-twisted Freebooter warbands beyond counting, while Ork armadas plough into 'swirly fings' all along the boundaries of the Great Rift. Some are never seen again, of course, but many more are spat out of Gork's maw, straight into the best fights of their lives.

Great Expectorations

Old Zogwort's Weirdwaaagh! is swallowed up by the trailing edge of the Abhorraxis warp storm. Weeks later, Imperial Astropaths in the Morrowgrym System experience a foul vision of the Ork god Mork letting fly with a mucosally eruptive sneeze all over their capital world of Morrowgrym Prime. This is rapidly followed by the arrival of Weirdwaaagh! Zogwort, whose warships burst from the empyrean coated in glowing green ectoplasm. Supercharged by their deity's revolting blessings, Zogwort's hordes utterly annihilate Morrowgrym's defenders.

An Enticing Prize
Mad Dok Grotsnik leads a warband of Painboyz, Cyborks and specially modified Killa Kans in an attack upon an isolated strike cruiser of the Silver Templars Chapter. He seizes a number of Primaris Space Marines alive, though what the deranged Ork intends to do with his captives is best not imagined.

Everywhere at Once
Conflicting reports by Imperial strategos concerning the location of Ghazghkull cause consternation at the highest levels of the Munitorum. The Grand Warlord is documented to be within the empire of Octarius, leading vast greenskin armies against Tyranid and Imperial forces in that region, and yet he is simultaneously sighted at the sacking of Cantissa, upon the killing fields of Aurochtha in the Imperium Nihilus, and joining the fighting around the forge world of Ryza. Punitive executions decimate the command staff charged with tracking Ghazghkull's movements, even after it is formally observed that as the greenskins of the Great Waaagh! are using warp storms to 'navigate' the galaxy, extreme empyric time dilation may be to blame for the confusion.

Triumphant Return
After seven years of brutal warfare, and thanks partly to the arrival of several companies of the Rift Stalkers Chapter, the forces of the Imperium finally defeat their Chaos foes in the Bargheist Stars. A grand triumph is held, with parades and martial celebrations spreading glory across a dozen loyalist worlds. Yet at the celebrations' height, Warboss Grukk Face-rippa appears at the head of a brand new Waaagh!. His greenskins flood the planets of Tremendix and Aposia before the horrified Imperial defenders can rally their forces, and plunge the beleaguered Bargheist Stars back into bloody war.

Da Green Fist
A warp anomaly resembling an immense green fist closes around the traitor world of Eisenfel. Freebooter warbands gather in the void aboard their kill kroozers, hoping to watch Gork's fist crush 'da Chaos gitz'. Instead, they are dragged in by the anomaly's gravitic fluctuations and plunged into a war with the planet's renegade rulers. So begins a frantic and madcap conflict upon a world that is being slowly crushed into rubble and ruin.

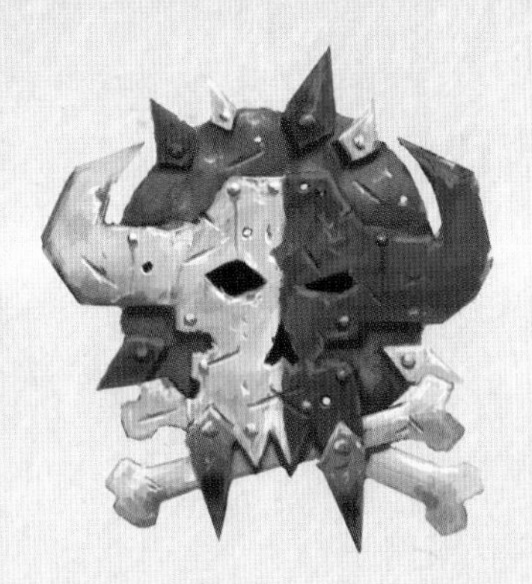

The Shootiest Boss
After a temporary parley with Badrukk's Freebooterz in the Trugruk System, Warlord Nazdreg turns his Waaagh! towards the Farsight Enclaves. The mighty Bad Moons war-leader has heard the tales of the War of Dakka, and is dead set on proving that his ladz are far shootier than 'sum shifty bunch of pirate gitz.' Besides which, Nazdreg has now heard of the Stormsurge artillery walker, and is intent on building one into a Stompa. Soon enough, Commander Farsight and his T'au followers find their worlds beset by this fresh new peril.

False Sanctuary
The Antonis Crusade gathers amidst the darkness of the Imperium Nihilus. After crushing the Orks of Antonis Delta into a mere fragment of their former might, the Imperial forces set forth to reclaim Antonis Enigma, Antonis Faraxis and Antonis Gemini. However, the arrival of several warbands of the Night Lords Traitor Legion sees the fighting go against the crusade. Falling back upon their safe haven of Antonis Delta, the crusade's leaders are horrified to find that tribe after tribe of resurgent Feral Orks have overrun their cities and strongpoints in the interim. Caught between the Heretic Astartes and Squiggoth-riding greenskin hordes, the Imperial forces are annihilated.

Rude Awakening
While attempting to loot the ancient treasures of a Necron tomb world, the Deathskulls of Waaagh! Zort trigger the planet's reanimation protocols. Canoptek constructs by the thousand surround the greenskin invaders, but far from being intimidated, the Deathskulls are delighted. Scavenging and stealing at will, the Orks cobble together hordes of Cyborks and Morkanauts, and ever-more improbable super-weapons, while using a hijacked Necron dolmen gate to ferry in wave upon wave of reinforcements. By the time Overlord Thanptek the Magnificent awakens to take command of his legions, he does so to the sight of a mob of leering Mekboyz standing over his sarcophagus, evil gleams in their eyes and revving power tools in their hands.

Vengeance for Rynn's World
Rejuvenated by a great influx of Primaris battle-brothers, the Crimson Fists declare a crusade of vengeance against the entire Ork race. Several Waaaghs! are diverted by their Warlords in the hopes of a truly apocalyptic punch-up.

Unlikely Saviours
The Imperial world of Jakhtor is on the verge of being overrun by Skull Knights Chaos Space Marines when a huge Blood Axe horde bursts from the warp and crushes the renegade force. The Orks then pull back to the fringes of the system. Surviving Imperial defenders are bemused, until they realise with dawning horror that their incoming reinforcements – called for by Astropaths almost a month earlier – will present the Orks with what they see as 'a proper scrap'. Desperate missives are fired out into the warp in the hopes of turning the reinforcement fleet aside, but with the empyrean churned to madness, they are lost. Just days later, a force of Space Wolves and Vostroyans arrive, and the Orks surge into battle once again.

Krooldakka's Onslaught
Warlord Krooldakka descends upon the Imperial world of Vigilus in the galactic north at the head of an enormous Speedwaaagh!. The planet's vast hivesprawls are protected by force fields, and its Imperial defenders drive off the initial greenskin assaults with comparative ease. Undeterred, the Orks build vast scrap cities in the desiccated wilds and engage in deadly races across the planet's dustbowl deserts. Word spreads of a world where Orks can find the best races, and fresh hordes flock to Vigilus by the week. So it is that, when the coming of the Great Rift collapses Vigilus' force fields, the subsequent greenskin invasions are catastrophically destructive.

Upon the world of T'ash'nuvar, the Fire caste of the T'au Empire attempted to purge the native Ork tribes in the name of settling and civilising the planet. What followed was a war of rising bloodshed and horror, in which the Goff hordes of Warboss Nurgbok overran one pacification contingent after another until the Fire caste were finally driven from the planet in disarray.

WARBOSSES

Ork Warbosses are the largest and most powerful of all the Orks in their tribe. Bloodthirsty and battle-hardened warriors, they are equipped with the best wargear that Meks can provide, and tower above the majority of greenskins. A Warboss achieves and maintains his position of power purely because of his size and prowess in the savage arts of war.

Though some Warbosses are cunning enough to plan a battle before the bullets start flying, it is on the front line that they truly excel. When the conflict is raging, these monstrous Orks give full rein to their battle-lust, charging into the ranks of the enemy and slaughtering everything in their path. The Warboss becomes a living embodiment of Orkdom, and commands respect and fear from all who behold him.

Particularly dominant Warbosses rise up to become Warlords. Army upon army will flock to the banner of a prominent Warlord, until he commands a horde of terrifying size. An Ork can rise to such exalted heights by showing no mercy in battle, as well as by brutally oppressing his lessers. Above all, greenskin leaders rise to the position of Warlord through a combination of bestial cunning, violence and deafeningly loud shouting, with intellect far from being a prerequisite for great power amongst the Ork race. In fact, many a Warboss is as thick as a bull grox, and will find subordinates to attend to the mundane tasks of battlefield organisation – such as knowing the whereabouts of the enemy and remembering to bring spare ammunition.

A Warboss is always intimidating in his war panoply, as a fierce appearance is essential when ruling with an iron fist. He will claim the lion's share of the spoils of war, even if it means strangling a few Deathskulls scavengers who have got to them first. Greenskin leaders often ride at the head of their armies, transported within clanking great battlewagons covered in personal glyphs and banners.

'Plan's dead simple, ladz. We go right up da middle, give 'em sum dakka on da way in, then get stuck in and give 'em sum boot-levva once we reach da trenches. Anyone don't like it, I'll kick yer teef in. Gottit?'

- Warboss Nurgok, noted Ork strategist

On the rare occasions that a Warboss is not asserting his status by breaking heads, he will hold court in a cavernous and foul-smelling hall, seated on a garish throne and surrounded by his Nobz and drinking cronies. Captured war banners hang above the Warboss' seat of power, each tattered and stained with the blood of those who once bore it into battle. It is from this lofty perch that the Warboss rules, glowering and yelling at his lackeys as he makes his grand plans of conquest and slaughter.

ORK TROPHIES

Orks judge the worth of a Warboss by the quantity and quality of the enemies he has overcome – and the martial trophies he has claimed from their corpses. These not only impress all who gaze upon them, but double up as handy blunt instruments with which to bludgeon anyone who draws the Warboss' ire.

Warbosses often adorn their thrones and trophy racks with the skulls of rival Orks, but as their reach extends beyond their original territories and into the stars, the Warboss has a far wider range of enemies to conquer. He will take great pleasure in twisting off the heads of his hardiest foes and displaying them for all to see, with Space Marine helmets especially occupying pride of place on a Warboss' trophy rack. To display the remains of the finest warriors of Humanity in this way is a great testament to a Warboss' prowess and right of leadership. Furthermore, Space Marine helmets come in a variety of bright colours that are irresistible to the more ostentatious of Warbosses.

NOBZ AND MEGANOBZ

Big, green and extremely mean, Nobz lord it over the rank-and-file Boyz. Whether riding to war in a smog-trailing Battlewagon, barrelling headlong into the enemy lines with choppas swinging, or clanking forwards in massive suits of mega armour, they are ferocious and resilient fighters whose assault can turn the tide of an entire battle.

NOBZ

The Orks call their ruling caste Nobz. Ork nobility is determined not by birth or a sparkly heirloom, but by sheer size and belligerence. Nobz delight in using their scarred fists and iron-shod boots to remind lesser greenskins of this fact.

Nobz often form a bodyguard for their Warboss, and should the Warboss fall, the largest of this entourage will take his place (after kicking in some heads to restore order, of course). Other Nobz prefer to lead mobs of Orks who they can boss around with impunity.

Arrogant in the extreme, Nobz revel in cruel and casual violence, delivering on-the-spot punishment to any lesser Ork, Gretchin or Snotling who annoys them. This punishment normally takes the form of a hefty whack on the head from a blunt instrument. Should the crime be a serious one, however – such as forgetting to bring the Nob's breakfast or reload his prized shoota – the blow will be administered with the business end of a choppa.

Alongside sheer body mass, decent weapons and armour are signs of high status amongst greenskins. No ordinary Ork is allowed to keep wargear better or more prestigious than that of his tribe's Nobz, and will quickly have such items 'confiscated'. As such, Nobz are usually equipped with a bewildering variety of killy stuff. All Nobz love to flaunt truly powerful guns, for example, and the richest can afford the much-feared kombi-weapons and kustom shootas: weapons capable of reducing everyone in their vicinity to bullet-riddled corpses or steaming piles of gore. Their tastes in melee weapons are equally as extravagant, with chain-bladed choppas and hydraulic power klaws being most popular of all.

MEGANOBZ

Ork veterans who value the thrill of close combat above all else often become Meganobz. They are characterised by their clanking suits of mega armour, and by a dogged belief in their own invulnerability.

A suit of mega armour comprises massive metal plates welded onto a piston-driven exoskeleton that boosts the wearer's strength to monstrous levels. Each suit of mega armour is individually 'tailored' by one of the tribe's Meks, who makes a great fuss of taking the customer's measurements before just hammering together whatever he has to hand. The end result is nevertheless a spectacular creation: a brutal suit bedecked with trophies and kill-markings, equipped with either the Meganobz' favourite shoota and a deadly set of limb-snipping shears, or a pair of roaring killsaws.

Mega armour is the ultimate status symbol. Meganobz see themselves as the elite warriors of the Ork tribe. Though other Ork Nobs sometimes mock their better-armoured brethren for going into battle with so much protective wargear, they do not do it within earshot, for a rampaging Meganob is an unstoppable opponent, and having an arm or two scissored or sawed off is a setback even for the toughest Nob.

On the field of battle, Meganobz form clanking mobs of heavily armed killing machines. Each Meganob weighs at least a ton, for unlike the armourers of the Imperium, the Ork Meks prefer quantity of material over quality. Though this slows the Meganobz' advance to the front line, the sheer impact of their combined charge is enough to crush most troops into a bloody paste.

While the Meganobz' immense bulk can be used to fearsome effect, it can also be a weakness. It is not uncommon to see a Meganob's comrades straining to get him back on his feet after a direct hit from enemy ordnance. Such is the resilience of greenskin engineering and physiology that the Ork in question will quickly be back in the fray, ready to wreak his bloody revenge.

PAINBOYZ

The chief passions of Painboyz, also known as Doks, are surgery and extreme dentistry. The latter is often carried out during the former, as the extracted teef pay for the exorbitant fees levelled at 'da kustomer'. Whilst the patient is safely strapped down, mouth wedged open and internal organs exposed, he is not really in a position to argue.

Painboyz learn their craft through a mixture of instinct, trial and error, and the time-honoured principles of 'Orky know-wotz'. Their greatest joy in life is 'eksperimentin', a mindset that creates a lot of common ground with Meks. Indeed, in many ways Painboyz are the Meks of the greenskin physique, in that they repair, maintain – and even improve upon – the Ork body itself. Woe betide those who seek treatment from a Painboy with spare time on his blood-slick hands; an Ork suffering from a nasty case of severed limb may risk employing a Dok to graft on a replacement, and end up with one of the local Mek's 'cuttin' edge' inventions. This can be distressing for the owner of, for instance, a Rutgot Mk II Exploding Leg, especially if it was his arm that needed the attention.

Indeed, Painboyz truly relish the implantation of the bioniks produced by Meks, and the professions occasionally work together to create Cyborks. These are unstable fusions of greenskin and machine, and range from Orks who have had damaged limbs replaced with whirring blades or tracks, to fully bionik Boyz who are more mechanism than Ork.

When his tribe is caught up in a Waaagh!, the battle raging and the wounded lying thick on the ground, a Painboy really comes into his own. This is a truly happy time for Doks. Never do they have a better opportunity to hone their skills, patching up the Orks in their care and giving them a quick shot from a rusty syringe to get them back into the fray. Needless to say, times of war are extremely lucrative for Painboyz; many only follow the richest Orks in battle, hoping their charges become grievously wounded enough to require their services.

Of course, Painboyz in battle aren't about to let the rest of the ladz have all the fun, and will cheerfully pile into the scrum of hand-to-hand combat. There they apply their anatomical knowledge, along with an array of surgical saws and blood-encrusted scalpels, to the task of vigorously dismembering the foe. Motorised separators are thrust into open wounds, tearing them wide and allowing the leering Painboyz to harvest choice 'squishy bits' from within their screaming victims. Fungal serums surge through the veins of luckless enemies until their blood congeals with spores. Clanking, syringe-festooned power klaws creak open and shut as the Painboyz fix their beady eyes upon hapless foes, kowing that soon enough their pneumatic blades will be slicing through flesh, bone and tendon. Grot orderlies descend upon the wounded, beady eyes and skinning tools glinting as they set to work. Anyone who has seen a Painboy wade through the enemy ranks and leave red ruin in his wake knows that Ork surgeons have little understanding of – and even less interest in – the notion of the sanctity of life.

These practitioners of indiscriminate surgery are never quite right in the head. They do not use anaesthetic, preferring to know that their patient is still alive and kicking. Painboyz burrow enthusiastically into their customers using oversized surgical implements; the sadistic glee with which they do so is particularly off-putting, especially for the patient. Still, such is the usefulness of the Painboy that such eccentricities are often overlooked, especially if the Warboss is the proud owner of a shiny new bionik limb.

BAD DOKS

The eccentricity of the Painboy is as nothing compared to that of a Bad Dok. These Orks are outcasts from their tribes, and are most often found practising their dubious arts within Freebooter warbands. Amongst such company, no questions are asked and a Bad Dok's past is his own business. Besides, Freebooterz are just mean and desperate enough to accept the surgical aid of any Oddboy who offers it, even if the risks are considerable.

Bad Doks practise deranged and disturbing surgeries upon their prey. Their patients can find themselves in possession of a set of mechanical lungs, sporting an extra head or limb, or even victims of the dreaded squig-brain transplant. Though Bad Doks never ask for payment, the price of seeking them out is high.

MEKANIAKS

Mekaniaks, also known as Mekboyz or Meks, are Orks with a natural gift for engineering. It is they who invent, build and maintain the machinery and weaponry of the greenskins, and for them, creating ever larger and more devastating engines of war to unleash upon the foe is an all-consuming obsession.

MEKS

Mekboyz are jovially imprecise craftsmen, content to weld, rivet and hammer away at chunks of scrap until they have patched together a chassis, gun barrel or bionik leg. As a result of this individualistic and unplanned approach, Ork technology develops in a ramshackle and exploratory way. This suits the Meks just fine, and the more inspired of their creations are just as deadly as the more aesthetically pleasing weapons created by the Aeldari or T'au.

Mekboyz are an essential part of every warband. Without Meks to keep the vehicles and spacecraft running, the greenskins would never be able mount a proper Waaagh!. Mobs of Burna Boyz and Lootas are often led by minor Mekboyz known as Spanners, whose talents keep the Orks' high-tech weapons working. Warbosses and Nobz who want a new wagon or weapon will go directly to a Mek and commission him to build it there and then. The result is never quite what the customer wanted, but is usually dead good anyway.

Meks like to take to the battlefield armed with their favourite invention. This is often an improbably complicated gun that crackles with barely harnessed power, such as a kustom mega-slugga, or else a howling killsaw more than capable of cutting the arm off a Space Marine in full armour.

BIG MEKS

Some Meks gain so much power that they slowly garner a following of acolytes, tread-heads and fellow Meks. These visionary Mekaniaks are known as Big Meks, and their mastery of Ork technology is second to none. Many wear hulking mega-armour of their own manufacture and wield weird wonder-weapons, and some even utilise force-field technology, protecting their creations with humming generators, or fashion teleport blastas that beam their victims – or at least their constituent parts – all over the battlefield and beyond.

The most infamous of all Mekboy weapons is the shokk attack gun, a bizarre device capable of opening holes in the very fabric of the material universe. This awesome power is used by Big Meks not to advance science or revolutionise travel, but to fire warp-crazed Snotlings into the enemy. Whirring up to speed, the gun carves out a short-lived shielded passage through the hellish dimension of the immaterium. With the tunnel's entrance created in front of the Big Mek, and the exit wherever he aims it, gleefully squealing swarms of specially accumulated Snotlings dash into the portal, expecting shiny rewards and food for their efforts. By the time they realise their mistake, the snots are scampering through a nightmarish passage lined with leering Daemons that drive them quite mad with terror. As the Big Mek does his best to place the exit hole in the exact location of the enemy forces, the resultant avalanche of screaming, clawing, defecating greenskins emerges not so much into the ranks of the foe as inside the foe themselves. There they obstruct vehicle workings, shred flesh and organs, trigger catastrophic meltdowns in plasma reactors, and create countless other hideous – and to the Big Mek, hilarious – consequences.

MEKBOY WORKSHOPS

All Mekboyz can perform battlefield repairs using no more than a weighty wrench-hammer, a sack of nails and a healthy dose of gumption, but most do their best work in the comfortably anarchic surrounds of their own workshop. The largest of these are sprawling fortress-factories stuffed with scrap, tools, chugging machineries and dozens of half-finished projects that the owner is 'still fiddlin' wiv'. Being industrious sorts, however, Meks are more than capable of cobbling together a small workspace from whatever is lying about, with rudimentary workshops often springing up from battlefield wreckage even while the bullets are still flying. Greenskin vehicles roar towards such teetering structures, their crews throwing sacks of teef at the resident Mek shortly before hollering impatiently. He and his grots get to work at once, hammering, welding and rewiring so that when the customers depart, they do so fully kustomised with snazzier guns, souped-up engines and extra armour plates.

WEIRDBOYZ

Weirdboyz are psychically powerful Orks who act as focal points for the energy subconsciously generated by their greenskin comrades, energy that binds them together with a common purpose. These Oddboyz resonate with the power of sheer Orkiness, and the more Orks there are nearby, the higher the charge held within their bodies.

Unfortunately, Weirdboyz struggle to control this build-up of psychic power. Even a close-run squig-eating contest between two rowdy Orks will cause waves of energy to pulse powerfully through any Weirdboy who strays near. Lights flash around his head, sparks fly from his eyes, and raw power starts to dribble from his mouth, nose and ears. Unless the Weirdboy finds some way to release this pent-up energy his head will explode, frequently detonating the heads of nearby Orks into the bargain. This can be highly inconvenient.

Any Weirdboy lucky enough to reach maturity will have learned how to release this power in controlled blasts. Though this makes the Weirdboy feel fantastic, it can cause a messy and untimely death for anyone in his vicinity. For this reason, Weirdboyz live in special huts away from the other Boyz, and are not allowed to wander about unless they are wearing warning bells and escorted by an entourage, which inevitably includes the strangest and most disturbed of all the greenskins in the tribe.

'Me brain's on fire! Feel da power of Gork and Mork you buncha gitz! Waaagh! Waaagh! Oh, zog me ladz, 'ang on, I fink I'm gunna… BLLLLEEEEERRRGGH!'

- Warphead Nurzag Wurrgit

When an Ork warband advances upon the enemy, there is much chanting, hurling of insults, stamping of feet, and bellowing of war cries. The surge of psychic energy generated by all of this behaviour resonates through a Weirdboy until, thrumming with power, he goes into a deep and terrifying battle-trance. His eyes pop and his limbs flail as he storms towards the enemy, Waaagh! energy crackling from his copper staff as the chanting increases in urgency and volume. When the surge reaches its excruciating peak, the Weirdboy will direct the resultant discharge to great effect. Crackling green energies blast enemies to pieces or stir the warlike nature of those greenskins nearby to a fever pitch. The Weirdboy can transport allies across the battlefield in an instant, or give voice to the terrifying roar of Mork himself. However the roiling Waaagh! energies are manifested, those Orks who accompany a Weirdboy to war are guaranteed a good show.

WARPHEADS

Warpheads are Weirdboyz who have survived enough battles for their minds to become totally saturated with psychic energy. Full of manic fervour and overconfidence, Warpheads recklessly plunge into the thickest fighting and discharge searing blasts of energy into the foe just for the hell of it.

Orks have severely addictive personalities that can swiftly lead them towards self-destructive tendencies. For Warpheads, this is expressed by a desire to experience the near-overwhelming build-up of Waaagh! energies as often as they can, riding the waves of annihilating power to the very brink before unleashing them in a spectacularly cathartic – and catastrophically obliterative – blast. Many Warpheads gather a following of like-minded Orks who are highly entertained by these destructive antics; these greenskins view the occasional case of exploding head as a small price to pay in order to watch Space Marines get stomped flat by giant green feet, Aeldari melted into glowing goo, and mobs catapulted into battle from thin air.

Most Warbosses will keep a Warphead or two about as living artillery pieces, or to restrict certain psychically potent enemies – such as the Aeldari – from 'tryin' funny stuff' during a battle. Other, more superstitious greenskin leaders – especially those of the Snakebites – even follow the Warpheads' ravings as sage strategic advice, believing their utterances to be sent from Gork and Mork themselves. Needless to say, this is a policy that meets with wildly varying levels of success.

BOYZ

Boyz are the rank and file of the Orks, with rank being the operative word. They go to battle in large, unruly mobs, and are usually led by a Nob who epitomises their skills – namely breaking skulls, kicking in teeth, blowing things up for the sake of it, and spraying dakka in all directions while bellowing in a loud, enthusiastic and semi-coherent fashion.

Tough, determined infantry, Boyz fall upon the enemy in a great howling tide of violence. Their battered and grubby armour usually consists of no more than a few scraps of flak jacket adorned with a shoulder or back plate bearing their insignia. Boyz place great pride in their weapons, though they are not above using their fists, claws and teeth when face-to-face with the enemy. They are generally armed with heavy solid-shot pistols known as sluggas and brutal-edged weapons called choppas. Though crude and varied in design, choppas are quite suitable for hacking off limbs and caving in skulls. When a large mob of Boyz armed with sluggas and choppas charge the foe, the mess they make of their enemies is quite terrifying.

Orks have a preference for crude, noisy weapons and find it difficult to believe a gun can inflict any real damage unless it makes a loud and terrifying noise. Those Boyz who have become addicted to the deafening roar of automatic weapons fire call themselves Shoota Boyz. These Orks form roving mobs that are continually on the lookout for something to kill, gleefully firing off ear-splitting fusillades of bullets whenever they see something moving up ahead. Though each Shoota Boy loves firing his sturdily constructed weapon, he often has more success when using his shoota to bash out the brains of his target.

Occasionally an Ork will manage to hang on to a heavy weapon that gives his mob some real anti-infantry or even anti-tank capability. The two favourites are the big shoota, beloved for its high rate of fire, and the trusty rokkit launcha. The larger the mob, the more likely they are to have these heavy weapon 'specialists' with them.

Some Boyz take to the field wearing scrap armour made up of thick plates of scavenged metal. These 'Ard Boyz are capable of enduring a greater degree of enemy fire and fending off lesser blows, and tend to look like walking magnets – although it is generally considered unwise to point this out.

'We don't fight fer food, or fer teef, or guns, or cos we'z told to fight. We fight cos we woz born to fight. And win.'

- Grukk, Ork Boy

BURNA BOYZ

Fire has an undeniable appeal to the greenskin race. The fascination with the ignoble art of setting things ablaze sometimes grows so profound in an Ork that he will find his way into the ranks of the Burna Boyz.

Dedicated arsonists all, Burna Boyz love nothing more than burning other people's stuff, and the owners into the bargain. The dual spectacle of leaping flame and frantically flailing victim is a thing of beauty to a Burna Boy, and they will seize any excuse to set someone on fire.

Burna Boyz are characterised by their welding masks and the long, stripped-down flamethrowers from which they take their name. These 'burnas' are able to spray great gouts of oily flame, and are linked to a sloshing tank of volatile promethium slung over the shoulder of the Burna Boy. A Burna Boy is given a wide berth on the field of battle, not only because of his acrid smell, but also because of the chance that a stray bullet will suddenly change him from cackling comrade to crackling conflagration.

No Warboss worth his teef would stand for the constant 'accidents' that accompany a mob of Burna Boyz without significant benefit, and so these pyro-addicts have to learn to adapt their behaviour to better serve Ork society. To this end, their burnas are modified with special nozzles and valves that allow the weapons to force out a fierce blue tongue of fire instead of a cloud of orange flame. This 'cuttin' flame' is powerful enough to slice through anything up to a metal bulkhead.

As a result, teams of Burna Boyz are invaluable during salvage operations and the creation of the larger Ork war machines, and will work under a Spanner's supervision for weeks on end to collect scrap for the Mekboy Workshops – just so long as they get plenty of metal to cut through and fungus beer to drink. When they march to war, they are accompanied by the same Spanners, who ensure the Burna Boyz do not get carried away and set light to the other Orks merely so they will 'do the burny dance'.

As with most Ork tools, the burna proves extremely useful in battle. When used as a flamethrower it is ideal for flushing out enemies hiding in ruined buildings and woods, especially when several Burna Boyz combine their firepower into a searing inferno. Drive-by immolations are equally a danger to those facing Burna Boyz, who delight in hanging off the sides of Trukks and Battlewagons as they race through the enemy lines, the Orks' weapons blanketing opponents with sheets of flames all the while. When facing heavily armoured opponents such as Space Marines, the Burna Boyz simply switch to their cuttin' flames, and use their burnas to slice apart the foe in melee. For this reason Burna Boyz are sometimes known as 'kan openers', and they prove invaluable upon the front line.

Sergeant Lassemer watched as the Ork tank crawled towards his men's position. The vehicle was burning, spewing smoke from where troopers Asmer and Shayl had put a lascannon blast through its hull. Its engine sounded to be on its last legs. Lassemer glanced at his squad, arrayed around him in textbook Mordian drill-formation. Their expressions were calm and confident. They held their lasguns at the ready.

'The moment that hatch opens up, give 'em a three-round volley, then switch to individual targeting,' ordered the sergeant. 'Let's do this quick and clean, gentlemen.'

The tank ground to a halt twenty yards from their line, and its huge boarding ramp – which jutted like a lantern jaw – slammed down. Orks bellowed, pounding out of the vehicle's smoke-filled interior. Lasguns flashed, once, twice, thrice. Shots found their mark, searing holes in green flesh and punching through rugged iron welding masks, yet to Lassemer's alarm only one of the Orks fell. The rest kept coming, lugging long-necked weapons with hissing pilot lights glowing at the ends of their barrels.

'Bring them down!' he barked, firing his laspistol. Yet the Orks weren't stopping. They barrelled forwards with maniacal enthusiasm, bellowing in excitement and shrugging off hit after hit. Lassemer's eyes widened as seven flamer muzzles were levelled at his squad.

'Emperor's bal—' The rest of his oath was lost amidst the guttural roaring of the Orks' weapons as they sent out a roiling wall of flame that consumed the Mordians. The last thing Sergeant Lassemer felt was white-hot agony before he was reduced to blackened ash.

LOOTAS

Lootas are the most heavily armed of all Orks, because they steal the best weapons from everyone else. They are light-fingered villains who will pinch anything that is not nailed down. Nothing is sacred to a mob of Lootas. Even a brief scuffle with a Loota over a stolen possession can lead to the previous owner finding that his lunch, his slugga and his gold teeth have also mysteriously gone missing. Many Lootas belong to the Deathskulls Clan who, being a dangerous band of grubby-fisted thieves, promote the kind of behaviours that Lootas epitomise.

A typical Loota has a very open-minded attitude regarding his possessions. If another Ork is skilled enough to steal from him, the Loota will not claim his possession back, at least not whilst the thief is still looking – it has been stolen fair and square. In turn, a Loota reacts to claims that he is a thief with a kind of offended innocence. The more cunning Lootas maintain that 'sharin' da welf' is an honourable and traditional part of Ork kultur. The other Orks maintain that the Lootas are a bunch of grasping, unscrupulous swine with no more concept of honour than a baked squig.

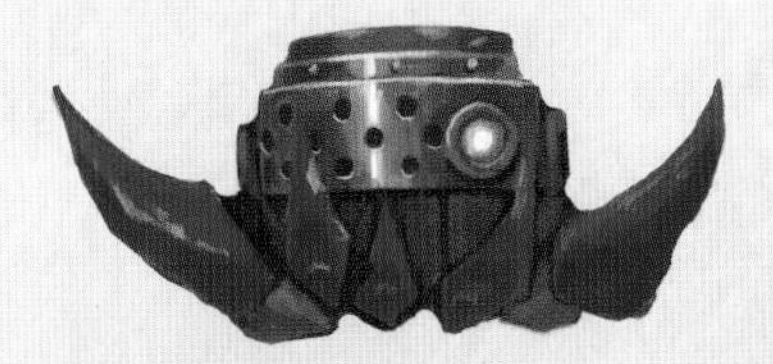

As a result of their constant quest to salvage, steal and stash anything they can lay their hands on, Lootas tend to be pretty well off by Orkish standards. They trade valuable 'shinies' in their hoard for progressively more powerful guns, forming the epicentre of a thriving arms trade that sees them befriend Meks and Spanners, who regard the Lootas as top-class customers and salvage workers.

Lootas use bribery and coercion as required in order to get their Mek comrades to build them one of the impressive shoulder-mounted weapons known as Deffguns. Each Deffgun is a fine example of the Mek's craft, cobbled together from heavy weaponry the Loota has salvaged. The Mek will make a series of 'adjustments' to the weapon during its construction, ranging from adding viewfinders and recoil compensators to cutting the weapon to pieces and rebuilding it from scratch. Spanners often accompany their Loota mates into battle, the better to see their creations in action. The exact nature and function of a Deffgun is always a bit of a lottery, but two things are always certain – it will deafen the owner and spell a violent death to anyone in its crosshairs.

When a mob of Lootas cuts loose, they do so in a pyrotechnic storm of bullets, rokkits and energy blasts that often surprises the Lootas themselves as much as their enemies. Ruins and undergrowth are blown apart in short order, and the infantry cowering behind them churned to blood-soaked pulp. Tanks shudder and grind to a halt under the relentless rain of impacts, hulls clanging and rattling as crews and systems are utterly perforated. Even aircraft can be torn from the skies by the raking fire of a Lootas mob, spiralling down to detonate in ferocious fireballs as though catastrophically swatted by the hand of Gork himself.

NARDRUK'S BLASTABOYZ

The Lootas mob known as Nardruk's Blastaboyz fight for Warboss Grubnutz of the Deathskulls, one of dozens of greenskin war-leaders currently invading the forge world of Ryza. Unscrupulous Spanner Nardruk has been known to take his tools to other Orks' equipment even while they are still using it, and has attracted a dubious gaggle of gits to fight at his side. The Blastaboyz think nothing of robbing both the enemy, whether living or dead, and fellow Orks in order to add more dakka to their monstrous deffguns. They are an insular bunch, unpopular amongst Grubnutz' tribe for their constant thievery. That said, few greenskins would challenge the Blastaboyz to their faces, lest they find the pins mysteriously stolen from their stikkbombs a moment before their explosive demise. Besides, once the bullets begin to fly and the Waaagh! energy starts flowing, there are few mobs more handy to have about in a fight. Daubed in lucky blue paint, feet braced and lips skinned back, the Blastaboyz level an endless hail of fire into the enemy, reaping such a fearsome tally that all previous indiscretions are quite forgotten by the rest of the tribe – at least until the next cache of shootas goes mysteriously missing, anyway.

TANKBUSTAS

Orks tend to fixate upon whatever they enjoy most, gathering together with others of a like mind and forming a specialist mob. The Tankbustas are a classic example of one of these subcultures. They are Ork Boyz who have experienced the undeniable thrill of scoring a direct hit upon an enemy tank and seeing the vehicle explode in flames.

If greenskins were given to musing upon such things, they might equate the rush felt by a successful Tankbusta to the elation felt by a Feral Ork who has managed to kill a rampaging Squiggoth or Megadon. An Ork finds something glorious in being able to boast about killing something twenty times his size. The victorious warrior becomes the focus of grudging admiration and envy from his fellows, a feeling to which a young Ork can easily become addicted. Just as a Feral Ork may take the talons, horns or skull from a great beast he has killed, a Tankbusta will invariably take a trophy from a vehicle he has destroyed and display it about his person. It is common for a Tankbusta to wear armour plates fashioned from pieces of a tank he has destroyed, sport nuts and cogs as crude jewellery, or to hammer rivets or bolts into his flesh as kill markings.

Rokkit launchas are the favoured weapons of these these anti-tank specialists, their range and destructive power making them ideally suited to the task. Some Tankbustas prefer to feel the shock waves from the explosions up close, using personalised methods of delivering munitions to the enemy. Tankhammers comprise a rokkit, or bundle thereof, strapped to the head of a big metal stick that can be swung into a tank's hull or an enemy's face. The resultant detonation tends to explosively incapacitate the tankhammer's wielder along with his luckless victim, but as is typical of Orks, Tankbustas never really think that far ahead. Bomb squigs, meanwhile, are trained to carry explosive payloads, bounding towards the nearest enemy vehicle before exploding messily, hopefully destroying their target in the process.

For close encounters, Tankbustas also carry heavy magnetic discs they call tankbusta bombs. These are attached to enemy vehicles with a great clang that heralds the detonation of the explosive charge inside. A whole mob using their tankbusta bombs on the same vehicle is almost certain to blow it to bits. This usually takes several Orks with it as shrapnel scythes through the air, but as the Tankbustas say, 'They knew da risks when they took da job'.

Not all of these self-proclaimed 'big-game huntas' have actually claimed their first tank kill. Aspirants tend to hang around more experienced Tankbustas, waiting for their own moment of glory. A Tankbusta who has succeeded in scoring his first confirmed kill of an enemy vehicle enjoys getting 'tanked up' after the battle, a ritual that involves devouring the wrecked tank's crew and drinking engine oil from the vehicle's smoking remains.

SQUIGS

Squigs are an integral part of the mobile and incredibly aggressive greenskin ecosystem. The squigs eat the refuse of the Orks (not to mention local plants, animals and quite often each other) and the Orks eat the squigs.

There are many forms of squig, and each variety incorporates many subtypes. Mekboyz squeeze viscous black lubricant from the snouts of oil squigs to keep gears and gubbinz working, and use porous sponge squigs to mop up flammable spills. Painboyz use medi-squigs to stitch wounds shut or suture limbs back in place. There are snackable squigs, parasite-hunting squigs, bag squigs, even rare and bizarre sets of musical squigpipes – whatever their biological quirks, all have their uses. The most enormous squigs are known as Squiggoths, and are ridden into battle by enterprising Orks who lash scrap-iron howdahs and field-guns to the belligerent monsters' backs.

Perhaps the most infamous squigs are the ravenous face-biters, which the Orks use in the same way humans might use attack dogs. Little more than a snapping, drooling mouth on legs, these attack squigs are a sign of status; many an Ork Warboss keeps a pet face-biter squig that dines upon those who have fallen out of favour with him. Other equally sharp-toothed squigs grow and breed in the sprawling cesspits of Ork settlements, lending an air of unpredictability and excitement to even the briefest trip to the drops.

TRUKKS

Many Boyz, especially those belonging to the Evil Sunz Clan, are addicted to speed. Being Orks, they are also addicted to smashing in heads, and ride to war in lightweight vehicles so that they can get to grips with the enemy as quickly as possible.

Trukks are built primarily for speed, and usually have little in the way of armour plating. A direct hit upon a Trukk can cause it to come apart in a clattering, cartwheeling pile of burning wreckage. Still, because Trukks are so light it is easy to bail out when they crash, and it is just as likely that incoming fire will merely smash apart some ablative wotsit that the driver only hammered into place so he could keep an eye on it.

Because Orks are so haphazardly inventive, no two Trukks ever look the same, though they typically have a large, loud engine and a flatbed enclosure. The vehicle's cab sometimes has a horned skull or jagged plate attached to it, a throwback to the old Ork practice of decorating their mounts with trophies. A Trukk is also fitted with rails and runners so that even the smallest vehicle can transport a mob of burly Boyz to the front line.

Orks will kustomise their Trukks in accordance with their clan's predilections. A Goff vehicle will be greasy and plain, with a large crew compartment and a heavy spiked wrecking ball for 'krumpin' enemy tanks. Evil Sunz Trukks almost always have turbo-charged engines and a red paint job, whereas the Snakebites decorate their vehicles to resemble their totem animals, and are not above patching them back together with old lengths of rope, squig-hide tarps and planks of wood. Deathskull Trukks tend to look suspiciously like hastily painted blue versions of those belonging to other clans, while Blood Axes daub their Trukks in garish camouflage patterns and have a habit of decking them out to look suspiciously Imperial (much as they might deny it). The most ostentatious are those used by the Bad Moons, which often sport squig-hide seats, deafening loudspeakers, smoking pipes and black and yellow flames along the bodywork. Meanwhile, the ragtag Trukks that carry Freebooter mobs into battle boast Jolly Ork glyphs, rusty hull-spikes and loot-hanging hooks in profusion. Some even mount rusted plank-and-winch arrangements that allow the rapacious greenskin pirates to pull alongside moving enemy vehicles and stage perilous, high-speed boarding actions. More than one packed troop-transport or lumbering battle tank has fallen foul of these deranged tactics, left blazing in the Freebooterz' wake as the Trukk roars away amidst the din of powerful engines and raucous space-shanties.

Some tribes make widespread use of Trukks to ferry greenskins into battle, fielding vast convoys that raise miles-wide dust trails in their wake. The impetus of these formations is terrifying; it is almost impossible to cause enough damage against such numerous, fast-moving armoured transports to halt the Ork assault before it connects. For every Trukk that comes apart in a shower of wreckage and greenskin corpses, another three swerve through the maelstrom of fire to crash into the enemy lines. Mob after mob of Orks barrel out of their blazing transports to bury the horrified foe, while those vehicles that have survived the reckless charge careen around the battlefield, guns blazing and crews whooping as they vent their fury on their overwhelmed opponents.

'Faster!' bellowed Grazbak, thumping his fist on the Trukk dashboard. 'Wossamatter Zaggit? Can't find the pedal? Krug's lot are beatin' us, ya useless grot-fondler!'

Zaggit shot Grazbak a manic look, eyes bulging behind his goggles, then stamped down with both feet on his oversized accelerator. The engine roared and the Trukk reared for a moment, the ladz in the back shouting in excitement and alarm. Then its front wheels slammed back down and it surged forwards at breakneck speed. Bullets, shells and las-blasts whipped around the Trukk as it hurtled towards the Imperial lines.

Krug's Trukk was still ahead of them, several of his ladz laughing and gesticulating rudely out the back as they neared the enemy's position. Grazbak howled in frustration, but the shout turned to one of surprise when Krug's Trukk vanished in a blinding white flash as a tank shell hit it square-on. Zaggit cursed and swerved as bits of Krug's vehicle rained down around them, and Grazbak laughed uproariously.

'That's wot ya get fer showin' off, eh Zaggit?' he roared. 'Now get us in there and let's get stompin'. WAAAGH!'

BATTLEWAGONS

Battlewagon is a catch-all term used by Orks to describe their tanks and heavy armoured transports. No two Battlewagons are ever precisely the same. However, most share certain distinguishing features that mean they fall broadly into one of a number of crude 'patterns' of Battlewagon that the Orks deploy to smash through the enemy lines, blast the foe to bits, and otherwise generally unleash mayhem.

The iron fists of the Ork warbands, Battlewagons fulfil many roles, but first amongst them is grinding the enemy into the ground. They are massive metal beasts that prowl through the greenskin hordes on great clanking treads. Some are mobile fortresses, packed to the gunnels with Ork warriors. Others bristle with ordnance and heavy weaponry.

Battlewagons are always large, heavily built and prestigious. These steel monsters belong to the most important and wealthy Orks. It is a rare Warboss indeed who does not own a Battlewagon or two, held at the ready for those occasions when he expects to encounter serious resistance or just fancies driving around his encampment, feeling important and shouting insults and orders at his underlings.

The Battlewagon is very sturdily armoured at its front, because that is the part the greenskins intend to ram into the enemy. These vehicles are often styled after the great beasts the Orks used to hunt in the wild, and frequently have an appropriate skull totem attached to their front. The Orks are convinced that this will make the vehicle fiercer and more effective in battle.

'They'z diggin' in up ahead ladz. Nargluk, get shootin' ya grot-brained git! Morgok, floor it and let's squash 'em into red paste! Waaagh!'

- Urglunk, Battlewagon Kommanda

Though Battlewagons vary tremendously in style, most are built with a certain battlefield role in mind. The Meks who build them delight in giving them grand and aggressive names, and – either through some quirk of racial memory or simply because Orks are not all that original – the most effective and widespread of these turn up time and time again in tribes all across the galaxy.

Assault vehicles such as the Gorespeeda, the Gutrippa and the Wheelz of Gork are the most common types of Battlewagons. Such contraptions are especially popular with the Evil Sunz and Goff Clans, though of course they find use amongst nearly all Ork warbands to one extent or another. They are geared towards taking large numbers of greenskins to the front line in the quickest possible time. Many Orks think of these

Battlewagons as great metallic Squiggoths, attaching sharpened tusks to the front and ensuring the vehicle growls gratifyingly when the engine is revved.

BONEBREAKAS

The Bonebreaka epitomises the popular subtype of Battlewagon known as Krushas. This family of wagons also includes such terrifying assault vehicles as the Bonecrusha, the Spleenrippa and the Gitmasher. The Bonebreaka combines armoured transport capabilities with an arsenal of heavy firepower and an enormous spiked deff rolla to create a versatile and enduringly popular Ork assault vehicle.

Often used to spearhead greenskin assaults, Bonebreakas lay down indiscriminate storms of fire from their lobbas and killcannons as they close with the enemy. Shells scream down, forcing infantry to dive for cover and blowing ragged holes in armoured vehicles and fortifications, with each fresh explosion raising a raucous cheer from the Bonebreaka's crew.

Yet it is when the Bonebreaka reaches the enemy lines that the real fun begins. As roaring Orks spill from its passenger compartment to charge into battle, the Bonebreaka rumbles right into the fight alongside them. Enemies vanish beneath the grinding spikes of the tank's deff rolla, with light vehicles, infantry and field artillery alike crushed to pulp. Bonebreakas plough red paths of ruin through the foe's lines, bursting from their rear covered in blood and viscera, the Ork crews cackling maniacally.

A lot of extra gubbinz and power are required to keep the deff rolla turning. This can make Bonebreakas somewhat prone to breaking down, but most crews are savvy enough to take preventative measures, perhaps dragging a dedicated grot rigger on-board to perform repairs mid-battle. Others reassure themselves by painting their vehicle with blue glyphs, hanging lucky squig's feet in the driver's cabin, or feeding captive grots and snots into the tank's workings so as to keep their Bonebreaka's belligerent beast-spirit satisfied.

GUNWAGONS

Gunwagons forego a substantial portion of their transport capability in order to mount artillery batteries' worth of big guns and many-barrelled wonder-weapons. Little more than armour-plated mobile arsenals, Gunwagons advance towards the enemy at a steady crawl, weapons hammering ceaselessly. Ensconced within their armoured cabins, the tanks' spotters peer through kustom lookin'-tubes and tele-gubbinz, calling out fresh targets to their gun crews with each passing moment. Explosions blossom amidst the enemy lines as the Gunwagons maintain their bombardment, what their gunners lack in accuracy more than made up for in sheer weight of fire.

The only real drawback to stuffing a wagon so full of ammunition and power cells is that – should the foe manage to inflict sufficient damage – it will detonate with jaw-dropping violence. Orks being Orks, this is seen as less of a drawback and more as a golden opportunity to 'take a few of da gitz wiv ya' by roaring into the enemy's midst before the Gunwagon explodes.

BLITZ BRIGADES

Orks have their own rough and ready approximations of the armoured formations fielded by other races. Known as Blitz Brigades, these spearheads consist of as many Battlewagons as can be massed together, crammed full of jubilant Orks and sent hurtling towards the enemy lines.

With formation names such as Gork's Green Fist, Killkrusha Brigade and Narmek's Treadz of Deff, Blitz Brigades are typically the pride and joy of the Meks who put them together and the Warbosses who order them into battle, and as the greenskin tank formations rumble into the fight, it is easy to see why. Treads and wheels churn up sprays of mud and gore as they grind over the screaming foe. Primitive glyphs and ragged banners display their allegiance and proclaim the might of those Ork leaders whose will they serve. Goffik rokk and feral battle-cries boom from their crude speakers, even as their guns thunder again and again. Howling mobs of Orks cling to their hulls and cram their troop compartments, the passengers' frenzied war chants rising to the war-torn skies. To see such a convoy of armour-clad death bearing down upon your lines is to know stark terror, which only redoubles as the Blitz Brigade ploughs through the fire levelled at it and slams into combat with a deafening crash.

Blitz Brigades are especially popular with the militarily minded Blood Axes and the speed-crazed Evil Sunz, though of course every clan makes use of such formations, and even Freebooter warbands can sometimes acquire enough wagons to roar into battle in style. Blitz Brigades vary wildly in size, from a few Battlewagons formed into an armoured fist, to rumbling nomadic tank-armies so vast that they raise fierce dust-storms in their wake.

Many Blitz Brigades boast outriders and supporting assets that add to their armoured might and strategic versatility. Trukks and assorted buggies roar alongside the larger Battlewagons, providing additional infantry or firepower as required. Skwadrons of Deffkoptas whirr through the air ahead of the Blitz Brigade's advance, scouting out enemy positions before returning to direct their ground-based brethren to the fight. Warbiker mobs serve a similar purpose, forming a vanguard force that can streak ahead or race back to aid the heavy tanks as required. Some Blitz Brigades are even spearheaded by super-heavy war engines; in such cases, monstrous and mobile battle fortresses such as the Skullhamma or Killbursta thunder along in the midst of the more conventionally sized wagons, unleashing enough firepower to reduce even the most determined defences to a smoking mountain of ruins and corpses.

WARBIKES AND DEFFKOPTAS

The Ork love of speed is nothing short of obsession. Many greenskins will take any excuse to hop aboard an overcharged and over-gunned Warbike or Deffkopta and go tearing off towards the enemy lines. Whether part of a larger Kult of Speed warband or acting as outriders for their foot-slogging brethren, these velocity-addicted maniacs run rings around the foe.

WARBIKES

An Ork warbike is far more than just a vehicle to its owner. A Warbiker treats his personalised steed with real care, because it is not only a thing of great prestige but also a direct conduit to the adrenalin-rich thrill of speed. Nothing short of dive-bombing the foe in a Blitza-bommer can compare to the raw excitement of hurtling towards the enemy on a bike with all guns blazing. This is why so many Speed Freeks and Evil Sunz are Warbikers.

The warbike is a single-seater attack bike armed with dakkaguns – massive, rapid-firing armaments that spray ragged bursts of armour-piercing shells with every pull of the trigger. Of course, fixing such devastating weaponry onto a bike poses a few problems, not least of which is the tendency for the vehicle to buck and spin wildly out of control when the guns are fired. The Orks find that this only adds to the appeal of the bike, making it more exciting to ride. Indeed, Warbikers are so reckless that they will even let go of the handlebars when careening into the enemy, better allowing them to lay about themselves with sluggas, choppas and improvised weapons.

Warbikers typically have a specific set to their features, especially after a really good battle. Their lips are drawn back in an ecstatic toothy grin, and their bloodshot and unfocused eyes are opened frighteningly wide. They often seem to shake for a good hour or two after leaving the saddle, for suspension is unheard of in Ork vehicles. Even in times of relative peace, Warbikers have a tendency to let loose the occasional whoop or cackle as they relive their glorious charges into the ranks of the foe.

Warbikers function as outriders and shock troops for the main horde. The pall of exhaust fumes thrown up by their vehicles helps obscure their advance, giving them a measure of protection from enemy guns. Some Warbiker tribes have even been known to use controlled skids to communicate messages back to their fellows by sending up clouds of dust. The Flaming Skull tribe go one step further, and are allegedly able to synchronise the skids of their bikes so precisely that when enemy aircraft pass overhead, they are greeted by trails of oily smoke and dust that spell out:

'ZOG OFF'.

WAZDAKKA GUTSMEK

Wazdakka Gutsmek, creator of the fabled Bike of the Aporkalypse, is said to be the greatest Ork Warbiker of them all. Greenskin legend tells of how Wazdakka was accused of cheating when he won the Race of da Burnin' Wheelz, and of how he levelled his tribe's settlement with his dakkacannons in response before roaring off in disgust.

From that day forth, or so the stories go, he has roamed the stars as a deadly Warbiker for hire. It is said that what began as aimless wandering has taken on overtones of a holy pilgrimage. More Speed Freeks flock to Wazdakka's banner with every battle and race he wins. Many mad-eyed Speed Freeks claim that Wazdakka is the greatest Speedboss of them all – after all, not only do the stories paint him as phenomenally fighty, spectacularly shooty and ruinously rich, but he is also by far and away the fastest Ork around. The devotees of Gutsmek claim that he will lead a smoke-belching and unstoppable Waaagh! from one end of space to the other. This is Wazdakka's Speedwaaagh!, the Speedwaaagh! that inspired all the others, and the greatest race in the history of time.

Most Orks have heard of Wazdakka Gutsmek, for his legend has spread through the tribes from one Ork empire to the next. Few can claim truthfully to have seen him, but a legend persists amongst the Nobz and Warbosses of the Kult of Speed that if an Ork travels fast enough, he may spot Wazdakka up ahead, a hurtling figure upon the horizon who can be chased all the way to the best fights in the galaxy.

DEFFKOPTAS

Deffkoptas are the lunatic inventions of Meks obsessed with flight. Each Deffkopta is a single-seater attack craft that has a set of whirring rotors mounted above the pilot's head and a jet booster at the rear. The rotors hold the Deffkopta aloft as the booster sends it screaming across the battlefield in the general direction of the enemy, its underslung weapons spitting death.

There have been countless instances of Ork Meks trying to master flight, but only a tiny fraction of them have achieved anything more than a spectacularly entertaining disaster. Still, Orks have a cheerful try-again attitude to technology, and there is never a shortage of willing test pilots amongst the ranks of the Speed Freeks. The Deffkopta was the result of decades of experimentation. Truth be told, it has remained the subject of rather a lot of experimentation to this day.

If there can be said to be a typical role for the Deffkopta, it is as a reconnaissance vehicle. Deffkoptas range ahead of the rest of the warband, locating victims for their brethren to fall upon. Once they have found an enemy force they will, with a supreme effort, turn their 'koptas around and head back to gather reinforcements. It is common for these returning Deffkoptas to then lead a Speed Freeks contingent onto the battlefield, with the main body of the warband following their exhaust trails to the front lines.

The problem with Meks is that they never make the same machine twice. Ever since the first Deffkopta was pioneered, Meks have devised more and more cunning ways to turn it from bizarre conveyance to lethal weapon. Early Deffkoptas were equipped with twin big shootas, but as the Meks have had their way with the Deffkopta design, it is just as common to see drums of rokkits at the front.

'Wot's fasta than a warbuggy, more killy than a warbike, and flies through da air like a bird? I got no bleedin' idea, but I'm gonna find out.'

- Kog da Flymek, pioneer of the Deffkopta

Such is the reckless madness of the average Deffkopta pilot that these ramshackle flying machines are often flown straight into enemy infantry, noses lowered so that the vehicles' rotor wings can be used as horrifyingly brutal and spectacularly messy weapons. Such tactics spread terror (as well as severed body parts) throughout the foe's ranks; it is a rare warrior indeed who can hold their nerve after an extremely low-flying Ork Deffkopta has lopped the head off their leader with its spinning blades, while the Speed Freek behind the controls laughs uproariously.

The main advantage of the Deffkopta over the warbike is that it can traverse absolutely any terrain. Though warbikes can attain great speeds over rolling plains, the only limit to the Deffkopta's theoretical velocity is the nerve of the Ork in the driving seat. As the pilot has to have a few screws loose to consider climbing into such a vehicle in the first place, this means that squadrons of Deffkoptas often pass their comrades in a kind of oily blur, their pilots howling in glee as they carve a path through the skies before slamming into the ranks of the foe.

Zodbrag clung, white-knuckled, to the controls of his Deffkopta. Jet acceleration pressed him back into his seat as he shot down the street between the ruined Imperial buildings. His vehicle's rotors thwopped noisily, the din blending with that of Nazrat and Gurzgrok's 'koptas to create a deafening cacophony that made Zodbrag laugh like a loon.

He saw an intersection ahead, criss-crossed by barricades. Imperial soldiers were crouched behind them, pouring fire into the Ork mobs trying to push up the street. Greenskin bodies were sprawled amidst the rubble.

Zodbrag gesticulated at the barricades, receiving toothy grins and thumbs-up gestures from Nazrat and Gurzgrok in response. Leaning over his controls, Zodbrag sent his 'kopta into a steep dive, his fellow Speed Freeks following close behind. Humie fire whipped around him, but the Imperials had spotted the threat far too late. Jinking madly through the hail of shots, Zodbrag squeezed his triggers and sent a volley of rokkits roaring down to explode amidst the foe. More detonations followed as his ladz added their own 'koptas' fire, and blew ragged holes in the enemy defences.

As he thrummed low over the blazing Imperial position, Zodbrag glanced back and saw mobs of Boyz surging forward, bellowing battle cries as they poured through the breach. That was more like it, he thought.

MEGATRAKK SCRAPJETS

Ork aircraft are the terror of the skies. Dakkajets hurtle through the clouds, blazing away madly at everything in their sights – be it friend, foe, or conveniently placed geographic feature – while bommers fly dangerously low over the battlefield as they look to deliver their devastating payloads. For all their brutal aggression and unbridled enthusiasm, however, many Ork Flyboyz lack a certain something in the fine art of not getting shot down.

Accordingly, after most battles Meks and enterprising Deathskulls can be seen securing the battered wrecks of numerous downed aircraft and hauling them away to be scrapped. Should the fuselage of such a craft be relatively intact, the more speed-crazed Meks will merrily weld onto it tracks, engines, guns and – ideally – the largest drill or cutting saw they can find. It is in this way that Megatrakk Scrapjets are made. It is considered unwise to point out that the wreck could simply have been rebuilt into another, functional aircraft – Meks do not like their work being called into question, and doing so is a quick route to a skull full of six-inch rivets, or else an involuntary ride in the 'test pilot's' chair.

Megatrakk Scrapjets are a favourite amongst Speed Freeks and grounded Flyboyz alike. They provide rocket-propelled acceleration, impressive firepower and the hilarious enjoyment of ramming through the enemy lines at the helm of what is essentially a giant, thrust-driven drill. Better yet, all this comes for substantially less teef than buying an actual Dakkajet. These vehicles further allow a downed Ork pilot to get back in the cockpit while simultaneously revelling in the half-remembered joys of mowing down the enemy at point-blank range. Of course, in some cases it was indulging in this very desire that caused the Flyboy to crash in the first place.

The array of weaponry welded, bolted and lashed onto Megatrakk Scrapjets is fearsome, allowing their drivers to perform ground-based strafing runs before slamming through any survivors with their nose drill screaming. Explosions blossom amidst the enemy lines as rokkits and wing-mounted missiles collide with their targets. Blood and viscera spray high into the air as squads of infantry are reduced to red pulp, and sparks fly as barricades and vehicle hulls are punched through with ease. All the while, grot tail-gunners strapped into the vehicles' rear-facing turrets blaze away with chattering big shootas, finishing off any shell-shocked victims – or at least making their corpses dance.

DROKK DA ROKKIT

The Blood Axe Ork known as Drokk da Rokkit was once one of his tribe's foremost Flyboyz. After one too many deck-hugging strafing runs in his prized Dakkajet, Drokk managed to rip the wings off his plane while chasing a group of Atillan Rough Riders down a narrow canyon. The spectacularly gory carnage that ensued as his hurtling fuselage ploughed through the luckless Imperial soldiers rekindled Drokk's love for butchering his enemies on the ground; the very next day, the Blood Axe spent every toof in his possession on having his wrecked plane kustomised by a Big Mek into a Megatrakk Scrapjet.

BOOMDAKKA SNAZZWAGONS

The roar of overcharged engines and the crackle of flames herald the arrival of the Boomdakka Snazzwagons. Lightly built speedsters based around looted vehicle frames, Snazzwagons are clad in hastily welded scrap armour. Their drivers go hell for leather, for they know that a single well-placed artillery shell is likely to blow their ride to smithereens. Of course, the enemy has to hit them first, and as the Snazzwagons fishtail and skid madly through hails of incoming fire, it quickly becomes apparent this is no mean feat!

Snazzwagon drivers race each other to the front lines, howling with glee as they pump their accelerators and coax ever more speed out of their jouncing, snarling rides. Meanwhile, their crew hang on for dear life, eyes wide with exhilaration as they prepare to unleash their vehicle's weaponry upon the foe.

Boomdakka Snazzwagons boast only a single primary armament. That said, the so-called Mek speshul is nothing to be sniffed at. Essentially an enormous gatling gun operated by a grinning lunatic, this cannon lays down howling hails of red-hot projectiles in a constant stream. Sawing storms of bullets precede the Snazzwagons into battle, shredding enemy infantry and chewing their armoured support vehicles to smoking scrap by dint of sheer weight of fire. Yet for all the carnage the Mek speshul can unleash, this is not the most feared weapon brought to bear by the Snazzwagon's crew.

There is a reason that these vehicles are popular with speed-crazed Burna Boyz, and that is the extensive cache of burna bottles crammed into every available nook and cranny of the Snazzwagon's ramshackle chassis. These simple and brutally effective weapons consist of a glass bottle – or occasionally a clay pot, in the case of Snakebite Snazzwagons – into which is poured volatile squig oil, filched promethium, and anything else the greenskins can think of that has a high probability of catching on fire.

Gangs of howling Burna Boyz cling to the Snazzwagons as they roar into battle, and as they speed through the enemy lines, these lunatics light their burna bottles and let fly. The resulting inferno is every bit as dangerous to the Snazzwagons as it is to their victims, but the sheer devastation such a drive-by-skorching can inflict on the foe – both in terms of casualties and morale – is more than worth a few exploding Snazzwagons. Even if it wasn't, the crew are usually having far too much fun to care about paltry concerns like getting cremated in a firestorm.

BIG PYRO

The deranged Deathskulls known as the Pyro-Mekaniaks are the hangers-on and toadies of the Snazzwagon-driving Mekboy Big Pyro. In their never-ending quest to attain pole position at the head of their mechanised warband's advance, they have achieved infamy for their apparent willingness to set everything around them – and occasionally themselves – on fire. Meanwhile, Big Pyro is diligent in keeping his Snazzwagon well stocked with burna bottles in preparation for the next fight.

KUSTOM BOOSTA-BLASTAS

LOCKJAW

The mangled Mekboy Lockjaw has oil running through his veins. Hailing from the world of Scalex VI, he was a crewman aboard a Great Gargant until it met an explosive demise beneath the guns of a Warlord Titan. The Gargant's destruction hurled Lockjaw through the air like a blazing comet, inadvertently fostering in him a passion for dangerous acceleration. Now, wired into his Boosta-blasta, Lockjaw mows down his victims and exults in the high-octane carnage.

The Kustom Boosta-blasta exemplifies everything that Speed Freeks look for in a vehicle. Ferociously fast, absurdly heavily armed, and boasting the capacity to set things on fire by simply overtaking them, this speedster is the favoured mount of those Meks for whom going fast and blowing things up has become the be-all and end-all. Such Mekaniaks are so obsessed with being in their vehicles that they may even build themselves into the chassis, essentially becoming particularly impressive centauroid Cyborks whose legs just happen to have been replaced by an entire warbuggy.

The main weapon of the Kustom Boosta-blasta is its enormous turret-mounted rivet gun. This fearsome tool-cannon launches heated rivets as long as a grown man's forearm, and does so at a truly impressive rate. Though not particularly accurate, the armament's weight of fire more than makes up for its imprecision, and with the heated rivets able to pierce through even power armour, this weapon has developed a dread reputation amongst those enemy forces who have encountered it.

Those fortunate enough to avoid the rivet kannon's fire should not consider themselves safe, for the Boosta-blasta is a swift and deadly buggy that has a vicious trick to play on enemies at point-blank range.

As the Boosta-blasta roars towards the enemy, its crew begin to chant 'Burn 'em up! Burn 'em up! Burn 'em up!'. Then, as the buggy roars past the foe at breakneck speed, the grot in the passenger seat pulls his fire-lever with an evil grin, causing the rows of exhausts lining the vehicle's flanks to project tongues of flame that engulf everything nearby. So do Kustom Boosta-blastas leave twin paths of flame in their wake as they hurtle across the battlefield, igniting ammo caches and fuel dumps in spectacularly explosive blasts. When an entire speed mob of these vehicles thunders through the enemy lines, they create a wide fiery trail that Speed Freeks refer to as 'da burnin' highway'.

The Kustom Boosta-blasta is seen in especially large numbers when the Evil Sunz go to battle, for it perfectly suits their way of war. Many of their warbands field multiple Boosta-blasta speed mobs that race across the battlefield amidst clouds of exhaust fumes, and spearhead massed charges by Evil Sunz Warbikers. Such mechanised forces steamroll everything before them amidst crashing gunfire and bestial roars of glee.

SHOKKJUMP DRAGSTAS

The Shokkjump Dragsta combines two of the foremost triumphs of the Mekaniak's art – recklessly fast speedsters and deranged weaponry. It is perhaps unsurprising that it has become the most popular form of transport amongst the Mekboyz of the Kult of Speed.

From a purely conventional point of view, the Shokkjump Dragsta is a formidably armoured fighting vehicle. Built tough enough to withstand incoming fire and high-speed crashes alike, the vehicle boasts a frankly suicidal capacity for acceleration in a straight line. Meanwhile, its rokkit launcha has the anti-armour punch to reduce vehicles of a commensurate weight class to blazing scrap, while the vehicle's vicious axle-saws are useful in scything the legs out from under enemy infantry.

For all this, the thing that makes the Shokkjump Dragsta truly terrifying is its incorporation of shokk-attack technology. Mounted on the vehicle's chassis – and augmented with a dedicated targeting squig – is a kustom shokk rifle. Eschewing the vicious reverse-snotectomies inflicted by the shokk attack gun, this weapon instead kills whatever falls under its sights by the simple expedient of opening micro-warp-rifts inside the victim.

The technology employed by the shokk rifle is used to far greater effect in the massive thrumming generator-assembly that gives the Shokkjump Dragsta its name and provides its most remarkable ability. By powering up the spinning drive apparatus at the Dragsta's rear, the crazed driver can punch a warp tunnel through reality, creating the entrance directly in front of his vehicle. He then roars through the resultant rift and bursts from the other end, having neatly bypassed any intervening enemies, defences and obstacles. Indeed, many an apparently impenetrable fortress has fallen to the sudden emergence of hurtling Shokkjump Dragstas within its walls.

'Nuffin' to it, just floor yer accelerator, drive straight at da fortress and hit da big green button. Let's face it, wevva da shokka works or not, yer goin' through dat wall!'
- Mekboy Sparknutz, something of an optimist

The Shokkjump Dragsta's capacity for winning races and fatally surprising friend and foe alike makes the vehicle extremely popular amongst greenskins of every stripe. And if repeated use of the shokker tends to send the driver a little odd? Well, most Orks would point out that Speed Freeks are not exactly the most stable individuals to begin with.

BOSS SHOKK

The Bad Moons Ork called Boss Shokk is a maniac with a mission. Inspired by (obsessed with might be a more accurate term) the legend of Wazdakka Gutsmek, Shokk seeks not only to catch up with this avatar of speed, but to leap ahead of him and thus win Wazdakka's Speedwaaagh!. To this end, he engages in constant races against friend and foe alike. Boss Shokk rarely leaves the seat of his Shokkjump Dragsta, except for when maintenance needs performing or an Grot Oiler needs strangling…

DEFFKILLA WARTRIKES

When Speed Freeks hurtle into battle, they are led by the fastest and killiest boss Orks around. Some of these prefer riding to war aboard a rumbling Battlewagon or Trukk with their entourage of burly Nobz around them, yet for the truly velocity-obsessed, nothing short of pole position will do. Such lunatic Speedbosses race into the fray aboard Deffkilla Wartrikes.

Fast-moving fighting platforms, Deffkilla Wartrikes make little concession to armoured protection for their riders. After all, what boss wants to be seen cowering behind slabs of scrap iron when he should be getting stuck in? Instead, Speedboss and driver both are exposed to the enemy, proving just how tough they are by braving incoming fire without so much as flinching.

The outsized boomstikks wielded by the Wartrike's crew should not be underestimated. Discharged at point-blank range, these stubby weapons kick like a Squiggoth, hit like a Trukk and can rip an armoured warrior in half with a single ragged blast. The deafening roar of boomstikks being fired is also deeply satisfying to any greenskins in earshot, for it bespeaks some serious dakka.

The main danger posed by the Deffkilla Wartrike comes from its monstrous passenger. An Ork Speedboss is a fearsome prospect at the best of times, but when mounted on the back of a hurtling trike, he becomes more terrifying still. With its outsized jet engine, the Deffkilla Wartrike can run down even the swiftest of prey, leaving behind a burning trail of flame that sets enemies ablaze. Wheel-scythes spinning, the trike rips a red path into the midst of the foe, where the bellowing Speedboss quickly gets krumpin'.

Sometimes a Wartrike simply ploughs headlong into the toughest-looking enemy formation its driver can see, at which point the Speedboss lays about himself with ferocious abandon. Warriors are hurled through the air like ragdolls, lifted from their feet and headbutted to death, or smashed into the floor by the enormous Ork's clubbing overhand blows. The Speedboss may even be overcome by the desire to give the enemy a good kicking, leaping down into their midst and going on the rampage before hopping back aboard his ride slathered in blood and guts.

In order to fight on the move without requiring the Wartrike to slow down, many Speedbosses go to battle equipped with the much-feared snagga klaw. This piston-powered battle-talon is every bit as vicious as a normal power klaw, but has the additional benefit of mounting a barbed grapnel attached to a cannon and several dozen feet of heavy iron chain. This allows the Speedboss to effectively harpoon victims as he zooms past, and either rip massive chunks out of them or – on a particularly good day – reel in his snagged victims and beat seven shades of squig-guts out of them at close quarters. Especially callous Speedbosses have been known to fire their snagga claws into choice victims and then 'ferget' to reel them in, leaving the target being chain-hauled helplessly across the battlefield at breakneck pace. It is an abuse that few foes can long survive.

Deffkilla Wartrikes are especially popular amongst Goffs and Evil Sunz. For the former, the appeal lies in getting to punch the enemy in the face as quickly as possible. The latter, meanwhile, prefer reaching the enemy as quickly as possible so as to punch them in the face. Such are the complex subtleties of greenskin kultur…

RUKKATRUKK SQUIGBUGGIES

The first Rukkatrukk Squigbuggies were invented by enterprising Snakebites in order to feed Speed Freeks on the move. Mobile pens full of edible squigs, the vehicles kept pace with the warband's Warbikers, buggies and Trukks while their grinning crews hawked their wares at the tops of their lungs. Once a suitable bag of teef was slung across to them by a hungry driver or passenger, choice squigs were loaded into the Rukkatrukk's squig launchas and fired into the hands – or even waiting gobs – of the hungry customers. Legend has it that it was only after a rabid attack squig was accidentally stuffed into the launcha and fired into a luckless Ork's face that the true potential of this mobile murder-menagerie was realised.

Nowadays, Rukkatrukk Squigbuggies are often seen muscling their way through their fellow Speed Freeks as they roar towards the front lines. Easily identified by their rugged construction, the throaty roar of their engines, and the anarchic masses of squigs and Orks riding aboard them, these vehicles employ close-range living artillery to wreak havoc amongst the enemy ranks.

Rukkatrukks typically mount both a squig launcha and a heavy squig launcha. The squig launcha is Ork-portable, often tossed between one crewman and another in order to quickly deliver the perfect squig into the middle of an enemy squad, bunker or transport as the Rukkatrukk rides past. By comparison, the heavy squig launcha is bolted securely to the Rukkatrukk's chassis, and is operated by the vehicle's leering gunner.

Though some Snakebite crews have been known to fire everything from buzzer-squig pots and bellow-lunged screech-squigs to the truly revolting – and panic-inducing – bowel-torrent squigs, three types of living ammunition are particular common: bitey squigs, bile squigs and boom squigs.

Bitey squigs include any squiggly beast with sufficient jaws, claws and stingers to savage the target and anything stood close by. Launched gnashing and snarling into the enemy, they latch onto the first thing they hit and do not stop chewing until they are bludgeoned, stomped or shot to death.

Bile squigs comprise any breed the crew can get hold of that squirt, spray or vomit harmful fluids. Typically launched by the handful, these disgusting creatures squeal and thrash while madly jetting acids, lubricants, poisons and flammable bio-slop in every direction. The foe are drenched in disgusting – and often harmful – slime, leading to much hilarity amongst the Rukkatrukk crew as their victims slip, skid, scream in pain, burst into flames, dissolve or worse.

The boom squig is infamous for its defence mechanism of violently exploding at the slightest provocation 'to warn off predators'. Typically triggered by direct physical contact or surprising loud noises – or sometimes even by its own bouts of indigestion – boom squigs detonate with such force that they kill or maim anything unlucky enough to be in the vicinity. Needless to say, these creatures not only make for excellent ammunition, but they are also dropped by the crew as living landmines, and are favourite props when it comes to greenskin practical jokes. Nothing provokes greater amusement amongst a Rukkatrukk crew than hiding a boom squig under their driver's seat, though this can prove inconvenient for everyone if it happens to trigger while the buggy is in full motion.

FLYBOYZ

It takes a special kind of Ork to strap himself into the pilot's seat of a ramshackle aircraft and hurtle into aerial combat – namely, a bonkers one! Renowned as frothing loons even amongst the Speed Freeks, these Ork aces scream through the skies at breathtaking velocities, and will cheerfully approach any target head-on – no matter how massive or dangerous.

DAKKAJETS

Streaking into battle through war-scorched skies, a Dakkajet's massive thruster leaves an oily contrail of black smoke in its wake while the plane's huge wing-mounted supa-shootas spit hails of bullets at the foe. Though not as nimble as the aircraft of some other races, Dakkajets are capable of an incredible turn of speed that makes them fearsome dogfighters. It also helps that Orks fly like complete lunatics, taking risks that Imperial pilots would see as pure insanity.

Dakkajet pilots are great believers in quantity over quality. As such, they ensure the Meks strap every gun available to the fuselages of their aircraft. In the heat of battle, while corkscrewing madly through formations of enemy aircraft, the Flyboyz cut loose with their full arsenal. They maintain that long, uncontrolled bursts are the best way to ensure the target goes down in a blazing ruin. Some Dakkajet pilots have even been known to smash out their cockpit glass with the butts of their sluggas in order to add their own pistol-fire to the barrage. This can have unforeseen and spectacular consequences for the pilots when attempted during void warfare.

Dakkajets fill the dual strategic niches of air-to-air dogfighters and air-to-ground assault craft, not least because their whooping pilots attack every target in sight with maniacal abandon. Armoured columns and infantry formations alike find themselves raked by furious firestorms as the Dakkajets hurtle low overhead, while enemy pilots feel panic building as jostling swarms of these ramshackle greenskin aircraft race towards them with absolutely no consideration for their own survival. Of particular note is the fearsome 'flyin 'eadbutt' favoured amongst the most deranged Flyboyz, who – unable to resist getting stuck-in at point-blank range – simply crank their throttles and soar headlong into their victims, bellowing Waaagh! all the way. Needless to say, the impact of several dozen tons of scrap metal, jet fuel and munitions moving at breackneck speed is enough to decapitate even an Imperial Titan on a good day, and a single such kamikaze manoeuvre has – on occasion – turned the course of an entire war.

BLITZA-BOMMERS

Even on their best day, the average Ork Flyboy has little patience for trajectories, payload arcs, and all the other 'borin' bits' involved in high-altitude bombing. Blitza-bommer pilots instead ensure that their massively unsubtle boom bombs land more or less on target by simply dropping them from point-blank range.

A Blitza-bommer pilot will throw their craft into a screaming nose-dive, their terrified grot crewman pulling the bomb-release lever at the last possible moment. After a loud clank and some alarming juddering, the payload plunges groundwards and explodes with a thunderous bang. Meanwhile, with his bomb away, the cackling Flyboy (hopefully) pulls up. Such manoeuvres do not always end well, and most grots have to be forcibly nailed into their bombardier's nests to avoid them bailing out before take-off.

That said, when a boom bomb does score a direct hit, the resultant carnage is more than worth the risks. These humongous explosives reduce fortifications to blazing rubble, turn tanks into craters, and generally rip enormous holes in the enemy lines for the foot-slogging Orks to pour through.

BURNA-BOMMERS

Burna-bommers are an inevitable by-product of the Orks' love for speed, fire, and the desire to combine these things while killing something. Strapped with as many incendiary bombs and rockets as is physically feasible, Burna-bommers streak low over the battlefield, raining conflagrant death upon enemy infantry. The wild-eyed Burna Boy pilots of these craft like to watch their targets burn 'up close an' crispy'. As such, they regularly return to base with their vehicle's undercarriage streaked with gore and scorch marks.

Burna-bommers sometimes carry skorcha missiles, 'fire and ferget' armaments that render them even more deadly. These corkscrewing warheads make a mockery of fortifications, exploding in pyrotechnic showers that drive their victims from cover, or else cook them alive within defences turned into deathtraps.

WAZBOM BLASTAJETS

When the blocky silhouettes of the Wazbom Blastajets fill the skies, any sane enemy knows to run for cover. Kustom-built airborne death-machines bristling with humming force fields and crackling madcap weaponry, Wazbom Blastajets are ferociously shooty and surprisingly resilient to incoming fire. They are built by demented Mekboy pilots who – fed up with seeing the Flyboyz having all the fun – build all the best scrap and kunnin' inventions into their own personal aircraft.

Wazbom pilots compete to see whose personalised creation can blow up the most targets the fastest, and in the most hilariously spectacular of ways. The Meks thoroughly enjoy such contests, for not only are they entertaining, but every successful kill ensures more scrap to be looted at the battle's end. The experience is somewhat less entertaining for the enemy, of course, who find themselves subjected to aerial bombardment by a bewildering array of lethal weaponry. Kustom mega-kannons spit searing streams of raw energy into the foe, blasting them to atoms, while underslung smasha guns snatch up their targets in localised force fields and squash them like a grot's skull under a Runtherd's boot. Some Blastajets mount tellyport mega-blastas, whose shimmering beams grab their victims and hurl them through the warp to either rematerialise high in the air, fatally emerge inside solid objects, or be torn apart and distributed liberally over a wide area. Meanwhile, return fire rattles from the Blastajets' thick armour or rebounds from the wobbling force-field bubbles they project.

FAMOUS FLYBOYZ

From one end of the galaxy to the other, deranged Ork Flyboyz hurtle into battle with the sole intent of creating as much high-speed carnage as they can. Many fly solo, giving themselves overblown names such as Kaptin Killwingz, Da Black Barun or Flyboss Dakkafrag in order to strike terror into their enemies and impress their peers. Others form entire skwadrons of ace Flyboyz and set out on sortie after madcap sortie, their legends growing with each retelling.

Amongst the most infamous of these aerial murder-mobs is the Deff Skwadron. Led by Flyboss Kommanda Uzgob, the Deff Skwadron is one of the most iconic formations of Ork Flyboyz in recent memory. Surviving dozens of sorties in the bloody war between Warbosses Badthug and Grimlug, Uzgob's airborne loons have been responsible for the deployment of the 'gantbuster bomb in Scrap Alley, the sinking of Warboss Grimlug's battleship – the imaginatively named Grimlug – and the aerial deployment of over five thousand angry squigs into Grimlug's main encampment.

There are many other famed skwadrons, of course. The Deathskulls aces known as the Blue Bommaz have been the terror of friend and foe alike above the jungles of Armageddon for three years now, their Blitza-bommer wings screaming down to scrape the canopy with every suicidal attack run. Madblag's Fireskull Flyaz are a band of gun-happy Evil Sunz pilots whose aerial races have been known to literally set the skies above Ryza on fire for miles in every direction. Meanwhile, the Imperial Knights of Q'unelen II learned to fear the short-lived but deadly Goff Flyboyz known simply as Da Nuttaz, whose repeated flying headbutts took a shocking toll on the ancient war engines of that world.

MEK GUNZ

Though no self-respecting Ork would ever admit it, there is undeniable strategic value to supporting close-quarters assaults with heavy ranged firepower. Batteries of grot-crewed Mek Gunz fill this role within many warbands, the enemy quickly learning that their ramshackle appearance belies the ability to rain ferocious salvoes of firepower down on all in their sights.

Orks tend to drag Mek Gunz to the battlefield behind speeding wagons before cutting them loose and leaving them in untidy heaps for the grots to sort out. The terrified gaggle of Gretchin 'krew' rarely know what each gun will do until they pull the firing lever and witness the destruction they wreak upon the enemy – or occasionally upon themselves.

Some Runtherds use the threat of serving in a Mek Gunz battery to instil discipline in their grot mobs, with rebellious or lazy runts being sent to 'shoot da gunz'. Should the miserable grot krews survive for long they will soon become deafened and have to resort to a rudimentary system of sign language. This is rarely successful, as there are only so many signs a grot can carry around with him.

Countless weird Mek Gunz have been fielded by greenskin warbands over the millennia, from shock-wave projecting pulsa rokkits and chain-and-shell-firing hopsplat guns, to the crude but effective squig catapult. Yet several types of Mek Gun are seen again and again. Most common are kustom mega-kannons, bulky energy weapons powered by crackling batteries, thrumming capacitors, and whirly gubbinz galore. Charged until their needles are dancing in the red, mega-kannons unleash raw power that annihilates everything caught in the blast.

Rather more unusual is the bizarre force-field projector known as the bubblechukka. This peculiar weapon generates clusters of energised spheres that vary wildly in size and solidity, and are sent drifting across the battlefield to rain down upon enemy positions. Some are as big as wrecking balls, yet impact with the force of a backhand slap, while others look no larger or more fearsome than a soap bubble yet hit hard enough to flip a Chimera onto its roof.

Force fields also feature in the operation of the smasha gun, which traps its target in a localised energy barrier, hoists them into the air, and then – if the gun keeps working long enough and the polarity does not catastrophically reverse – crushes them like a massive invisible fist. The traktor kannon, meanwhile, fires its thrumming energies far further, and is often used as an anti-aircraft weapon. Targets caught in its beam are reeled in and smashed against the ground with killing force, at least on those occasions that the kannon does not inadvertently get pulled skywards instead, its shrieking crew still clinging to it as it sails through the air to detonate some distance away.

ORKY KNOW-WOTZ

Although Orks rarely find applications for them beyond the battlefield, many greenskin technologies are surprisingly advanced. A warband benefiting from the services of a Big Mek or two are likely to find themselves with access to energy weapons, mass transportation beams and all manner of other strange devices. A good proportion of these are too bulky to be mounted on anything smaller than a spacecraft or super-heavy war engine, yet still they remain popular inventions that can play a significant role in battle.

The force fields deployed by Mekaniaks have frustrated the efforts of many an Imperial gun-line, and can be used in both offensive and defensive capacities – either trapping, crushing or hurling the foe, or deflecting and dissipating incoming fire. Teleportation is another area in which Orky know-wotz proves remarkably effective. Greenskins have been known to teleport even Titan-class war engines, such as Gargants, directly into the fray, as well as delighting in beaming their enemies – or at least, constituent bits of them – all over the battlefield at every opportunity they get.

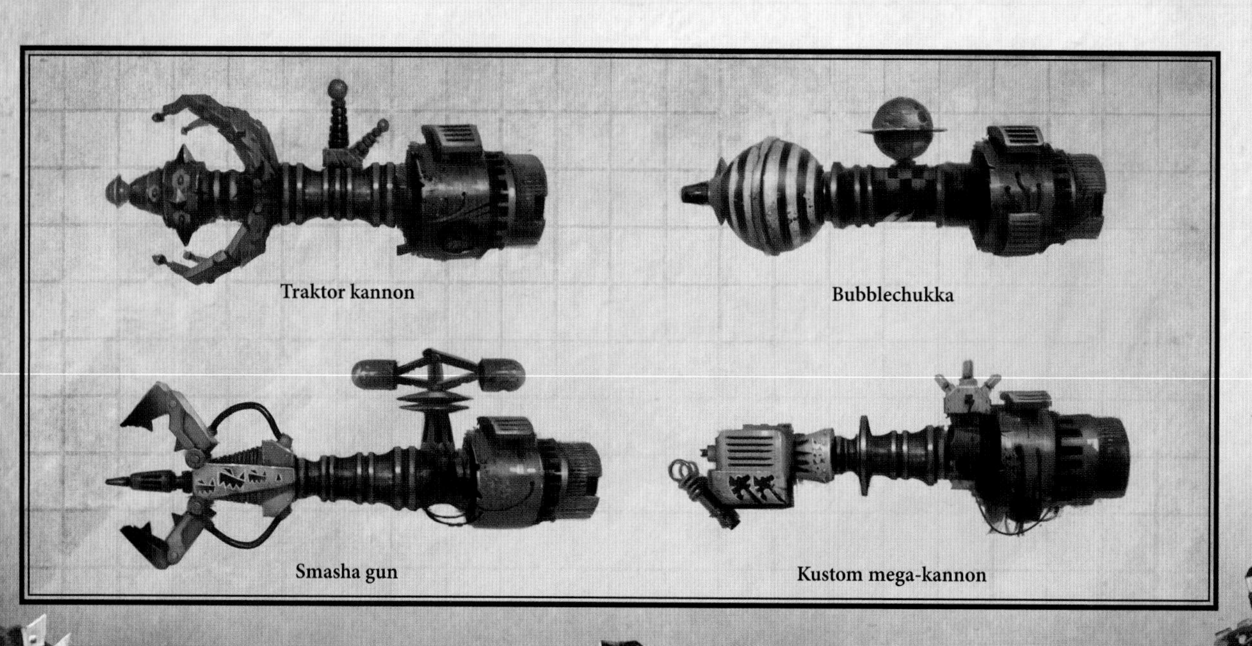

Traktor kannon

Bubblechukka

Smasha gun

Kustom mega-kannon

GRETCHIN AND RUNTHERDS

As the downtrodden underclass of greenskin society, Gretchin – or grots – get herded into battle whether they wish to be there or not. Though far from natural warriors, they are at least passable shots, and can prove surprisingly dangerous in large numbers. Coupled with their vicious streak, this makes Gretchin mobs more of an asset than they might first appear.

GRETCHIN

Gretchin mobs make up for their shocking lack of quality with sheer quantity. The natural cowardice and feeble-limbed incompetence of the Gretchin sub-species does not predispose them to the arts of war, and a typical grot would prefer to have his head buried in a sporehole than to actually participate in a proper battle. There do exist Gretchin with a little more backbone, though, and when emboldened by the possession of a gun of their own, these diminutive greenskins can be enlisted with promises of plunder or, when that fails, threats of a beating.

The short-ranged nature of the ramshackle weapons typically afforded to Gretchin mobs – rusted pistols, simple knives and occasionally blunderbusses – encourages them to get into the thick of the fighting. Gretchin are actually pretty decent marksmen, and were the Orks to allow them better firearms they might even pose a credible threat to the enemy. The sad reality, however, is that grot mobs rarely win any glory on the battlefield, as they are used by the Orks as a combination of cannon fodder, bullet shields, mine clearance devices and living carpets.

A mob of Gretchin is generally several-dozen strong, the grots bickering and shrieking as they scamper towards the foe. Some are savvy enough to recognise there is no point in trying to defy their Ork masters, acknowledging that their best chance of survival lies in showing willing; these grots are allowed to at least pick and choose where and who they fight on the battlefield. As for the rest of their kind, their reluctance to see frontline action is usually remedied by a swift boot up the backside from the nearest Runtherd.

RUNTHERDS

Runtherds are tough and leathery old Oddboyz with a strange predisposition towards the control and well-being of their tribe's grots. Far from seeing this as a chore, they relish their work, for theirs is an ancient and well respected Ork profession with the added perk that a snack is never far away.

Runtherds often cement their natural control over the lesser greenskins with a large spiked claw on a pole. Affectionately known as a grabba stikk, a deft Runtherd can catch a fleeing grot with the tool of his trade and hurl the offending runt into a nearby minefield with one fluid motion. Many Runtherds will have their local Mekboy carry out a snazzy upgrade on their stikk, modifying it into a crackling grot-prod that can be used to deliver a nasty jolt to squigs, runts and anything else in reach. Needless to say, these Oddboyz delight in the sight of enemy warriors doubled over in convulsions as high-voltage current runs through their bodies. Only once the foe is down for the count do the Runtherds release their voracious squig hounds to finish the job.

ZOGROD WORTSNAGGA

Zogrod Wortsnagga is one of the most infamous Runtherds in recent history, and a ruthless Freebooter possessed of a very specific – and frankly, slightly weird – set of skills. While still a yoof, Zogrod showed remarkable talent in the field of taking even the most timorous runt and turning them into a steely-eyed (albeit still weedy and often incontinent) killer. Wortsnagga soon got a bit of a reputation amongst the Snakebites of his tribe for his so-called 'kommando runts', who scurried into battle with something akin to actual bravery and could drag down surprisingly formidable targets. Zogrod's rise to prominence hit something of a snag when he became a bit too attached to his charges, and started losing his temper when seeing other Orks 'wastin' 'em'. Zogrod finally flipped at the Battle of Gimbli's Bunker, and fired a particularly wasteful Mekboy through the tunnel created by his own shokk attack gun; he and his precious runts were banished from the tribe as punishment. Zogrod has wandered the space-lanes ever since, hiring out his ferocious packs of kommando runts to any Warboss desperate or downright odd enough to pay.

KILLA KANS

A Killa Kan is outwardly similar to its larger cousin, the Deff Dread. They are both essentially giant metal canisters on piston-driven legs, sporting vicious weaponry such as powered shears, blood-encrusted buzz saws, and high-calibre ranged weapons. However, it is inside these walkers that the differences becomes more pronounced, for Killa Kans are piloted by grots rather than Orks.

Kans tend to operate in loose groups of two or three. This is because their pilots still retain a good degree of Gretchin cowardice, finding it hard to overcome their natural instincts even when hardwired into a ten-foot-tall killing machine. As a result they still believe in safety in numbers, and harbour none of the delusions of invincibility common to Deff Dreads. It is not unheard of for Killa Kans to become paralyzed with shell shock at the first sign of danger or waddle off in panic when the going gets tough, despite the fact their metal carapaces make them all but invulnerable to small arms fire.

Gretchin practically queue up for the chance to become a Killa Kan pilot. After a lifetime of menial tasks punctuated by casual violence, the idea of striding about in a hulking metal body and lording it over his Ork oppressors is irresistible to a grot. Nothing short of actually witnessing the horrific implantation process can deter a downtrodden runt from pursuing his destiny as a Kan pilot. Such is the competition that the more organised grot groups hold loosely regulated lotteries to determine who gets to be wired into the shiny new killing machine when a Mekboy has finished building a Killa Kan.

Once the grot pilot is in place, he will often wreak his revenge on those who have bullied him in the past, smashing into their residence in the night with a terrible shriek or stomping them into a bloody paste in front of their mates. The Meks and Painboyz responsible for the grot's 'upgrade' look upon these spectacles with a kind of paternal pride before leading the rogue Kan back to its pen. There it will stand dormant amongst its metal-clad brethren, emitting the odd snore until it is time to march to battle.

'Fink yer big, do ya? Fink yer bigger than Buggit, ya zoggin' gitz? Well yer not! NOT ANY MORE! Now Buggit's da big one, and he's gonna stomp ya good! WAAAGH!'

- 'Scrawny' Buggit, Killa Kan pilot

When that time comes, Killa Kans can wreak a terrifying degree of havoc amongst the foe. Years of repression and misery find their expression in an explosively gory rampage as the Kans are set loose upon the enemy lines.

They clank and waddle their way across no man's land, and as they go they let fly with an assortment of heavy weaponry that – thanks to the grots' reasonable marksmanship skills – score more hits than misses. Rokkit launchas send blunt-nosed projectiles roaring in to blow enemy vehicles apart in roiling fireballs and reduce fortifications to rubble. Skorchas spit out thick tongues of flame that engulf the foe and send them reeling away as living torches, much to the high-pitched glee of the Kans' pilots. Yet perhaps the most feared of all Killa Kan armaments is the grotzooka; essentially an enormous blunderbuss fed from a bulky hopper built into its breach, the grotzooka is stuffed liberally with scavenged scrap-metal, bits of masonry, nails, screws, bullets, broken tools, shards of glass, bewildered squigs, and – more often than not – the remnants of the loader's discarded lunch. Fired from mid-to-close range, the grotzooka fills the air with a whizzing cloud of lethal shrapnel that can reduce entire squads of infantry to a red mist in a heartbeat.

Those Killa Kan pilots who do not lose their nerve or get blown to scrap by the foe's guns typically charge their walkers into close combat with tinny metal screams of 'Waaagh!'. Once there, they cause every bit as much carnage as they did at range, going about their bloody work with a range of vicious industrial-looking tools attached to their long hydraulic limbs. Piston-driven klaws shear through heavily armoured foes, howling buzz saws create showers of gore with each wide swing, and vicious drillas punch through vehicle hulls to destroy vital systems and bore through terrified crew. So armed, the Killa Kans rampage their way through the enemy's position, working out their anger and spite amidst the screams of their victims.

DEFF DREADS

Deff Dreads epitomise the three main ideals of Ork warfare: big, shooty and stompy. They thunder and clank across the battlefield, limbs waving as heavy weapons spit death into the enemy ranks and powered shears snip excitedly in anticipation of the hideous bloodletting to come.

An Ork who dreams of finding a shortcut to power will sometimes make the terrible mistake of volunteering to be a Deff Dread pilot. He believes that once he is in control of an enormous metal machine bristling with the deadliest of greenskin weaponry, nothing can stand in his way. However, he soon finds out that the disadvantage to being permanently wired into an enclosed metal can is being permanently wired into an enclosed metal can. This realisation tends to drive the pilot a bit crazy, and hence new Deff Dreads need 'runnin' in' – often at the expense of any nearby life forms and buildings.

Painboyz have an important role to play in any warband that includes Deff Dreads. Dread pilots have to be interfaced with the crude circuitry of the machine itself. Meks lack the surgical skill for such a feat, and only the Painboyz have the requisite know-how to jam the wires into roughly the right areas of the pilot's brain (after all, you can't just nail the pilot into the Dread's interior and hope for the best – though that doesn't mean this hasn't been tried). The Deff Dread pilot will also need regular medical attention in the long term, as wires tend to pull out under the stress of battle.

Despite this, Deff Dreads are an extremely powerful asset to an Ork army. Their wheezing, piston-driven limbs can rip a human in two or smash through a reinforced wall, often at the same time. A Dread can storm into an enemy squad with impunity, the blows of its opponents bouncing harmlessly from its thick metal shell whilst it scissors through their ranks with its buzz saws and power shears. Deff Dreads have been sighted with all manner of different weapon loadouts; some are kitted out entirely with saws and klaws, while others pack skorchas, chattering big shootas and multiple rokkit launchas in various configurations. Unsubstantiated rumours describe far stranger engines carrying outsized siege weaponry or rolling along on high-speed tracks. Knowing Orks, such adaptations are entirely likely.

Deff Dread pilots revel in demolishing and killing things, taking out their rage at being incarcerated upon anything that strays too close whilst bellowing 'Waaagh!' through the Dread's speaker grilles. This anger eventually simmers down to a normal level of Orkish bloodthirst as the new occupant acclimatises. Still, a Deff Dread's pilot will take any opportunity to display the destructive power of his new metal body, if only to make himself feel better about the fact he has to eat his meals through a straw.

DREAD MOBS

Some Meks become obsessed with making the stompiest war machines ever known to the Ork race. They daydream about leading hordes of Killa Kans and Deff Dreads into battle, an army of walkers just as numerous as the hordes of Boyz that their Warboss leads into battle. This accomplishment is well within the capacity of the most gifted Ork Meks, who often turn renegade as their single-minded quest to create more and more walkers consumes their tribe's time and resources.

One particularly well-known example of this is related in the story of Bugnutz, a Big Mek who disassembled a Battlewagon and used the scrap metal to create a trio of Killa Kans for his faithful Grot Oilers. Unfortunately the Battlewagon belonged to 'Krusha' Kilskarr, Warlord of the Gore-wheels, and he was not well pleased.

Bugnutz ended his days nailed upside down to the front of the wagon he was forced to build as a replacement. To this day the story of Bugnutz acts as a cautionary tale for those Meks whose ambition far outweighs their common sense (i.e. all of them).

GORKANAUTS AND MORKANAUTS

The ground shakes and deafening metallic shouts of 'Waaagh!' ring out as Gorkanauts and Morkanauts stomp into battle. Sitting in a weight category somewhere between Deff Dread and Stompa, these lumbering bipedal war-engines combine the strengths of combat walkers and battle-tanks to great effect.

Over twenty feet in height and Orkoid in appearance, Gorkanauts and Morkanauts are war effigies that echo aspects of Gork or Mork respectively. A Gorkanaut is typically piloted by a Nob, while a Morkanaut will instead be operated by the Mek who built it. Either way, this pilot has chosen to go it alone aboard his enormous armoured war-suit in a bid to make a name for himself.

An Ork typically takes this rather drastic step after seeing visions of the Ork gods bellowing at him to march out into the stars and join the Great Waaagh!. Sometimes these are experienced as a result of swirling Waaagh! energy coursing through the greenskin's brain, instigated by localised warp storm activity or overspill from a nearby Weirdboy having 'a funny five minutes'. At other times it is more likely the result of a bang on the head or a dodgy batch of fungus brew, but the upshot is the same: the Ork pilot goes on the warpath, accompanied by whatever loyal or well-paid ladz he can scrounge up. Some vanish without trace, swallowed up by the dark void, but others – such as Nardzog the Stompanator or Kaptin Killgubbinz – have won infamy and renown. Since the Great Rift split the galaxy, instances of such Ork folk-heroes setting off for battle and glory have increased enormously. Entire nomadic warbands of Gorkanauts and Morkanauts have been seen rampaging throughout Imperial space and beyond, bellowing through their speakers of the Great Waaagh! and the coming of Gork and Mork. They typically leave little but blazing devastation in their wake.

GORKANAUTS

Gorkanauts are all about raw killing power. Every bit as subtle as a sledgehammer to the face, they act as line-breakers, spearheading Ork infantry assaults to great effect. One of their arms ends in a huge hydraulic klaw of Gork, a weapon capable of caving in a fortress wall or gutting a tank with a single blow. Their other primary armament is the enormous dakka-maker known as the deffstorm mega-shoota. Comprising six triple-barrelled big shootas mounted on a rotating armature, the deffstorm whirls up to speed with a deafening howl before spraying a truly breathtaking amount of bullets into everything in its path. Infantry, vehicles and buildings alike are chewed apart by this relentless hail, and as its barrels spin to a halt it is common to see ragged corridors of corpses and wreckage stretching away from the Gorkanaut for hundreds of feet.

MORKANAUTS

Where Gorkanauts epitomise the unsubtle brutality of almighty Gork, a Morkanaut displays all the lethal kunnin' of equally almighty Mork. The Mekboyz who build and pilot Morkanauts pack them with all manner of energy weapons and glowy gubbinz. Their salvoes of rokkits, shoota shells and kustom mega-zappa blasts can reduce swathes of the enemy to ruin in moments, while their crushing klaws of Mork make short work of any who survive. Many Morkanauts also mount kustom force fields, the better to ward off the return fire of the enemy as they wreak devastation across the battlefield.

Morkanaut pilots – like their Gorkanaut equivalents – are often outcasts. Some feel the call of the Great Waaagh! and set out to cause carnage in the name of Mork. Others fight for Freebooter warbands, hunting like violent magpies for the technological secrets of other races. Such Badmeks have usually been ejected from their tribe for crimes such as using the local Weirdboy's hut for target practice. These rogue pilots are especially dangerous, and often begin their wanderings by flattening their former tribe's settlement by way of revenge.

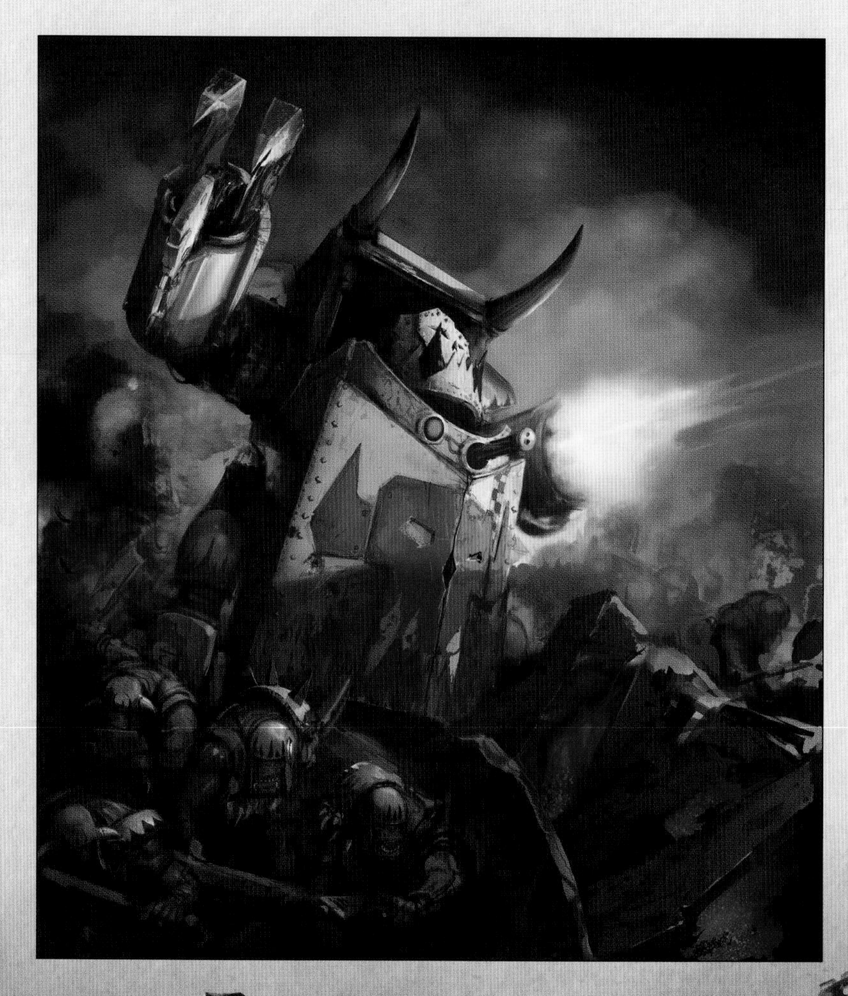

STOMPAS

Stompas are enormous walking fortresses. Clad in layer upon layer of scrap-iron armour, bristling with dakka and massive motorised combat weapons, they live up to their name by stomping across the battlefield and annihilating everything in their path.

Every Stompa is a unique creation, usually the product of several Mekaniaks' fevered brains and countless hours of grot slave-labour. However, as they rise up within their teetering scaffolds and approach a state of completion, certain key similarities manifest in nearly all Stompas.

First and foremost, these super-heavy walkers are all built as fat-bellied and belligerent Orkoid figures, effigies of the Ork gods Gork and Mork that stand as tall as a hab-block. They are usually powered by massive internal boilers and furnaces that link to a forest of enormous smokestacks and vents, which bristle from the Stompa's back. One arm is a gangling hydraulic affair the size of a docking crane, which ends in a monstrous chainsaw known as a mega-choppa. This weapon can obliterate entire squads of infantry with a single swing, or carve super-heavy battle-tanks apart with a sustained assault.

The Stompa's other arm usually comprises an intimidating mass of artillery. The largest of these weapons is the deffkannon, a breathtakingly huge gun that launches armour-piercing high-explosive shells with a devastating yield. So destructive is a blast from this weapon that even the Ork gunners' questionable accuracy is unlikely to spare any unfortunates caught beneath its sights.

Every bit as terrifying is the Stompa's supa-gatler, a preposterously huge gatling cannon that spits streams of high-calibre shells at an astonishing rate. When a supa-gatler cuts loose it can rapidly annihilate swathes of infantry and light vehicles; often, the slaughter only stops when the ammunition runs dry. Supported by a battery of long-range supa-rokkits and an array of hull-mounted heavy weaponry, these primary armaments allow a single Stompa to kick out the firepower of a small army.

As they lumber into battle with black smoke billowing from their stacks, Stompas carry mobs of Orks aboard their cramped transport decks. Once amongst the enemy lines, they disgorge their bellowing passengers to wreak havoc before stomping towards the biggest enemy they can see and barging into it with the force of an avalanche. Few are the foes who can survive such a crushing charge, and even these will soon be torn apart by the combined fury of the Stompa and the frenzied greenskins who boil around its feet. So do Stompas vent the wrath of Gork and Mork upon the battlefield.

STORMBOYZ

Stormboyz, the shock troops of many successful warbands, are far too efficient and disciplined by the standards of right-thinking greenskins. Their contrary stance to the good old-fashioned values of anarchy and disorder manifests in a desire to be organised and obedient. Nevertheless, they are still Orks, and share the Orkish desire to get into battle as quickly as possible. To this end they go to war strapped to rokkit packs that, when activated, propel their wearers forwards on great tongues of oily black flame.

Greenskins grow up faster than humans, but young Orks sometimes take a year or so to find their place in society. This can lead to feelings of rebelliousness and anger in an Ork yoof, and he may run off to join a Stormboy camp, especially if he is a military-minded Goff or Blood Axe. These camps provide direction for greenskins who are sick of being told they can do whatever they like. Young Orks can become addicted to the regimented life of a Stormboy, and dedicate their lives to the time-honoured martial practices of drilling, marching and hurtling through the air.

Forethought and planning are avoided by most Orks, who much prefer to just make it up as they go along and do not see the need for discipline. The Stormboyz are the exception to this rule, and have actual respect for authority. The battle-gear of the common Ork tends to be individualistic and tattered, whereas Stormboyz revel in sporting uniform colours and equipment. Stormboyz are also obsessed with the trivial details of warfare, such as the strength and location of the foe. The older Orks view all this parading, boot-polishing and voluntary obedience with something between amusement and contempt, but the Stormboyz take it very seriously indeed.

Despite their strange ways, the Stormboyz are a force to be reckoned with upon the battlefield. They are always eager to prove their prowess to friend and foe alike by putting their battle-drills into practice, and use their rokkit packs to ensure they are the first to get stuck in. Flying into battle is seen as undignified by the older Ork warriors, who far prefer to charge headlong into the enemy while waving their arms and shouting at the top of their lungs. Still, even really old greenskins realise that airborne nutcases are invaluable when attacking Imperial bastions and defence lines. After all, a hurtling great lump of rocket-powered Ork can be a very effective weapon in itself.

Unfortunately for the Stormboyz, the volatile jump-packs made by those rare Mekboyz willing to work for them are anything but reliable – a Mek finds the image of a malfunctioning rokkit pack as amusing as the next Ork. It is a common sight to see a Stormboy corkscrewing into the distance or ploughing into the ground, much to the entertainment of his comrades. Despite their proclamations of military genius, Stormboy battlefield doctrine is very much a case of pull the lever, shout 'ere we go!' and hope for the best…

MADBOYZ

Madboyz are those Orks whose minds didn't develop quite right, or who have been driven insane by the energies of Gork's Grin. Though they are physically identical to other Orks, the fact they wear outlandish garb and carry everything from rusty buckets to stuffed squigs into battle proves they are different in all sorts of entertaining ways. Madboyz often form informal retinues for Weirdboyz, and live apart from other Orks in small shanty towns. Mobs of Madboyz are considered to be lucky, their presence a sign of good fortune. However, this does entail a degree of inconvenience, such as when they decide to hold impromptu shouting contests in the middle of a night raid, or pelt the foe with a volley of stikkbomb pins before waiting expectantly for the loud bangs to start. The fact remains that Madboyz are a surprisingly potent asset on the battlefield, for their antics confound the foe. Even the most gifted tactician cannot predict the anarchic movements of Madboyz caught up in the excitement of battle. After all, how can you second-guess an enemy who is as likely to tear apart an infantry platoon with their bare hands as they are to mill about picking snot-grubs out of each other's noses?

BOSS ZAGSTRUK

DA BOSS

A merciless killer and a fanatical disciplinarian, Boss Zagstruk is the much-feared leader of a band of Stormboyz known as the Vulcha Squad. He despises weakness and loves nothing more than bullying those smaller than him into doing precisely what they are told. Zagstruk's mood swings between foul temper and murderous fury at the slightest provocation.

The Vulcha Squad hold their leader in high esteem, and fear his famous rages far more than any enemy. Da Boss, as his disciples call him, never lowers his voice beneath a shout. Worse still, he executes on the spot any who show insubordination or cowardice. This tends to keep even the largest and most truculent of the Orks under his charge in check.

The rumour is that Zagstruk was born in the centre of a human settlement, and that he quickly throttled his way across the hinterlands to his parent tribe. His warriors say that every day since his birth Zagstruk has made at least one kill, and that he takes any excuse for a fight. The petrifying look in Zagstruk's eye is testament to this, and many of the Vulcha Squad swear blind that they have seen Da Boss stare down Warlords, gnarwolves and Squiggoths alike.

The Vulcha Squad get their name from Zagstruk's personal aircraft, *Da Vulcha*. This huge red fightabomma is an antique by the standards of modern Ork aircraft. Nevertheless it still packs a fearsome payload, not least of which are the Vulchas themselves. At the climax of a battle, Boss Zagstruk and his ladz will fly in a low attack run over the front line, riding in the belly of the thundering Vulcha. At a barked command from Zagstruk, the Vulcha's primary bomb bays fall open and send the cargo of Stormboyz plummeting towards the battle below. At the last minute Zagstruk will order his Boyz to fire up their rokkit packs, sending the Orks into the enemy boots-first even as the blitz missiles slung under the fins of Zagstruk's own pack whistle in to blast craters in the foe's lines.

This signature attack is made all the more devastating by Zagstruk's own wargear, the bioniks known as Da Vulcha's Klaws. Zagstruk had these made for him after his own legs were ripped off by a Space Marine Dreadnought, whose wiring systems he subsequently gnawed through until the machine was incapacitated. These piston-driven and power-clawed augmetics enhance Zagstruk's formidable strength to the extent that when he makes contact with the enemy, it is invariably with a sickening crunch.

Since Gork's Grin split the stars, Zagstruk's ladz have noticed a distinct change in Da Boss. Although he has always been driven, the Ork leader has become downright ambitious. He is gathering ever more Stormboyz to his banner, as well as warbands of Blood Axes and Goffs that he has kicked savagely into line, for Zagstruk is embarking on a Stormwaaagh! to end all Stormwaaaghs!. Already he has conquered the Imperial shrine world of St Rezmond's Hope, and remade the planet in his own uncompromising image, but the mad gleam in Zagstruk's eye tells his followers all they need to know – Da Boss has far grander ambitions than conquering a single planet…

PLANET ZAG

Once, St Rezmond's Hope was a paradise of marble shrineplexes and prayer gardens. The coming of Zagstruk's Stormwaaagh! reduced it to ruins, which have since been looted to rebuild the world in a form more pleasing to Da Boss. Now known as Planet Zag, it is a place of gun-fortresses, military encampments, Mekaniak factories and enough parade grounds and firing ranges to satisfy even the most obsessive Stormboy. Its armour-plated capital, Da Bossfort, is overlooked by a huge – and formerly holy – mountain that has been painstakingly carved by captive Imperial sculptors into a series of titanic likenesses of Zagstruk's face. Beneath the lowering glares of these stone visages, Zagstruk's followers drill all the harder in his name.

'I DUNNO WOT YOU BEEN TOLD,
STORMBOY MOBS IS MIGHTY BOLD,
WE'RE DA HARDEST OF DA LOT,
WE MAKE YOU LOT LOOK LIKE GROTS.'

- Stormboy drill-chant

KOMMANDOS

'Half-glimpsed shadows? Orks wearing camouflage? Do you take us for imbeciles? Orks are barbaric and entirely single-minded. Army dogma, which has served us well for ten thousand years, teaches us this. Greenskins come on in a great horde, they do not slink and sneak in the shade.

Guards! Take the prisoner to the holding cells to await execution for cowardice and incompetence.'

- Provost-Major Kyne, at the court martial of Lt Gordo

Kommandos epitomise the Orky virtue of low cunning. Nothing makes a Kommando happier than creeping up on an unsuspecting enemy, his mates slithering through the undergrowth at his side. When the time is right, the Kommandos will burst from their hiding places, slashing, stabbing and shooting at their stunned prey before they have a chance to strike back.

Kommandos are viewed with suspicion by the majority of Boyz, on the rare occasions they are viewed at all. These specialists do not socialise with other greenskins; they sometimes go into self-imposed exile for months at a time, and in more extreme cases even permanently divorce themselves from their tribe. Kommandos prize intelligence and initiative, and some of them are even able to read. Not for them the thrill of a massed charge or a turbo-powered race to the front line in a badly made Trukk. Instead a Kommando gets his kicks from slitting throats and spreading panic behind enemy lines before launching a perfectly timed ambush. The horrified look on the faces of their prey, who assumed they would be able to see the Ork attack a mile off, is tremendously rewarding to the members of a Kommando mob. These scare tactics are epitomised by Snikrot of the Red Skull Kommandos, whose name is a byword for terror upon Armageddon.

On the field of battle, Kommandos will assassinate sentries and destroy gun emplacements to give the rest of the ladz a better chance of reaching the enemy lines unscathed. It is common for each Kommando to have a specialist role within the mob, and have a nickname appropriate to his role, such as 'Fireboy' or 'Throatslit'. This organised and militaristic outlook means that young Stormboyz often develop into Kommandos instead of rejoining the right-thinking Ork Boyz at the heart of each warband.

The tools of the Kommando's trade are subtle by Ork standards. They place great faith in soot-blackened blades and camouflage, painting their skin with stripes of blood, dirt and dung so that they blend in with their surroundings. This practice is shocking to a normal Ork, who considers the idea of covering up his greenness unnatural. Only the Blood Axes truly see the value of such caution. Some Kommandos are even more inventive with their camouflage, attaching foliage to their uniforms or employing cunning disguises (cunning by Orky standards, anyway). Kommandos do occasionally employ heavy weapons, which they reveal only when they are in position to cripple a battle-tank or slaughter an enemy squad that has broken from cover.

Gurzak crawled through the underbrush, a knife clenched in his jaws. The Kommando stopped, peering through the foliage at the enemy beyond. The T'au had dismounted from their battlesuits to effect field repairs. They bent over flashing systems and open inspection hatches, intent on their work. Gurzak leered, his power klaw flexing in anticipation. They believed they were safe this far behind the front lines. Time to prove them wrong. The Nob motioned with his free hand, signalling the rest of the ladz to form up on his position. He held up three fingers, then two, then one. As the last digit dropped he launched himself forwards, the rest of the Kommandos following closely behind him as his hand fell to his sidearm. Sluggas and Orks roared. Stikkbombs sailed through the air. The T'au barely had time to cry out before the first choppa sank home...

BOSS SNIKROT

DA GREEN GHOST

The infamous Ork Hunters of the Armageddon Imperial Guard are afraid of one Ork and one Ork alone. In the dark nights of the equatorial jungles between Prime and Secundus, these grizzled veterans whisper tales of Boss Snikrot, the Stalker. They tell of a killer who slips through the jungle like a ghost, who can pass through throttlevine groves without disturbing a single leaf. They tell of a savage hunter who lives for vengeance, whose eyes blaze with the devilish light of hatred. Finally, they tell of his victims, left to bleed to death with their eyes put out and their scalps ripped free from their skulls.

Boss Snikrot was a Kommando in high regard at the time of Ghazghkull's original invasion, and his was amongst the first of the Ork tribes to navigate the green hell that separates Armageddon Prime from Armageddon Secundus. The sea of jungle was vast, and Snikrot's Kommandos soon separated from the main tribe. Straying towards Cerberus base, the majority of his tribe fell foul of the Imperial Guard jungle-fighting specialists stationed in the heart of the verdant realm. Snikrot ordered his Boyz to withdraw, vowing to conquer the environment before they turned their attention to the human bases.

Snikrot had learnt his lesson well. He pledged to fight a guerrilla war from the heart of the jungle, stripping his kit down to the bare minimum so that the colour of his skin blended in with the jungle itself. He and his Kommandos became one with the tangled vegetation, their tough hides and strong metabolism giving them a natural resistance to the lethal defences of the nightmarish environment. Snikrot and his ladz refined their already prodigious abilities in stealth and sabotage until they were able to slip into an Astra Militarum barracks and kill the residents in their sleep. Thus began a campaign of terror and psychological warfare that has plagued the Imperial war effort upon Armageddon ever since.

Snikrot's Red Skull Kommandos, so called because of their habit of scalping their victims and spreading the hot blood onto their own heads, were still at large when Ghazghkull returned fifty years later. By this time the legend of Snikrot had spread to the furthest hives. Some spoke of a ghost who drank the blood of his victims in the dark of the night. Some told of a murderous beast who wore the dog tags of his numerous victims upon his chain-wrapped forearms so he could whisper their names to the jungle moon. Some told of his deadly knives, and how they had tasted the throats of colonels, nobles and courtesans alike.

All across Armageddon, in the flickering twilight of the hives, mothers scare their children into obedience with stories about the stalker Snikrot. Each of the gruesome tales has a basis in truth. To this day, Snikrot is one of the most feared of all greenskins, and even the Ork Hunters pray to the Emperor that it is not their neck that Snikrot buries his knives in next.

Of late, a surprising number of Orks have been given cause to hope for the same thing. With the Daemons of Chaos spilling onto Armageddon, Imperial and greenskin forces have been compelled, in a few extreme cases, to temporarily set aside hostilities to fight off the greater threat. Snikrot is disgusted by such compromise, seeing it as weakness, and is quick to punish those Ork leaders guilty of it. More than one Nob has been dragged into the shadows, his severed head turning up on a spike shortly afterwards as a warning against 'mobbin' up wiv humies'.

'Ghazghkull led us to Armageddon. Ghazghkull told us ta stomp da oomans and knock da cities down. Where's Ghazghkull now? Zogged off across da galaxy when da goin' got tough, dat's where.

Don't matter. We ain't goin' anywhere, ladz, and when Armageddon belongs to da Orks, it won't be Ghazghkull's world. It'll be mine...'

- Boss Snikrot

FLASH GITZ

The richest and most obnoxious of all Orks are indisputably the Flash Gitz. These unsavoury individuals pursue a life of conquest and pillage, plying the stars in grotesquely ornamented Kill Kroozers and attack craft. The Flash Gitz take every opportunity they can to fight alongside the rest of the Boyz, if only to flaunt their revoltingly powerful weaponry in front of their less fortunate brethren.

Arrogant and wilful, the Flash Gitz believe that they are at the top of the pecking order of Ork society. This means that many Flash Git mobs are booted out of their tribes for giving the Warboss too much cheek or just being a bunch of smug show-offs. Others voluntarily pursue the life of the Freebooter so that they can get their hands on even more booty without having to share a single tooth.

Flash Gitz love accumulating treasure and are constantly on the lookout for opportunities to raid and pillage. They are so obsessed with upgrading their wargear that they will do almost anything to increase their wealth, including committing acts of theft, treachery and murder, and hiring out their services to various Warbosses or even alien races.

The Gitz are instantly recognisable by their ostentatious apparel and air of swaggering self-importance. Each is festooned with piercings, medallions, trophies, animal furs and gilded glyphs proclaiming the greatness of their owner, usually topped off by an extravagant hat. Many Flash Gitz are from the Bad Moons Clan, and the two factions always enjoy a good brag over barrels of the finest fungus rum that teef can buy.

The arrival of a Flash Gitz mob is usually announced by the jingle and clank of their many possessions. They love parading their wealth in front of other Orks, and want everybody to know about it when they do so. Even attendant grots are heavily ornamented and well dressed, and take great pride in boasting of their master's exploits.

If there is one thing the Flash Gitz like more than strutting their stuff, it is using their highly kustomised shootas to vaporise their enemies. The so-called snazzguns used by the Flash Gitz vary tremendously in design, but because bucketfuls of teef tend to encourage a Mek to produce his best work, they are all uniformly deadly. Woe betide the fool who gives a Flash Git the excuse to test out his latest purchase.

The Flash Gitz seen amongst the hordes of most Ork tribes are there as mercenaries. However, they also form the mainstay of many Freebooter warbands; mob upon mob of Flash Gitz will rally beneath the banner of a suitably intimidating Freebooter Warboss in the name of rampaging around space, blowing things up, and grabbing as much loot as they can carry.

Amongst such Flash Git crews, boisterous competition quickly reaches unhealthy levels. With so many aggressive and mean-spirited show-offs jostling for their share of the loot, infighting and one-upmanship become endemic. Finding expression through acts of sabotage, not-so-friendly fire, races to grab loot and even good-old-fashioned brawling, such disciplinary issues can cause the Freebooter warband to implode altogether if left unchecked.

When directed by the iron will of a sufficiently merciless Freebooter Warboss, this mutual antipathy instead becomes a powerful asset. Knowing that openly battering one another will only draw their Warboss' ire, the Flash Gitz instead redouble their efforts to show their rivals up through spectacular deeds of reckless destruction and pillaging. Roaring space shanties at the tops of their lungs, they storm into the fight with their snazzguns blazing and sweep the horrified enemy away in a tide of enthusiastic savagery. And if a few rival mobs get blown up in the process, well, that just proves they couldn't 'handle their dakka'.

KAPTIN BADRUKK

DA FREEBOOTER KING

Kaptin Badrukk is the most infamous Freebooter of all. A legend amongst his own cut-throat subculture, Badrukk has plied the stars in his steel-jawed Kill Kroozer *Da Blacktoof* for several blood-soaked decades. The Kaptin leads a vicious band of villains known as Badrukk's Flash Gitz, and has fought at the side of every major Warlord in recent history. He maintains that without the devastating weapons of his Gitz, many of those Warlords would have been long dead – a claim that any who have seen them in action can well believe.

Badrukk is a typical Freebooter Warboss only in that his personal appearance is ostentatious in the extreme. Ugly as a bull grox, his bald and heavily scarred head is decorated with medals taken from defeated Imperial admirals whose ships he has ransacked and left for dead. Badrukk's teeth, so numerous that his face is permanently split by a hideous rictus grin, are plated with an alloy of adamantium and priceless ur-gold stolen from the Palace of Undying Light.

The Kaptin's gilded armour is tarnished only by the blood of his most recent victims, and his back banners proclaim his supreme abilities as a fighter and a conqueror. A lead-lined greatcoat protects Badrukk from the radiation generated by his beloved weapon, Da Rippa, a gun so dangerous that merely standing near it is tantamount to a death sentence. The weapon once belonged to the Ogryn bodyguard of a sub-sector governor, and the Kaptin has since modified it to fire unstable plasma canisters instead of high-calibre bullets so that each hit detonates with incredible power.

Badrukk was chased out of his tribe by his fellow Bad Moons on charges of having too many teef for his own good. From the day of his exile, the Kaptin's accomplishments have far outstripped those of his fellow Freebooter Warbosses. Fighting alongside the fleet of Warlord Garaghak, Badrukk blunted a tendril of the Tyranid Hive Fleet Kraken with a daring raid on the Norn Queen at its heart. During the War of Dakka, his warriors out-shot a T'au Empire Hunter Cadre, and some even claim that the Kaptin has personally slain a void-whale.

For an Ork, Badrukk is an excellent strategist, and acts as an advisor for any Warlord rich enough to meet his exorbitant fees. After the battle, he and his Flash Gitz usually 'persuade' their employers to give them the lion's share of the booty before climbing back aboard *Da Blacktoof* and heading off in search of more carnage. Many Warlords see this as a price well worth paying for the sake of a good scrap and the unforgettable sight of Badrukk and his Flash Gitz unleashing their deadly weaponry upon the panicking foe.

Badrukk's attacks have become especially daring and spectacular in recent years, making use of tellyporta strikes to drop his Flash Gitz precisely where they need to be. Directed force-bubble weaponry traps enemies in the kill-zone with them. This is thanks to the efforts of Badmek Mogrok, a flashy Bad Moons Big Mek who owes Badrukk his life. The Kaptin rescued Mogrok from the disastrous conclusion of the war on the Knight world of Alaric Prime, and has been wringing the Badmek dry for his technological know-wotz ever since. With Mogrok's grudging aid, Badrukk has successfully raided the Necron treasure world of Tanhotep, ransacked several isolated planets in the Imperium Nihilus and defeated the so-called Grand Guard of the Chaos Warlord Nahsghar the Unrepentant. These victories have swelled Badrukk's coffers like never before, and seen *Da Blacktoof* transformed into a gunned-up kustom monster capable of reducing a hive city to ruins all by itself.

MAD DOK GROTSNIK

DA PAINBOSS

Grotsnik always had a morbid fascination with rooting around in other people's heads. When an ugly Goff called Ghazghkull stumbled into Grotsnik's medical tent holding his brain in place with both hands, the Dok saw a great opportunity. Two hours later Ghazghkull staggered out again, this time clutching a skull of shining adamantium.

Ghazghkull's rise to Grand Warlord took less than a week. Suddenly extremely popular, Grotsnik looked at the mob of Orks waiting outside his tent and saw another great opportunity. He convinced the richest Nobz of his tribe that they too should have 'a Ghazghkull special'. What Grotsnik didn't tell them was that each cranium contained a portion of high explosive, and that he had a remote trigger hidden away for each of them. The work kept rolling in, and if a Nob with a metal cranium offended Grotsnik, well, later that day he might come down with a nasty case of exploding head.

Eventually the Nobz figured out what was happening. Realising they could not tackle Grotsnik face-to-face, they organised a little accident for him. Grotsnik was called out to take a look at the wiring of a faulty Deff Dread, but he was in for a nasty surprise. Grabbing Grotsnik with a pincer, the Dread held him down in the dirt and used its massive circular saw to cut open the Dok's head before stomping off into the distance.

As Grotsnik's Gretchin orderlies looked down upon their dying master, they too saw a great opportunity. They dragged the Dok all the way back to the medical tent, and soon the sounds of bone saw, hammer and drill began to drift across the sleeping camp.

During that long night, one of the Gretchin lost his lunch whilst elbows-deep in Grotsnik's brain pan. The other lost a pet spider that scurried into the warmest, softest place it could find: the Dok's hinged-open head. Grotsnik died several times that night, but he was brought back to life by an inventively applied grot-prod. In the small hours of the morning, Grotsnik staggered out of the tent clutching his new metal skull-plate, alive but quite, quite mad. Filled with manic glee, the Dok danced and sang in the moonlight, grisly explosions playing counterpoint to his operatic efforts as he triggered the Nobs' explosive craniums one by one.

Since that day, Grotsnik's tastes in surgery have become even more bizarre. He has cut off several of his own limbs 'just to keep his hand in', replacing them with grafts from customers who have been overcome with generosity whilst out cold on the slab. He has lobotomised a fair number of the brave and the foolish coming to his tent, only to replace their brains with live squigs. It is even rumoured that he is building his own composite super-Ork out of organs and body parts 'donated' by his customers. Many believe that without Ghazghkull's patronage the Dok would have been properly killed long ago, but the fact remains that the Dok is as tough as nails and a fearsome fighter to boot.

Grotsnik long ago grasped that staying in Ghazghkull's good books was his ticket to glory. When Gork and Mork called the Grand Warlord away from Armageddon 'fer greater fings', Grotsnik went along for the ride. As Ghazghkull subjugates rival Warlords and adds their forces to his own, so Grotsnik picks over the casualties and takes the best of the defeated Nobs for his own nefarious projects. Grotsnik even bullies rival Painboyz into working for him as orderlies, much to their chagrin. Most of these press-ganged Painboyz vanish altogether when the Dok tires of their grumbling, and rumours persist of Grotsnik's ghoulish 'brain-bot', in which he supposedly preserves the accumulated know-wotz of his failed orderlies for later reference.

Ghazghkull knows of his Mad Dok's excesses, and the growing resentment for them amongst his subservient Warbosses, yet he has taken no action to curb Grotsnik's enthusiasm. For many this raises the question of what precisely the Dok is working on for his master, and what manner of horrors may be revealed when Grotsnik finally considers his magnum opus to be complete.

DA CORPSE LOOTAS

Dok Grotsnik may have spent many years in the company of Goffs, but he has always been a Deathskull at heart. Of late, he has returned to his roots by gathering a warband of Deathskulls, Painboyz and Freebooterz and setting out to harvest not scrap-metal, but corpses from the battlefield. His Corpse Lootas typically prefer to get stuck in and generate a solid body-count before picking over the dead and wounded and dragging away all those that catch Grotsnik's eye. This warband boasts many Cyborks, along with biologically 'kustomised' monsters that Grotsnik has taken to calling his 'Stitchboyz'. With killsaws screaming and syringes flashing, the Corpse Lootas rampage from one battlefield to the next, cannibalising everything in sight and packing their 'meat wagonz' with raw materials for Dok Grotsnik's horrible experiments.

'Operate! Operate! Still time to operate!'

- Mad Dok Grotsnik

GHAZGHKULL THRAKA

PROPHET OF GORK AND MORK

Ghazghkull Mag Uruk Thraka is a mighty prophet of the Waaagh!, capable of rousing entire planetary populations of Orks into a frenzy of conquest and bloodshed. He is the single most influential greenskin in the galaxy, and billions march to war in his name. But it was not always this way.

Ghazghkull started his career as a common Goff warrior on the backwater planet of Urk. During a raid upon a Space Marine command sanctum, Ghazghkull caught a bolter shell to the face that pulped a large area of his cranium and caused extensive brain-damage. A Deathskulls Painboy called Mad Dok Grotsnik was close to hand, and replaced part of Ghazghkull's cerebellum with bioniks made from adamantium.

It may be that these bioniks triggered some latent psychic power, or perhaps their recipient simply suffers from delusions, but for whatever reason, from that point on Ghazghkull claimed to be in direct contact with the Ork gods Gork and Mork.

Some dark power certainly favoured Ghazghkull, for his rise to power amongst the tribes of Urk was meteoric. He fought his way through the ranks until he achieved the position of supreme planetary Warlord. Orks respect strength, courage and battle prowess, and it could not be denied that Ghazghkull possessed all of these qualities in abundance. In addition, he had something that most Warlords lack: vision. He stirred the Orks of his home world with impassioned speeches, telling them it was their mission to conquer the galaxy. Wherever Ghazghkull went he united warring tribes with an overwhelming sense of destiny.

All this might have come to nothing had not Urk's sun started to flicker and die. Ghazghkull told the Orks that this was a sign from Gork that the time had come to launch a Waaagh! bigger than any seen before or since. Those who wished to join the crusade could follow Ghazghkull; those who disobeyed would die. To an Ork they chose to follow their prophet. They would conquer the known galaxy or die in the attempt.

Since that time, Ghazghkull's list of conquests has grown ever-longer. He crushed the defenders of the Seven Systems. He looted the forge world of Dynostix V, and annihilated the Astral Drakes Chapter to the last man. He has twice invaded the world of Armageddon – though that one planet has resisted Ghazghkull's every attempt at final victory.

Now, with Gork's Grin splitting the stars, Ghazghkull's conquests have grown tenfold. Some say that the powerful vision that led him away from Armageddon was caused by the warp energies building up to the opening of the Great Rift, others that it truly was Gork and Mork speaking to him through his captive Weirdboyz. Whatever the truth, Ghazghkull now leads Da Great Waaagh! across the stars, and his visions from his gods come with ever-greater frequency and ferocity. It is whispered amongst the Runtherds that Ghazghkull has even gained the ability to witness and influence events unfolding far away 'through da Great Green'; if this is so, he has become a graver threat to the galaxy than ever before.

'We'z gonna stomp da universe flat and kill anyfing dat fights back.

We'z da Orks, and we woz made to fight and win!'

- Grand Warlord Ghazghkull Mag Uruk Thraka, prophet of Gork and Mork, leader of Da Great Waaagh!

THE ART OF WAAAGH!

Ork armies are sprawling, anarchic forces of vibrantly colourful and dangerously ramshackle war-engines and warriors that pour across the battlefield to bury their foes. These pages show examples of the brutish and tribal greenskin panoply.

Ghazghkull Thraka

Warboss with power klaw, kombi-weapon with rokkit launcha, and attack squig

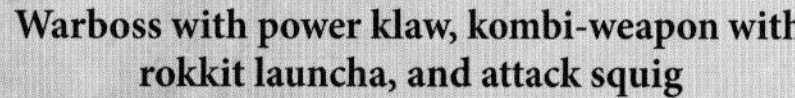

Upon the killing fields of Armageddon, Warlord Ghazghkull Mag Uruk Thraka leads a vast Goff horde into battle with Imperial forces. The ground shakes beneath the pounding of their boots as the foe are swept away upon a green tide.

The ordered gun-line of the T'au Empire is overwhelmed by the sheer aggression of the Ork charge. With Dakkajets roaring low overhead, Goff Nobz and Stormboyz spearhead the bloody breakthrough.

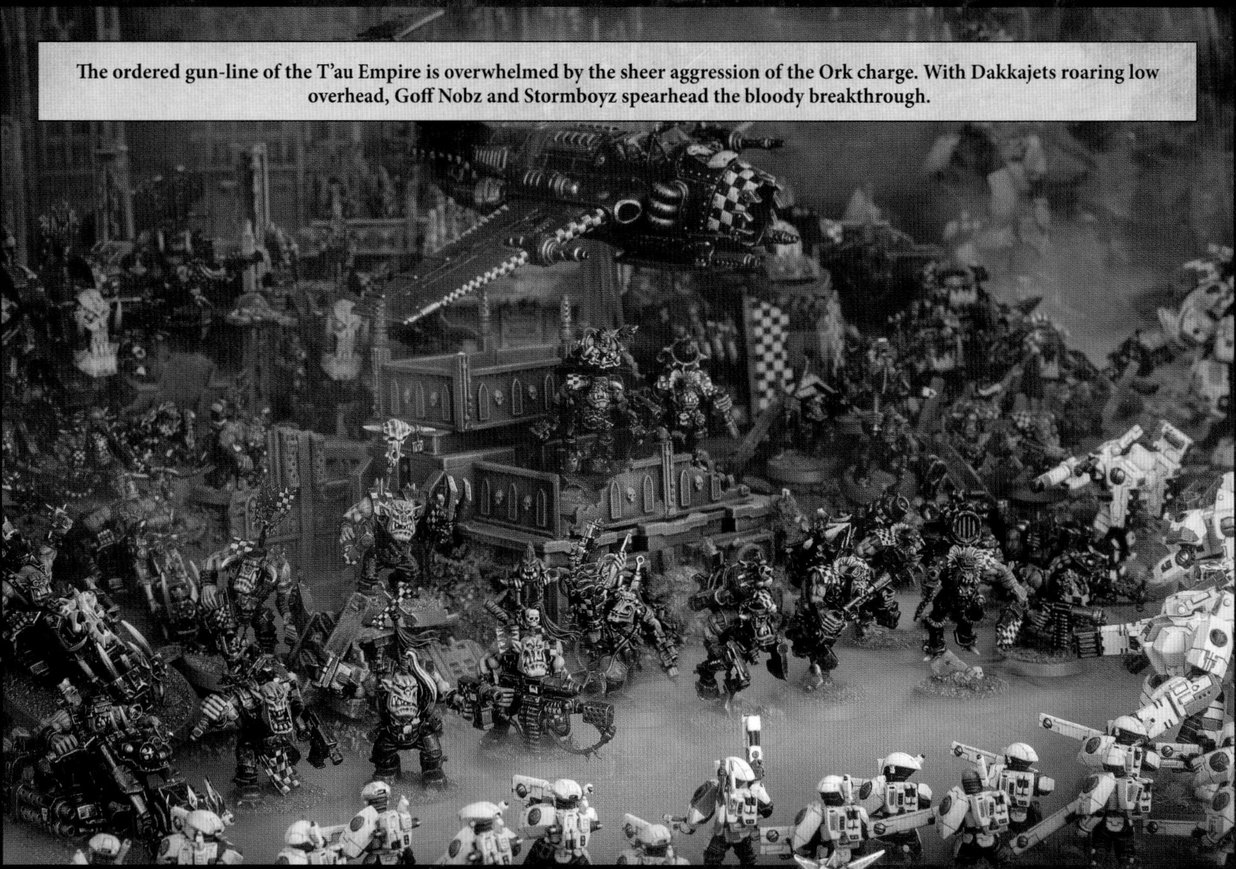

Painboy with power klaw and 'urty syringe

Weirdboy

Big Mek in Mega Armour with power klaw, kustom force field and kombi-weapon with rokkit launcha

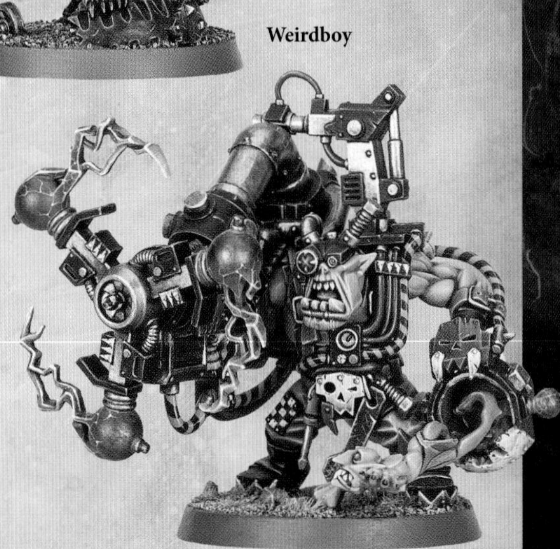

Big Mek with shokk attack gun

Evil Sunz Kustom Boosta-blasta

Meganob with kustom shoota and power klaw

Dust clouds billow to the skies and the roar of engines rises to a deafening crescendo as Evil Sunz Speed Freeks and Flyboyz barrel headlong into the fray.

Bad Moons Big Mek with tellyport blasta

Meganob with killsaws

Mek with choppa and kustom mega-slugga

Protected by the kustom force-shield projected by their Big Mek, a clanking mass of Bad Moons Gorkanauts, Morkanauts, Deff Dreads and Meganobz meet the Terminator elites of the Space Wolves in a crunching battle to the death.

Spent shell-casings fall like rain as the Lootas and Gunwagons of a Deathskulls warband open fire. Salvo after salvo of hot lead and whistling munitions hammers the enemy lines, blowing them to shreds in a storm of dakka!

Deathskulls Nob with choppa and slugga

Snakebite Nob with choppa and slugga

Blood Axe Nob with choppa and slugga

A fast-moving force of Blood Axes strikes suddenly at the advancing Thousand Sons. Even as the mechanised elements of the force hit the Chaos warriors from the front, the wily Boss Snikrot slips around their flank, Mork's Teeth raised in preparation for the slaughter

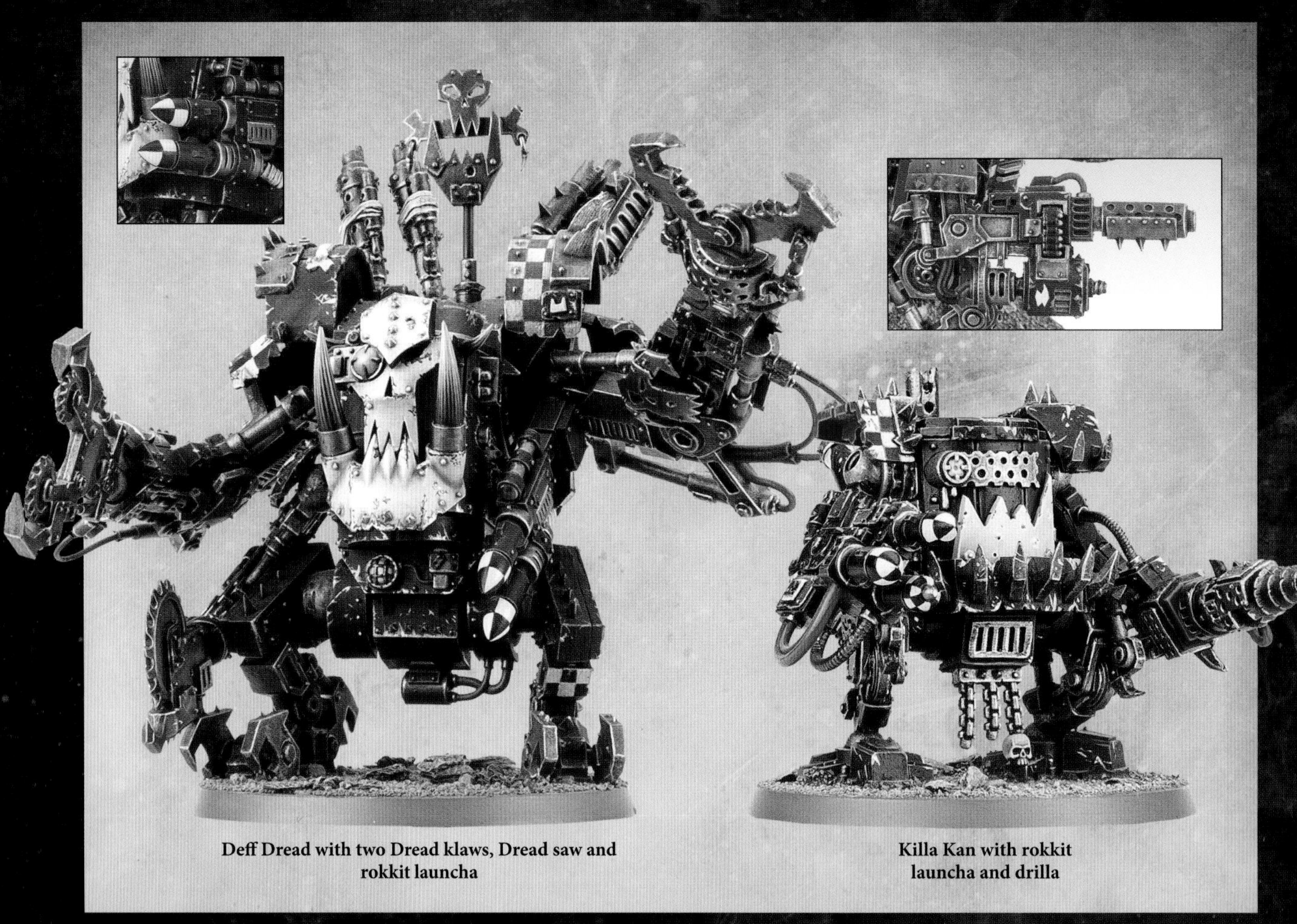

Deff Dread with two Dread klaws, Dread saw and rokkit launcha

Killa Kan with rokkit launcha and drilla

Greenskin Deff Dreads and Killa Kans are powerful combat walkers cobbled together from scrap metal and heavy weaponry. These deadly contraptions are typically daubed in the colours of their clan, and decorated with iconography.

Kaptin Badrukk

Flash Gitz Kaptin

Flash Git

Goff Deffkilla Wartrike

Snakebite Rukkatrukk Squigbuggy

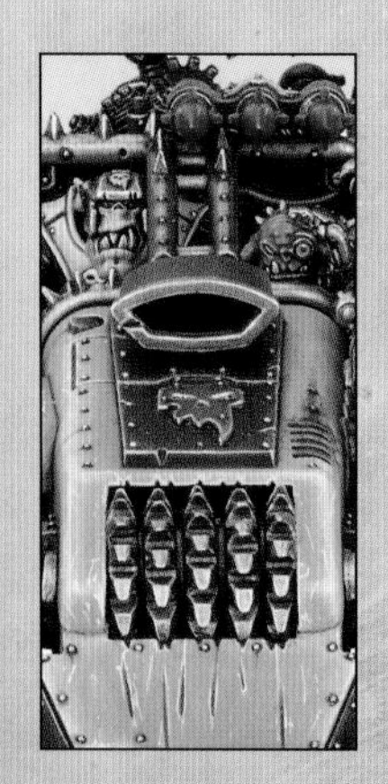

Bad Moons Shokkjump Dragsta

ON THE WARPATH

Ork armies are incredibly varied, as likely to boast massed infantry as squadrons of aircraft or columns of armoured fighting vehicles. This variation is well illustrated by the two starting forces presented below.

A large number of Ork warbands are built around a solid core of foot-slogging infantry. This is doubly true for Orks from the Goff Clan, who specialise in burying their enemies beneath an avalanche of brutish greenskin warriors. The first of these two forces is built to reflect this, being based around a solid core of Ork infantry under the leadership of a Big Mek with Shokk Attack Gun. While the Big Mek's bizarre heavy weapon provides firepower and a Painboy stands ready to perform battlefield surgery, a mob of Ork Boyz and a mob of burly Nobz storm towards the enemy, led into the fight by a heavily armoured Deff Dread. This force can be fielded as a Patrol Detachment, as detailed in the *Warhammer 40,000* rulebook.

The second starting force is a very different proposition, being formed almost entirely from highly mobile vehicles and bikes to create a small but effective Outrider Detachment. Hailing from the Evil Sunz Clan and led by a Deffkilla Wartrike, this force fills three Fast Attack choices with a Boomdakka Snazzwagon, a Kustom Boosta-blasta and a mob of Warbikers, adding in a monstrous Bonebreaka that transports the force's Boyz into battle.

Both of these forces are Battle-forged, meaning that their owning player benefits from Command Points to spend on powerful Stratagems. As the collections expand, they will generate even more Command Points to spend.

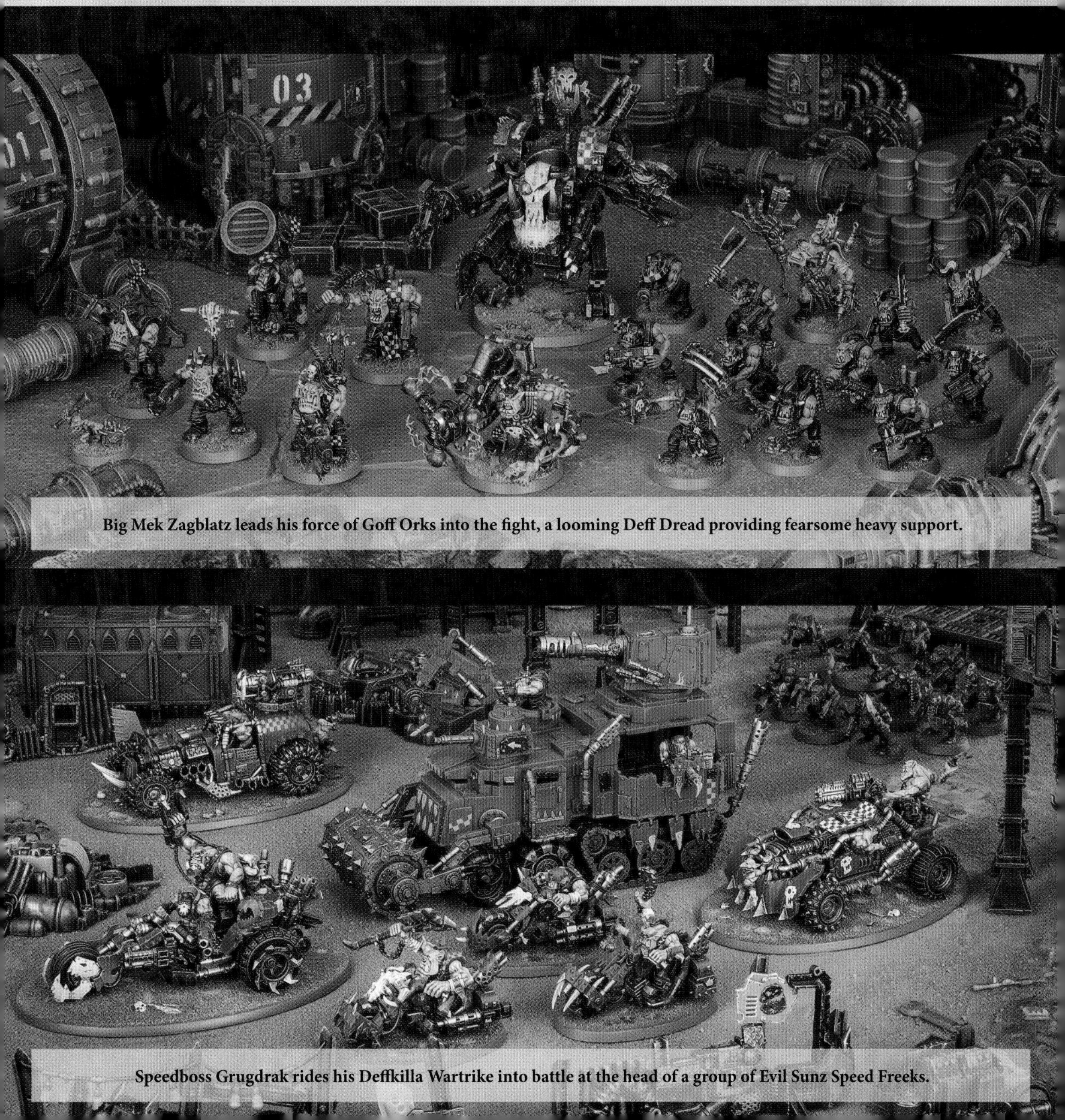

Big Mek Zagblatz leads his force of Goff Orks into the fight, a looming Deff Dread providing fearsome heavy support.

Speedboss Grugdrak rides his Deffkilla Wartrike into battle at the head of a group of Evil Sunz Speed Freeks.

THE WARBAND ASSEMBLES

By adding more Citadel Miniatures to your Orks collection, your army can grow in countless different and exciting ways. Pictured above is a Bad Moons force that combines infantry, buggies, aircraft and even a lumbering super-heavy Stompa to create a truly formidable warband.

This Bad Moons warband is led by the mighty Warboss Borgok Badklaw, and is known in typically direct Orkish fashion as Badklaw's Blitzboyz. Even the toughest Warboss needs some Oddboyz to provide the kunnin' behind his throne; in this case, those Oddboyz are the mega-armoured Big Mek Krugg and ectoplasmically flatulent Weirdboy Wurrgutz. The beating heart of the Blitzboyz is formed of Boyz mobs who can spill across the battlefield to seize objectives and kick the enemy's teeth in. Arik's Gitstompas are armed with sluggas and choppas for maximum close-quarters killing power, while in typical Bad Moons fashion, Drogg's Dakkaboyz and Nagrat's Ladz are packing shootas for additional firepower. These Boyz are spearheaded into battle by the hulking forms of the Meganobz known as Badklaw's Bossboyz, who are every bit as feared by their own ladz as they are by the enemy!

Having lots of extra teef to throw about, Warboss Badklaw has ensured his warband benefits from plenty of armoured back-up. The Shokkjump Dragsta known as *Badwheelz* and the Megatrakk Scrapjet known as *Da Wingless Wunda* provide fast-moving ground-based firepower; during battle they come hurtling out of Krugg's Mekboy Workshop with fresh kustom-jobs to try out on the enemy. The Wazbom Blastajet *Mork's Thunda* and the

Blitza-bommer *Gitbusta* ensure the skies belong to Borgok, while a Morkanaut and Gorkanaut – *Nurbok's Revenge* and *Da Mad Mangler* – back the Boyz up with some heavily armoured line-breaking might. Looming over the rest of the warband – and most likely all of their enemies – is the terrifying Stompa known as *Megakrusha*. By far the biggest, most deadly and ostentatious battle engine in the warband, this lumbering war effigy often transports Badklaw and his Bossboyz in style.

With three HQ choices, three Troops choices, an Elites choice, two Fast Attack choices, two Heavy Support choices, two Flyers, one Fortification plus a Lord of War, Badklaw's Blitzboyz form a Battalion Detachment, Super-Heavy Auxiliary Detachment and Fortification Network Detachment. Along with being Battle-forged, this gives the army an impressive eight Command Points to spend on the sorts of powerful Stratagems that – if used at the right time – can change the entire course of the battle!

1. **Warboss Borgok Badklaw**
2. **Big Mek Krugg Kogfang**
3. **Weirdboy Wurrgutz**
4. **Ork Boyz mob, Arik's Gitstompas**
5. **Ork Boyz mob, Drogg's Dakkaboyz**
6. **Ork Boyz mob, Nagrat's Ladz**
7. **Meganobz mob, Badklaw's Bossboyz**
8. **Shokkjump Dragsta, *Badwheelz***
9. **Megatrakk Scrapjet, *Da Wingless Wunda***
10. **Mekboy Workshop**
11. **Wazbom Blastajet, *Mork's Thunda***
12. **Blitza-bommer, *Gitbusta***
13. **Morkanaut, *Nurbok's Revenge***
14. **Gorkanaut, *Da Mad Mangler***
15. **Stompa, *Megakrusha***

WARRIORS OF GORK AND MORK

This section contains all of the datasheets that you will need in order to fight battles with your Ork miniatures. Each datasheet includes the characteristics profiles of the unit it describes, as well as any wargear and special abilities it may have. Some rules are common to several Ork units, and are described on these pages and referenced on the datasheets themselves.

KEYWORDS

Throughout this section you will come across a keyword that is within angular brackets, specifically **<Clan>**. This is shorthand for a keyword of your own choosing, as described below.

<Clan>

All Orks belong to a clan, a group of like-minded greenskins that share a propensity for a certain kind of warfare.

Some datasheets specify what clan the unit is drawn from (e.g. Ghazghkull Thraka has the **Goff** keyword, so is from the Goff Clan). If an Ork datasheet does not specify which clan it is drawn from, it will have the **<Clan>** keyword. When you include such a unit in your army, you must nominate which clan that unit is from. You then simply replace the **<Clan>** keyword in every instance on that unit's datasheet with the name of your chosen clan.

For example, if you were to include a Warboss in your army, and you decided he was from the Bad Moons Clan, his **<Clan>** Faction keyword is changed to **Bad Moons** and his Breakin' Heads ability would then say 'If a **Bad Moons** unit fails a Morale test within 3" of a friendly **Bad Moons Warboss**, the Warboss can restore order with a brutal display of violence. If they do so, the unit suffers D3 mortal wounds but the Morale test is then considered to have been passed.'

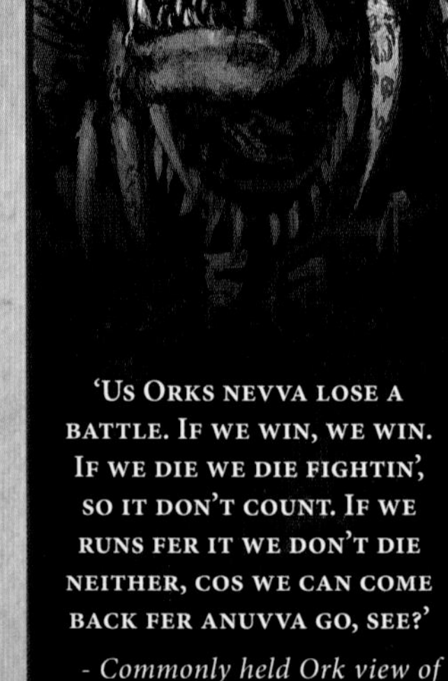

'Us Orks nevva lose a battle. If we win, we win. If we die we die fightin', so it don't count. If we runs fer it we don't die neither, cos we can come back fer anuvva go, see?'

- Commonly held Ork view of Ork warfare

ABILITIES

The following abilities are common to several Ork units:

Dakka! Dakka! Dakka!

Nothing aids accuracy like the simple expedient of firing so many shots that you just can't miss.

Each time you roll an unmodified hit roll of 6 for an attack with a ranged weapon made by a model in this unit, that hit roll succeeds regardless of any modifiers. In addition, immediately make an additional hit roll against the same target using the same weapon. These additional hit rolls cannot themselves generate any further hit rolls. When firing a weapon with randomly determined characteristics (e.g. a bubblechukka), any additional hit rolls use the same characteristics as the hit roll that generated the additional hit roll. This ability does not affect weapons that automatically hit their target.

'Ere We Go!

Once a mob of Orks builds up a good head of steam, their sheer momentum carries them into the fight like a green avalanche.

You can re-roll charge rolls for this unit. When doing so, you can re-roll all or any of the dice.

Mob Rule

The more Orks in one place, the more the Waaagh! energy flows, and the more fearless they all become.

When using the Leadership characteristic of this unit, you can use either its own Leadership characteristic, or you can choose for the characteristic to be equal to either the number of models in the unit or the number of models in another friendly unit within 6" that has this ability.

Speed Mob

Ork buggies and trikes gather in mobs at the battle's start, making boastful wagers before tearing away in a frenzy.

The first time this unit is set up on the battlefield, all of its models must be placed within 6" of at least one other model from the unit. From that point onwards, each model operates independently and is treated as a separate unit for all rules purposes.

ORK WARGEAR LISTS

Many of the units you will find on the following pages reference one or more of the following wargear lists (e.g. Nob Weapons). When this is the case, the unit may take any item from the appropriate list below. The profiles for the items in these lists can be found in the appendix (pg 119-121).

BATTLEWAGON EQUIPMENT

- Grabbin' klaw
- Grot rigger
- Lobba
- Stikkbomb chukka
- Wreckin' ball

SHOOTY WEAPONS

- Kombi-weapon with rokkit launcha
- Kombi-weapon with skorcha
- Kustom shoota

NOB WEAPONS

Up to two weapons can be chosen from the following list:

- Big choppa
- Choppa
- Killsaw
- Power klaw
- Power stabba
- Slugga

One weapon can be chosen from the following list:

- Kombi-weapon with rokkit launcha*
- Kombi-weapon with skorcha*

*Cannot be taken by a Nob on Warbike or Boss Nob on Warbike

12 POWER

GHAZGHKULL THRAKA

NAME	M	WS	BS	S	T	W	A	Ld	Sv
Ghazghkull Thraka	5"	2+	5+	6	6	8	5	8	2+

Ghazghkull Thraka is a single model armed with a twin big shoota, kustom klaw and stikkbombs. Only one of this model can be included in your army.

WEAPON	RANGE	TYPE	S	AP	D	ABILITIES
Twin big shoota	36"	Assault 6	5	0	1	-
Kustom klaw	Melee	Melee	x2	-3	3	-
Stikkbomb	6"	Grenade D6	3	0	1	-

ABILITIES

'Ere We Go, Mob Rule, Dakka! Dakka! Dakka! (pg 82)

Great Waaagh!: Friendly **ORK INFANTRY** units within 6" of Ghazghkull Thraka at the start of the Charge phase can charge even if they Advanced this turn. In addition, add 1 to the Attacks characteristic of models in friendly **ORK INFANTRY** units if they made a charge move this turn and Ghazghkull Thraka is within 6" of that unit when they are chosen to fight.

Prophet of Gork and Mork: Ghazghkull Thraka has a 4+ invulnerable save.

The Boss is Watchin': If a friendly **ORK** unit fails a Morale test while it is within 6" of Ghazghkull Thraka, he can restore order with a brutal display of violence. If he does so, the unit suffers D3 mortal wounds but the Morale test is then considered to have been passed.

FACTION KEYWORDS ORK, GOFF

KEYWORDS CHARACTER, INFANTRY, MEGA ARMOUR, WARBOSS, GHAZGHKULL THRAKA

'Da humies fink da galaxy got torn in two cos of da Chaos Gods. Dem Chaos boyz and da pointy-earz fink so too. Troof is, dey'z all wrong. I'm da prophet of da Waaagh! and I'm tellin' you now, dat fing rippin' da galaxy in 'arf is Gork's big green grin. And why's he grinnin', ladz? Cos it's our time! Gork's grinnin' cos its da hour of da Ork, and we'z gunna stomp da stars flat! WAAAGH!'

- Ghazghkull Thraka

Ghazghkull Thraka stomps into battle, as hulking as the Killa Kans that lumber alongside him.

4 Power

WARBOSS

NAME	M	WS	BS	S	T	W	A	Ld	Sv
Warboss	5"	2+	5+	6	5	6	4	8	4+

A Warboss is a single model armed with a kombi-weapon with rokkit launcha, power klaw, two sluggas and stikkbombs.

WEAPON	RANGE	TYPE	S	AP	D	ABILITIES
Kombi-weapon with rokkit launcha	When attacking with this weapon, choose one or both of the profiles below. If you choose both, subtract 1 from all hit rolls.					
- Rokkit launcha	24"	Assault 1	8	-2	3	-
- Shoota	18"	Assault 2	4	0	1	-
Slugga	12"	Pistol 1	4	0	1	-
Attack squig	Melee	Melee	4	-1	1	Each time a model with an attack squig fights, it can make 2 additional attacks with this weapon.
Big choppa	Melee	Melee	+2	-1	2	-
Power klaw	Melee	Melee	x2	-3	D3	When attacking with this weapon, you must subtract 1 from the hit roll.
Stikkbomb	6"	Grenade D6	3	0	1	-

WARGEAR OPTIONS

- This model may replace its kombi-weapon with rokkit launcha with a weapon from the *Shooty Weapons* list.
- This model may replace its power klaw with a big choppa.
- This model may take an attack squig.

ABILITIES

'Ere We Go, Mob Rule, Dakka! Dakka! Dakka! (pg 82)

Waaagh!: Friendly <Clan> Infantry units within 6" of this model at the start of the Charge phase can charge even if they Advanced this turn.

Breakin' Heads: If a <Clan> unit fails a Morale test while it is within 3" of a friendly <Clan> Warboss, the Warboss can restore order with a brutal display of violence. If they do so, the unit suffers D3 mortal wounds but the Morale test is then considered to have been passed.

FACTION KEYWORDS Ork, <Clan>

KEYWORDS Character, Infantry, Warboss

An Ork Warboss advances in the midst of his brutal green horde, bellowing orders as they close in upon the foe.

4 POWER

BIG MEK

WITH SHOKK ATTACK GUN

NAME	M	WS	BS	S	T	W	A	Ld	Sv
Big Mek with Shokk Attack Gun	5"	3+	5+	5	4	4	3	7	4+
Grot Oiler	5"	5+	4+	2	2	1	1	4	6+

A Big Mek with Shokk Attack Gun is a single model armed with a shokk attack gun and stikkbombs. It may be accompanied by a Grot Oiler.

WEAPON	RANGE	TYPE	S	AP	D	ABILITIES
Shokk attack gun	60"	Heavy D6	2D6	-5	D6	Before firing this weapon, roll once to determine the Strength of all its shots. If the result is 11+ each successful hit inflicts D3 mortal wounds on the target in addition to any normal damage.
Stikkbomb	6"	Grenade D6	3	0	1	-

ABILITIES

'Ere We Go, Mob Rule, Dakka! Dakka! Dakka! (pg 82)

Big Mekaniak: At the end of your Movement phase, this model can repair a single friendly <CLAN> VEHICLE model within 3". That model regains D3 lost wounds. A model can only be repaired once per turn.

Grot Oiler: Once per battle, a Grot Oiler can assist its master in making repairs. If it does so, the model being repaired regains 1 additional lost wound.

When rolling to wound this unit, use the Big Mek's Toughness while it is on the battlefield. The death of a Grot Oiler is ignored for the purposes of Morale tests. The Grot Oiler is considered to have the CHARACTER keyword for the purposes of shooting attacks.

FACTION KEYWORDS	ORK, <CLAN>
KEYWORDS (BIG MEK)	CHARACTER, INFANTRY, BIG MEK
KEYWORDS (GROT OILER)	INFANTRY, GRETCHIN, GROT OILER

'Travellin' through space is boring. Well, boring unless da hulk yer on is full of dem gene-sneakers, or a base fer da Chaos ladz wiv da spikes, or already has Boyz on it. Or if humie lootas come callin', that's always good fer a bit a sport. Or unless yer have a mutiny or two to pass da time, or unless strange fings start happenin', which dey usually do when yer out in da warp. One time we had some bloody great ugly fing come straight out of Weird Lugwort's 'ed! It butchered half da ladz, that was pretty entertainin'. Come ter fink of it, space is a pretty good larf. And that's before yer find yerself a nice new world ta crush!'

- Bigmaw, Ork Runtherd

Thrumming energies crackle around the Big Mek's kustom force field generator, deflecting enemy shots.

6 Power

Big Mek

in Mega Armour

NAME	M	WS	BS	S	T	W	A	Ld	Sv
Big Mek in Mega Armour	4"	3+	5+	5	4	5	3	8	2+
Grot Oiler	5"	5+	4+	2	2	1	1	4	6+

A Big Mek in Mega Armour is a single model armed with a kustom mega-blasta and power klaw. It may be accompanied by a Grot Oiler.

WEAPON	RANGE	TYPE	S	AP	D	ABILITIES
Kustom mega-blasta	24"	Assault 1	8	-3	D6	If you roll one or more unmodified hit rolls of 1, the bearer suffers 1 mortal wound after all of this weapon's attacks have been resolved.
Tellyport blasta	12"	Assault 3	8	-2	1	If a model suffers any unsaved wounds from this weapon and is not slain, roll a D6 at the end of the phase. If the result is greater than that model's Wounds characteristic, it is slain.
Killsaw	Melee	Melee	x2	-4	2	When attacking with this weapon, you must subtract 1 from the hit roll.
Power klaw	Melee	Melee	x2	-3	D3	When attacking with this weapon, you must subtract 1 from the hit roll.

WARGEAR OPTIONS

- This model may replace its kustom mega-blasta with a killsaw or one item from the *Shooty Weapons* list.
- This model may take either a tellyport blasta or a kustom force field.

ABILITIES

'Ere We Go, Mob Rule, Dakka! Dakka! Dakka! (pg 82)

Grot Oiler: Once per battle, a Grot Oiler can assist its master in making repairs. If it does so, the model being repaired regains 1 additional lost wound.

When rolling to wound this unit, use the Big Mek's Toughness while it is on the battlefield. The death of a Grot Oiler is ignored for the purposes of Morale tests. The Grot Oiler is considered to have the CHARACTER keyword for the purposes of shooting attacks.

Kustom Force Field: If this model is equipped with a kustom force field, friendly ORK units have a 5+ invulnerable save against attacks made with ranged weapons while they are wholly within 9" of it. While a model equipped with a kustom force field is embarked, the vehicle transporting it has a 5+ invulnerable save against attacks made with ranged weapons instead.

Big Mekaniak: At the end of your Movement phase, this model can repair a single friendly <CLAN> VEHICLE model within 3". That model regains D3 lost wounds. A model can only be repaired once per turn.

FACTION KEYWORDS: ORK, <CLAN>

KEYWORDS (BIG MEK): CHARACTER, INFANTRY, MEGA ARMOUR, BIG MEK

KEYWORDS (GROT OILER): INFANTRY, GRETCHIN, GROT OILER

WEIRDBOY

3 POWER

NAME	M	WS	BS	S	T	W	A	Ld	Sv
Weirdboy	5"	3+	5+	5	4	4	3	6	6+

A Weirdboy is a single model armed with a Weirdboy staff.

WEAPON	RANGE	TYPE	S	AP	D	ABILITIES
Weirdboy staff	Melee	Melee	+2	-1	D3	-

ABILITIES

'Ere We Go, Mob Rule, Dakka! Dakka! Dakka! (pg 82)

Waaagh! Energy: Add 1 to Psychic tests taken for this model for every 10 ORK models (excluding GRETCHIN) within 10" of it when the roll is made, to a maximum of +3. If the result of the test is 12+ this model immediately suffers Perils of the Warp.

PSYKER

This model can attempt to manifest one psychic power in each friendly Psychic phase, and attempt to deny one psychic power in each enemy Psychic phase. It knows the *Smite* psychic power and one psychic power from the Power of the Waaagh! discipline (pg 129).

FACTION KEYWORDS ORK, <CLAN>

KEYWORDS CHARACTER, INFANTRY, PSYKER, WEIRDBOY

'Weirdboyz is alright, just don't stand too near to 'em less ya want yer bonce to go bang like a bomb squig under a Battlewagon. Don't hang about in front of 'em either, finkin' about it, cos if one of 'em chukz up on ya, yer face is gettin' melted off quicker than a grot in a fungus-brew chuggin' contest. In fact, Weirdboyz is alright, just so long as yer stays as far away from 'em as ya can get...'

- Narklob, Bad Moons Boss Nob

BOSS SNIKROT

4 POWER

NAME	M	WS	BS	S	T	W	A	Ld	Sv
Boss Snikrot	6"	2+	5+	6	5	6	6	7	6+

Boss Snikrot is a single model armed with Mork's Teeth and stikkbombs. Only one of this model can be included in your army.

WEAPON	RANGE	TYPE	S	AP	D	ABILITIES
Mork's Teeth	Melee	Melee	User	-1	2	-
Stikkbomb	6"	Grenade D6	3	0	1	-

ABILITIES

'Ere We Go, Mob Rule, Dakka! Dakka! Dakka! (pg 82)

Kunnin' Infiltrator: During deployment, you can set up Boss Snikrot in hiding instead of placing him on the battlefield. At the end of any of your Movement phases, Snikrot can stalk from his hiding place – set him up anywhere on the battlefield that is more than 9" away from any enemy models.

Terrifying Killer: Subtract 1 from the Leadership characteristic of enemy units while they are within 6" of Boss Snikrot.

Throat Slitta: Add 1 to wound rolls for attacks made with Boss Snikrot's melee weapons when targeting enemy units wholly within or on a terrain feature.

Red Skull Kommandos: Re-roll hit rolls of 1 in the Fight phase for attacks made by friendly BLOOD AXE KOMMANDOS units while they are within 6" of Boss Snikrot.

Sneakiest Git: Add 3 instead of 1 to saving throws for Boss Snikrot while he is receiving the benefit of cover.

FACTION KEYWORDS ORK, BLOOD AXE

KEYWORDS CHARACTER, INFANTRY, KOMMANDO, BOSS SNIKROT

5 POWER

BOSS ZAGSTRUK

NAME	M	WS	BS	S	T	W	A	Ld	Sv
Boss Zagstruk	12"	2+	5+	6	4	6	6	7	4+

Boss Zagstruk is a single model armed with Da Vulcha's Klaws, a slugga, choppa and blitz missiles. Only one of this model can be included in your army.

WEAPON	RANGE	TYPE	S	AP	D	ABILITIES
Blitz missiles	18"	Assault 1	6	-1	D3	-
Slugga	12"	Pistol 1	4	0	1	-
Choppa	Melee	Melee	User	0	1	Each time the bearer fights, it can make 1 additional attack with this weapon.
Da Vulcha's Klaws	Melee	Melee	+2	-3	D3	Each time the bearer fights, it can make no more than 3 attacks with this weapon.

ABILITIES

'Ere We Go, Mob Rule, Dakka! Dakka! Dakka! (pg 82)

Full Throttle: When Boss Zagstruk Advances, you can add 6" to his Move characteristic instead of rolling a dice, but if you do, roll a D6 at the end of the phase; on a 1, he suffers 1 mortal wound.

Cybork Body: Each time Boss Zagstruk loses a wound, roll a D6; on a 5+ that wound is not lost. You cannot make a Dok's Tools roll for this model if you do so.

Drill Boss: Friendly Goff Stormboyz units automatically pass Morale tests while they are within 6" of Boss Zagstruk.

Stormboyz Strike: During deployment, you can set up this model flying high in the skies instead of placing it on the battlefield. At the end of any of your Movement phases this model can plummet onto the battlefield – set it up anywhere on the battlefield, more than 9" away from any enemy models.

FACTION KEYWORDS: Ork, Goff

KEYWORDS: Character, Infantry, Stormboy, Jump Pack, Fly, Boss Zagstruk

6 POWER

DEFFKILLA WARTRIKE

NAME	M	WS	BS	S	T	W	A	Ld	Sv
Deffkilla Wartrike	14"	2+	5+	5	6	8	5	7	4+

A Deffkilla Wartrike is a single model equipped with a killa jet. The crew is armed with a snagga klaw and three twin boomstikks.

WEAPON	RANGE	TYPE	S	AP	D	ABILITIES
Killa jet	When attacking with this weapon, choose one of the profiles below.					
- Burna	8"	Assault D6	5	-1	1	This weapon automatically hits its target.
- Cutta	8"	Assault 2	8	-4	D6	If the target is within half range of this weapon, roll two dice when inflicting damage with it and discard the lowest result.
Snagga klaw (shooting)	8"	Assault 1	4	0	1	You can re-roll wound rolls for attacks made with this weapon.
Twin boomstikk	12"	Assault 2	5	0	1	If the target is within half range, add 1 to hit rolls for this weapon.
Snagga klaw (melee)	Melee	Melee	+2	-2	D3	You can re-roll wound rolls for attacks made with this weapon.

ABILITIES

'Ere We Go, Mob Rule, Dakka! Dakka! Dakka! (pg 82)

Speedwaaagh!: Friendly <Clan> Biker and Vehicle units within 6" of this model at the start of the Charge phase can charge even if they Advanced this turn.

Fuel-mixa Grot: Once per battle, when this model Advances, add 6" to its Move characteristic for that Movement phase instead of rolling a dice.

Explodes: If this model is reduced to 0 wounds, roll a D6. On a 6 it explodes, and each unit within 3" suffers 1 mortal wound.

FACTION KEYWORDS: Ork, <Clan>

KEYWORDS: Character, Vehicle, Speed Freeks, Speedboss, Deffkilla Wartrike

5 POWER

KAPTIN BADRUKK

NAME	M	WS	BS	S	T	W	A	Ld	Sv
Kaptin Badrukk	5"	2+	4+	5	4	6	4	8	3+
Ammo Runt	5"	5+	4+	2	2	1	1	4	6+

Kaptin Badrukk is a single model armed with a slugga, choppa, stikkbombs and Da Rippa. He may be accompanied by an Ammo Runt. Only one of this unit can be included in your army.

WEAPON	RANGE	TYPE	S	AP	D	ABILITIES
Da Rippa	When attacking with this weapon, choose one of the profiles below.					
- Standard	24"	Heavy 3	7	-3	2	-
- Supercharge	24"	Heavy 3	8	-3	3	If you roll one or more unmodified hit rolls of 1, the bearer suffers 1 mortal wound after all of this weapon's attacks have been resolved.
Slugga	12"	Pistol 1	4	0	1	-
Choppa	Melee	Melee	User	0	1	Each time the bearer fights, it can make 1 additional attack with this weapon.
Stikkbomb	6"	Grenade D6	3	0	1	-

ABILITIES

'Ere We Go, Mob Rule, Dakka! Dakka! Dakka! (pg 82)

Goldtoof Armour: Kaptin Badrukk has a 5+ invulnerable save.

Flashiest Gitz: Re-roll hit rolls of 1 in the Shooting phase for friendly FLASH GITZ units while they are within 6" of Kaptin Badrukk.

Ammo Runt: If Kaptin Badrukk is accompanied by an Ammo Runt, you can re-roll one hit roll each time he shoots.

When rolling to wound this unit, use Badrukk's Toughness while he is on the battlefield. The death of an Ammo Runt is ignored for the purposes of Morale tests. The Ammo Runt is considered to have the CHARACTER keyword for the purposes of shooting attacks.

FACTION KEYWORDS ORK, FREEBOOTERZ

KEYWORDS (BADRUKK) INFANTRY, CHARACTER, FLASH GITZ, KAPTIN BADRUKK

KEYWORDS (AMMO RUNT) INFANTRY, GRETCHIN, AMMO RUNT

Kaptin Badrukk fixes his ladz with a beady eye to make sure they unleash maximum dakka upon the enemy.

4 POWER

BOYZ

NAME	M	WS	BS	S	T	W	A	Ld	Sv
Ork Boy	5"	3+	5+	4	4	1	2	6	6+
Boss Nob	5"	3+	5+	5	4	2	3	7	6+

This unit contains 10 Ork Boyz. It can include up to 10 additional Ork Boyz (**Power Rating +3**) or up to 20 additional Ork Boyz (**Power Rating +7**). A Boss Nob can take the place of one Ork Boy. Each model is armed with a slugga, choppa and stikkbombs.

WEAPON	RANGE	TYPE	S	AP	D	ABILITIES
Big shoota	36"	Assault 3	5	0	1	-
Rokkit launcha	24"	Assault 1	8	-2	3	-
Shoota	18"	Assault 2	4	0	1	-
Slugga	12"	Pistol 1	4	0	1	-
Choppa	Melee	Melee	User	0	1	Each time the bearer fights, it can make 1 additional attack with this weapon.
Stikkbomb	6"	Grenade D6	3	0	1	-
Tankbusta bomb	6"	Grenade D3	8	-2	D6	-

WARGEAR OPTIONS
- Any Ork Boy may replace its choppa and slugga with a shoota.
- For every 10 models in the unit, one Ork Boy may take a tankbusta bomb.
- For every 10 models in the unit, one Ork Boy may replace its choppa and slugga with a rokkit launcha or big shoota.
- The Boss Nob may replace its slugga and choppa with items from the *Nob Weapons* list.

ABILITIES
'Ere We Go, Mob Rule, Dakka! Dakka! Dakka! (pg 82)

Green Tide: Add 1 to the Attacks characteristic of models in this unit while it contains 20 or more models.

FACTION KEYWORDS ORK, <CLAN>

KEYWORDS INFANTRY, BOYZ

1 POWER

GRETCHIN

NAME	M	WS	BS	S	T	W	A	Ld	Sv
Gretchin	5"	5+	4+	2	2	1	1	4	6+

This unit contains 10 Gretchin. It can include up to 10 additional Gretchin (**Power Rating +1**), or up to 20 additional Gretchin (**Power Rating +3**). Each model is armed with a grot blasta.

WEAPON	RANGE	TYPE	S	AP	D	ABILITIES
Grot blasta	12"	Pistol 1	3	0	1	-

ABILITIES
Dakka! Dakka! Dakka! (pg 82)

Surprisingly Dangerous in Large Numbers: Add 1 to hit rolls for attacks made by models in this unit while it contains 20 or more models.

FACTION KEYWORDS ORK, <CLAN>

KEYWORDS INFANTRY, GRETCHIN

MAD DOK GROTSNIK

5 POWER

NAME	M	WS	BS	S	T	W	A	Ld	Sv
Mad Dok Grotsnik	5"	2+	5+	5	5	4	4	8	4+

Mad Dok Grotsnik is a single model armed with a slugga, power klaw and 'urty syringe. Only one of this model can be included in your army.

WEAPON	RANGE	TYPE	S	AP	D	ABILITIES
Slugga	12"	Pistol 1	4	0	1	-
Power klaw	Melee	Melee	x2	-3	D3	When attacking with this weapon, you must subtract 1 from the hit roll.
'Urty syringe	Melee	Melee	User	0	1	Each time the bearer fights, it can make 1 additional attack with this weapon. This weapon always wounds on a 4+ unless it is targeting a VEHICLE or TITANIC unit, in which case it wounds on a 6+.

ABILITIES

'Ere We Go, Mob Rule, Dakka! Dakka! Dakka! (pg 82)

Cybork Body: Each time Mad Dok Grotsnik loses a wound, roll a D6; on a 5+ that wound is not lost. You cannot make a Dok's Tools roll for this model if you do so.

One Scalpel Short of a Medpack: At the start of the Charge phase, if Mad Dok Grotsnik is not within 3" of another friendly ORK INFANTRY unit, not within 1" of an enemy unit, and is within 12" of an enemy unit, he will automatically attempt to charge the nearest enemy unit. He can do so even if he Advanced or Fell Back in the same turn.

Dok's Tools: Roll a D6 each time a friendly ORK INFANTRY or BIKER unit loses a wound while it is within 3" of Mad Dok Grotsnik. On a 6 the wound is not lost. This is not cumulative with other Dok's Tools.

Sawbonez: At the end of your Movement phase, Mad Dok Grotsnik can attempt surgery on a single friendly ORK INFANTRY or BIKER model within 1" of him. If he does so, roll a D6 to determine if the surgery is successful. On a 1 the surgery fails, and the model you were attempting to heal loses a wound. On a 2+ the surgery succeeds, and that model regains D3 lost wounds. A model can only be the target of a surgery attempt once per turn.

FACTION KEYWORDS: ORK, DEATHSKULLS

KEYWORDS: CHARACTER, INFANTRY, PAINBOY, MAD DOK GROTSNIK

'Da battlefield is a land of rich opportunities if yer smart, kunnin' and remember to duck. Stuff blowin' up all over, ladz gettin' 'emselves torn up and chopped apart and goin' on fire and gettin' run over and wotnot. Loadsa potential kustomers, and most of 'em too far gone to fight back or complain about da goin' rate in teef. I mean, if yooz gonna risk yer neck fixin' da ladz up, it's only right you charge a bit extra in danger munny, innit? An' if dey's ever stoopid enough to kick up a fuss, well, ladz, dat's when ya gets to bring yer biggest needles out...'

- Dok Stitchiz to his orderlies, before the Battle of Moslok

PAINBOY

3 Power

NAME	M	WS	BS	S	T	W	A	Ld	Sv
Painboy	5"	3+	5+	5	4	4	4	6	6+

A Painboy is a single model armed with an 'urty syringe and power klaw.

WEAPON	RANGE	TYPE	S	AP	D	ABILITIES
Power klaw	Melee	Melee	x2	-3	D3	When attacking with this weapon, you must subtract 1 from the hit roll.
'Urty syringe	Melee	Melee	User	0	1	Each time the bearer fights, it can make 1 additional attack with this weapon. This weapon always wounds on a 4+ unless it is targeting a **VEHICLE** or **TITANIC** unit, in which case it wounds on a 6+.

ABILITIES

'Ere We Go, Mob Rule, Dakka! Dakka! Dakka! (pg 82)

Sawbonez: At the end of your Movement phase, this model can attempt surgery on a single friendly **<CLAN> INFANTRY** or **BIKER** model within 1" of it. If it does so, roll a D6 to determine if the surgery is successful. On a 1 the surgery fails and the model you were attempting to heal loses a wound. On a 2+ the surgery succeeds and that model regains D3 lost wounds. A model can only be the target of a surgery attempt once per turn.

Dok's Tools: Roll a D6 each time a **<CLAN> INFANTRY** or **BIKER** unit loses a wound while it is within 3" of any friendly **<CLAN> PAINBOYZ**. On a 6 that unit does not lose that wound.

Grot Orderly: Once per battle, you can re-roll the dice when this model is attempting to heal a model using its Sawbonez ability, either when determining if the surgery is successful or when determining the number of lost wounds regained.

FACTION KEYWORDS: ORK, <CLAN>

KEYWORDS: CHARACTER, INFANTRY, PAINBOY

Leering with evil intent, a Painboy decides which of his wicked surgical implements to stick his victims with first.

MEK

2 POWER

NAME	M	WS	BS	S	T	W	A	Ld	Sv
Mek	5"	3+	5+	4	4	3	2	6	6+
Grot Oiler	5"	5+	4+	2	2	1	1	4	6+

A Mek is a single model armed with a kustom mega-slugga, choppa and stikkbombs. It may be accompanied by a Grot Oiler.

WEAPON	RANGE	TYPE	S	AP	D	ABILITIES
Kustom mega-slugga	12"	Pistol 1	8	-3	D6	If you roll one or more unmodified hit rolls of 1, the bearer suffers 1 mortal wound after all of this weapon's attacks have been resolved.
Choppa	Melee	Melee	User	0	1	Each time the bearer fights, it can make 1 additional attack with this weapon.
Killsaw	Melee	Melee	x2	-4	2	When attacking with this weapon, you must subtract 1 from the hit roll.
Stikkbomb	6"	Grenade D6	3	0	1	-

WARGEAR OPTIONS
- This model may replace its choppa with a killsaw.

ABILITIES

'Ere We Go, Mob Rule, Dakka! Dakka! Dakka! (pg 82)

Mekaniak: At the end of your Movement phase, this model can repair a single friendly **<CLAN> VEHICLE** model within 1". That model regains 1 lost wound. A model can only be repaired once per turn.

Grot Oiler: Once per battle, a Grot Oiler can assist its master in making repairs. If it does so, the model being repaired regains 1 additional lost wound.

When rolling to wound this unit, use the Mek's Toughness while it is on the battlefield. The death of a Grot Oiler is ignored for the purposes of Morale tests. The Grot Oiler is considered to have the **CHARACTER** keyword for the purposes of shooting attacks.

FACTION KEYWORDS: ORK, <CLAN>

KEYWORDS (MEK): CHARACTER, INFANTRY, MEK

KEYWORDS (GROT OILER): INFANTRY, GRETCHIN, GROT OILER

RUNTHERD

2 POWER

NAME	M	WS	BS	S	T	W	A	Ld	Sv
Runtherd	5"	3+	5+	4	4	4	3	7	6+

A Runtherd is a single model armed with a slugga and grabba stikk.

WEAPON	RANGE	TYPE	S	AP	D	ABILITIES
Slugga	12"	Pistol 1	4	0	1	-
Grabba stikk	Melee	Melee	+1	0	1	Each time the bearer fights, it can make 1 additional attack with this weapon.
Grot-prod	Melee	Melee	+2	-1	1	-

WARGEAR OPTIONS
- This model may replace its grabba stikk with a grot-prod.
- This model may take either a grot lash or a squig hound.

ABILITIES

'Ere We Go, Mob Rule, Dakka! Dakka! Dakka! (pg 82)

Runtherd: If your army is Battle-forged, you must include at least one unit comprised entirely of **GRETCHIN INFANTRY** in a Detachment for each **RUNTHERD** unit in that Detachment. **RUNTHERD** units do not take up slots in a Detachement.

Squig Hound: If a unit comprised entirely of **GRETCHIN INFANTRY** fails a Morale test while it is within 3" of any friendly **RUNTHERD** models with a squig hound, ignore the result. D3 models from the unit are slain instead.

Grot Lash: Re-roll hit rolls of 1 in the Fight phase for attacks made by units comprised entirely of **GRETCHIN INFANTRY** while they are within 3" of any friendly **RUNTHERD** models with a grot lash.

FACTION KEYWORDS: ORK, <CLAN>

KEYWORDS: CHARACTER, INFANTRY, RUNTHERD

A mob of Burna Boyz hustle enthusiastically toward the enemy, eager to set light to everything in sight.

3 POWER

BURNA BOYZ

NAME	M	WS	BS	S	T	W	A	Ld	Sv
Burna Boy	5"	3+	5+	4	4	1	2	6	6+
Spanner	5"	3+	5+	4	4	1	2	6	6+

This unit contains 5 Burna Boyz. It can include up to 5 additional Burna Boyz (**Power Rating +3**) or up to 10 additional Burna Boyz (**Power Rating +6**). For every 5 models in the unit, a Spanner can take the place of one Burna Boy. Each Burna Boy is armed with a burna and stikkbombs. Each Spanner is armed with stikkbombs and either a kustom mega-blasta, big shoota or rokkit launcha.

WEAPON	RANGE	TYPE	S	AP	D	ABILITIES
Big shoota	36"	Assault 3	5	0	1	-
Burna (shooting)	8"	Assault D3	4	0	1	Before a unit fires this weapon, roll once for the number of attacks and use this for all burnas fired by the unit until the end of the phase. This weapon automatically hits its target.
Kustom mega-blasta	24"	Assault 1	8	-3	D6	If you roll one or more unmodified hit rolls of 1, the bearer suffers 1 mortal wound after all of this weapon's attacks have been resolved.
Rokkit launcha	24"	Assault 1	8	-2	3	-
Burna (melee)	Melee	Melee	User	-2	1	-
Stikkbomb	6"	Grenade D6	3	0	1	-

ABILITIES

'Ere We Go, Mob Rule, Dakka! Dakka! Dakka! (pg 82)

Pyromaniaks: If this unit destroys an enemy unit in the Shooting phase, it automatically passes Morale tests until the start of your next turn.

Mekaniak: At the end of your Movement phase, a Spanner can repair a single friendly <CLAN> VEHICLE model within 1". That model regains 1 lost wound. A model can only be repaired once per turn.

FACTION KEYWORDS ORK, <CLAN>

KEYWORDS INFANTRY, BURNA BOYZ

TANKBUSTAS

4 POWER

NAME	M	WS	BS	S	T	W	A	Ld	Sv
Tankbusta	5"	3+	5+	4	4	1	2	6	6+
Boss Nob	5"	3+	5+	5	4	2	3	7	6+
Bomb Squig	5"	2+	2+	3	4	1	1	4	6+

This unit contains 5 Tankbustas. It can include up to 5 additional Tankbustas (**Power Rating +4**) or up to 10 additional Tankbustas (**Power Rating +9**). A Boss Nob can take the place of one Tankbusta. For every 5 Tankbustas and/or Boss Nobz in the unit, it may be accompanied by up to 2 Bomb Squigs. Each Tankbusta and Boss Nob is armed with a rokkit launcha, stikkbombs and tankbusta bombs. Each Bomb Squig carries a squig bomb.

WEAPON	RANGE	TYPE	S	AP	D	ABILITIES
Pair of rokkit pistols	12"	Pistol 2	7	-2	D3	-
Rokkit launcha	24"	Assault 1	8	-2	3	-
Squig bomb	18"	Assault 1	8	-2	D6	This weapon cannot target units that can FLY. After making an attack with this weapon, the bearer is slain.
Tankhammer	Melee	Melee	-	-	-	Each time the bearer fights, it can only make a single attack with this weapon. If the attack hits, the target suffers D3 mortal wounds and the bearer is slain.
Stikkbomb	6"	Grenade D6	3	0	1	-
Tankbusta bomb	6"	Grenade D3	8	-2	D6	-

WARGEAR OPTIONS

- For every five Tankbustas and/or Boss Nobz in the unit, one Tankbusta may replace their rokkit launcha with a tankhammer.
- For every five Tankbustas and/or Boss Nobz in the unit, one Tankbusta may replace their rokkit launcha with a pair of rokkit pistols.

ABILITIES

'Ere We Go, Mob Rule, Dakka! Dakka! Dakka! (pg 82)

Tank Hunters: You can re-roll hit rolls for attacks made by this unit that target VEHICLE units.

Bomb Squig: The death of a Bomb Squig is ignored for the purposes of Morale tests.

FACTION KEYWORDS: ORK, <CLAN>

KEYWORDS (TANKBUSTAS): INFANTRY, TANKBUSTAS

KEYWORDS (BOMB SQUIGS): INFANTRY, SQUIG, BOMB SQUIGS

Emerging from the roiling dust clouds of the greenskin advance, the Tankbustas prepare to let fly with their deadly payloads.

NOBZ

7 Power

NAME	M	WS	BS	S	T	W	A	Ld	Sv
Nob	5"	3+	5+	5	4	2	3	6	4+
Boss Nob	5"	3+	5+	5	4	2	3	7	4+
Ammo Runt	5"	5+	4+	2	2	1	1	4	6+

This unit contains 1 Boss Nob and 4 Nobz. It can include up to 5 additional Nobz (**Power Rating +7**). Each Nob and Boss Nob is armed with a slugga, choppa and stikkbombs. For every 5 Nobz and/or Boss Nobz in the unit, it may be accompanied by 1 Ammo Runt.

WEAPON	RANGE	TYPE	S	AP	D	ABILITIES
Slugga	12"	Pistol 1	4	0	1	-
Choppa	Melee	Melee	User	0	1	Each time the bearer fights, it can make 1 additional attack with this weapon.
Stikkbomb	6"	Grenade D6	3	0	1	-

WARGEAR OPTIONS
- Any model may replace its slugga and choppa with items from the *Nob Weapons* list.
- For every 5 Nobz and/or Boss Nobz in the unit, one Nob or Boss Nob may have a Cybork body.

ABILITIES

'Ere We Go, Mob Rule, Dakka! Dakka! Dakka! (pg 82)

Ammo Runt: Each time this unit shoots, you can re-roll one hit roll for each Ammo Runt accompanying it.

When rolling to wound this unit, use the Nobz' or Boss Nob's Toughness while they are on the battlefield. The death of an Ammo Runt is ignored for the purposes of Morale tests.

Keepin' Order: Roll a D6 for each model that flees from a <Clan> unit that is within 3" of any friendly <Clan> units with this ability when the Morale test is taken. On a 6 that model does not flee.

Cybork Body: Each time a model with a Cybork body loses a wound, roll a D6; on a 6 that wound is not lost. You cannot make a Dok's Tools roll for this model if you do so.

FACTION KEYWORDS: Ork, <Clan>

KEYWORDS (NOBZ): Infantry, Nobz

KEYWORDS (AMMO RUNTS): Infantry, Gretchin, Ammo Runts

NOB
with Waaagh! Banner

4 Power

NAME	M	WS	BS	S	T	W	A	Ld	Sv
Nob with Waaagh! Banner	5"	3+	5+	5	4	4	3	6	4+

A Nob with Waaagh! Banner is a single model armed with a Waaagh! banner, kustom shoota, choppa and stikkbombs.

WEAPON	RANGE	TYPE	S	AP	D	ABILITIES
Kustom shoota	18"	Assault 4	4	0	1	-
Choppa	Melee	Melee	User	0	1	Each time the bearer fights, it can make 1 additional attack with this weapon.
Waaagh! banner	Melee	Melee	+2	0	2	-
Stikkbomb	6"	Grenade D6	3	0	1	-

ABILITIES

'Ere We Go, Mob Rule, Dakka! Dakka! Dakka! (pg 82)

Waaagh! Banner: Add 1 to hit rolls in the Fight phase for attacks made by <Clan> units while they are within 6" of any friendly Nobs with Waaagh! Banners.

Keepin' Order: Roll a D6 for each model that flees from a <Clan> unit that is within 3" of any friendly <Clan> units with this ability when the Morale test is taken. On a 6 that model does not flee.

FACTION KEYWORDS: Ork, <Clan>

KEYWORDS: Character, Infantry, Nob

A mob of Evil Sunz Meganobz hiss and clank their way towards the enemy as fast as they can, power klaws snapping in anticipation.

6 POWER

MEGANOBZ

NAME	M	WS	BS	S	T	W	A	Ld	Sv
Meganob	4"	3+	5+	5	4	3	3	6	2+
Boss Meganob	4"	3+	5+	5	4	3	3	7	2+

This unit contains 1 Boss Meganob and 2 Meganobz. It can include up to 7 additional Meganobz (**Power Rating +2 per model**). Each model is armed with a kustom shoota, power klaw and stikkbombs.

WEAPON	RANGE	TYPE	S	AP	D	ABILITIES
Kombi-weapon with rokkit launcha	When attacking with this weapon, choose one or both of the profiles below. If you choose both, subtract 1 from all hit rolls.					
- Rokkit launcha	24"	Assault 1	8	-2	3	-
- Shoota	18"	Assault 2	4	0	1	-
Kombi-weapon with skorcha	When attacking with this weapon, choose one or both of the profiles below. If you choose both, subtract 1 from all hit rolls.					
- Shoota	18"	Assault 2	4	0	1	-
- Skorcha	8"	Assault D6	5	-1	1	This weapon automatically hits its target.
Kustom shoota	18"	Assault 4	4	0	1	-
Killsaw	Melee	Melee	x2	-4	2	When attacking with this weapon, you must subtract 1 from the hit roll. If a model is armed with two killsaws, add 1 to its Attacks characteristic.
Power klaw	Melee	Melee	x2	-3	D3	When attacking with this weapon, you must subtract 1 from the hit roll.
Stikkbomb	6"	Grenade D6	3	0	1	-

WARGEAR OPTIONS	• Any model may replace its kustom shoota and power klaw with two killsaws. • Any model may replace its kustom shoota with a kombi-weapon with skorcha or kombi-weapon with rokkit launcha.
ABILITIES	**'Ere We Go, Mob Rule, Dakka! Dakka! Dakka!** (pg 82) **Keepin' Order:** Roll a D6 for each model that flees from a <Clan> unit that is within 3" of any friendly <Clan> units with this ability when the Morale test is taken. On a 6 that model does not flee.
FACTION KEYWORDS	Ork, <Clan>
KEYWORDS	Infantry, Mega Armour, Nobz, Meganobz

NOBZ
ON WARBIKES

NAME	M	WS	BS	S	T	W	A	Ld	Sv
Nob on Warbike	14"	3+	5+	5	5	3	3	6	4+
Boss Nob on Warbike	14"	3+	5+	5	5	3	3	7	4+

This unit contains 1 Boss Nob on Warbike and 2 Nobz on Warbikes. It can include up to 3 additional Nobz on Warbikes (**Power Rating +7**), or up to 6 additional Nobz on Warbikes (**Power Rating +12**). Each model is armed with a choppa, and rides a warbike equipped with two dakkaguns.

WEAPON	RANGE	TYPE	S	AP	D	ABILITIES
Dakkagun	18"	Assault 3	5	0	1	-
Slugga	12"	Pistol 1	4	0	1	-
Choppa	Melee	Melee	User	0	1	Each time the bearer fights, it can make 1 additional attack with this weapon.
Stikkbomb	6"	Grenade D6	3	0	1	-

WARGEAR OPTIONS
- Any model may take a slugga and/or stikkbombs.
- Any model may replace its choppa and slugga with items from the *Nob Weapons* list.

ABILITIES

'Ere We Go, Mob Rule, Dakka! Dakka! Dakka! (pg 82)

Keepin' Order: Roll a D6 for each model that flees from a <CLAN> unit that is within 3" of any friendly <CLAN> units with this ability when the Morale test is taken. On a 6 that model does not flee.

FACTION KEYWORDS ORK, <CLAN>

KEYWORDS BIKER, SPEED FREEKS, NOBZ

KOMMANDOS

NAME	M	WS	BS	S	T	W	A	Ld	Sv
Kommando	6"	3+	5+	4	4	1	2	6	6+
Boss Nob	6"	3+	5+	5	4	2	3	7	6+

This unit contains 5 Kommandos. It can include up to 5 additional Kommandos (**Power Rating +2**) or up to 10 additional Kommandos (**Power Rating +4**). A Boss Nob can take the place of one Kommando, and is armed with a power klaw, slugga and stikkbombs. Each Kommando is armed with a choppa, slugga and stikkbombs. One Kommando in every 5 models is also armed with a tankbusta bomb.

WEAPON	RANGE	TYPE	S	AP	D	ABILITIES
Slugga	12"	Pistol 1	4	0	1	-
Choppa	Melee	Melee	User	0	1	Each time the bearer fights, it can make 1 additional attack with this weapon.
Power klaw	Melee	Melee	x2	-3	D3	When attacking with this weapon, you must subtract 1 from the hit roll.
Stikkbomb	6"	Grenade D6	3	0	1	-
Tankbusta bomb	6"	Grenade D3	8	-2	D6	-

ABILITIES

'Ere We Go, Mob Rule, Dakka! Dakka! Dakka! (pg 82)

Kunnin' Infiltrators: During deployment, you may set up this unit in hiding instead of placing it on the battlefield. At the end of any of your Movement phases, this unit can stalk from their hiding place – set them up anywhere on the battlefield that is more than 9" away from any enemy models.

Sneaky Gits: Add 2 instead of 1 to saving throws for models in this unit while it is receiving the benefit of cover.

Throat Slittas: Add 1 to wound rolls for attacks made with this unit's melee weapons when targeting enemy units wholly within or on a terrain feature.

FACTION KEYWORDS ORK, <CLAN>

KEYWORDS INFANTRY, KOMMANDOS

Evil Sunz Warbikers roar into the fight, raising a vast cloud of dust and smoke as they surge toward the enemy lines.

'Mekboy Gogrut built dis bike fer me. Painted it proppa red just like I told 'im, stuck da biggest guns on wot he could find an' covered it wiv spikes. Job's a good 'un, right? Trouble is, cheeky zogger stuck brakes on it, like fer stoppin' wiv! Wot did he fink I am, sum kinda grot? Needless to say, I knocked his block off. Dat's his skull on da front there.'

- 'Firewheelz' Frazgat, Bad Ork Bikeboy

4 POWER

WARBIKERS

NAME	M	WS	BS	S	T	W	A	Ld	Sv
Warbiker	14"	3+	5+	4	5	2	2	6	4+
Boss Nob on Warbike	14"	3+	5+	5	5	3	3	7	4+

This unit contains 3 Warbikers. It can include up to 3 additional Warbikers (**Power Rating +3**), up to 6 additional Warbikers (**Power Rating +7**) or up to 9 additional Warbikers (**Power Rating +10**). A Boss Nob on Warbike can take the place of one Warbiker. Each model rides a warbike equipped with two dakkaguns.

WEAPON	RANGE	TYPE	S	AP	D	ABILITIES
Dakkagun	18"	Assault 3	5	0	1	-
Slugga	12"	Pistol 1	4	0	1	-
Choppa	Melee	Melee	User	0	1	Each time the bearer fights, it can make 1 additional attack with this weapon.
Stikkbomb	6"	Grenade D6	3	0	1	-

WARGEAR OPTIONS
- Any model may take a slugga and/or choppa.
- The Boss Nob on Warbike may replace his choppa and slugga with items from the *Nob Weapons* list.
- Any model may take stikkbombs.

ABILITIES: **'Ere We Go, Mob Rule, Dakka! Dakka! Dakka!** (pg 82)

FACTION KEYWORDS: ORK, <CLAN>

KEYWORDS: BIKER, SPEED FREEKS, WARBIKERS

5 POWER

KUSTOM BOOSTA-BLASTAS

NAME	M	WS	BS	S	T	W	A	Ld	Sv
Kustom Boosta-blasta	12"	4+	5+	5	6	8	4	6	4+

This unit contains 1 Kustom Boosta-blasta. It can include 1 additional Kustom Boosta-blasta **(Power Rating +5)** or 2 additional Kustom Boosta-blastas **(Power Rating +10)**. Each model is equipped with a rivet kannon and four burna exhausts, and each model's crew is armed with stikkbombs and a grot blasta.

WEAPON	RANGE	TYPE	S	AP	D	ABILITIES
Burna exhaust	8"	Assault D3	4	0	1	This weapon automatically hits its target.
Grot blasta	12"	Pistol 1	4	0	1	-
Rivet kannon	36"	Assault 6	7	-2	2	-
Stikkbomb	6"	Grenade D6	3	0	1	-

ABILITIES

'Ere We Go, Mob Rule, Dakka! Dakka! Dakka!, Speed Mob (pg 82)

Grot Gunner: Add 1 to hit rolls for attacks made with this model's grot blasta.

Riding Shotgun: When this model shoots, it can throw a Grenade and shoot with its Pistol(s) in addition to any other weapons.

Spiked Ram: Each time this model finishes a charge move, select an enemy unit within 1" of it and roll a D6; on a 4+ that unit suffers D3 mortal wounds.

Explodes: If this model is reduced to 0 wounds, roll a D6. On a 6 it explodes, and each unit within 6" suffers D3 mortal wounds.

FACTION KEYWORDS ORK, <CLAN>

KEYWORDS VEHICLE, SPEED FREEKS, KUSTOM BOOSTA-BLASTAS

6 POWER

SHOKKJUMP DRAGSTAS

NAME	M	WS	BS	S	T	W	A	Ld	Sv
Shokkjump Dragsta	14"	4+	5+	5	6	8	4	6	4+

This unit contains 1 Shokkjump Dragsta. It can include 1 additional Shokkjump Dragsta **(Power Rating +6)** or 2 additional Shokkjump Dragstas **(Power Rating +12)**. Each model is equipped with a kustom shokk rifle, rokkit launcha and saw blades.

WEAPON	RANGE	TYPE	S	AP	D	ABILITIES
Kustom shokk rifle	24"	Assault 2	8	-3	D6	If you roll one or more unmodified hit rolls of 1 for this weapon, the bearer suffers 1 mortal wound after all of this weapon's attacks have been resolved. Each time you make a wound roll of 6+ for this weapon, the target suffers 1 mortal wound in addition to any other damage.
Rokkit launcha	24"	Assault 1	8	-2	3	-
Saw blades	Melee	Melee	+1	-1	1	

ABILITIES

'Ere We Go, Mob Rule, Dakka! Dakka! Dakka!, Speed Mob (pg 82)

Shokk Tunnel: If you roll a 4+ when Advancing with this model, remove it from the battlefield and set it up again anywhere on the battlefield more than 9" away from any enemy units. After doing so, roll a D6; on a 4+ the model suffers 1 mortal wound.

Grot Gunner and Targetin' Squig: Add 2 to hit rolls for attacks made with this model's kustom shokk rifle.

Explodes: If this model is reduced to 0 wounds, roll a D6. On a 6 it explodes, and each unit within 3" suffers D3 mortal wounds.

FACTION KEYWORDS ORK, <CLAN>

KEYWORDS VEHICLE, SPEED FREEKS, SHOKKJUMP DRAGSTAS

5 POWER

BOOMDAKKA SNAZZWAGONS

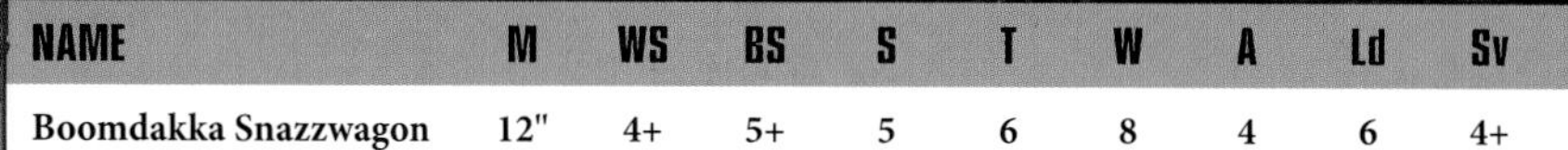

NAME	M	WS	BS	S	T	W	A	Ld	Sv
Boomdakka Snazzwagon	12"	4+	5+	5	6	8	4	6	4+

This unit contains 1 Boomdakka Snazzwagon. It can include 1 additional Boomdakka Snazzwagon (**Power Rating +5**) or 2 additional Boomdakka Snazzwagons (**Power Rating +10**). Each model is equipped with a Mek speshul and big shoota, and each model's crew is armed with burna bottles and a grot blasta.

WEAPON	RANGE	TYPE	S	AP	D	ABILITIES
Big shoota	36"	Assault 3	5	0	1	-
Grot blasta	12"	Pistol 1	3	0	1	-
Mek speshul	24"	Assault 9	5	-2	1	-
Burna bottles	6"	Grenade 2D6	4	0	1	Units do not receive the benefit of cover to their saving throws for attacks made with this weapon.

ABILITIES

'Ere We Go, Mob Rule, Dakka! Dakka! Dakka!, Speed Mob (pg 82)

Grot Gunner: Add 1 to hit rolls for attacks made with this model's big shoota and grot blasta.

Billowing Fumes: Subtract 1 from hit rolls for attacks made with ranged weapons that target this model.

Riding Shotgun: When this model shoots, it can throw a Grenade and shoot with its Pistol(s) in addition to any other weapons.

Explodes: If this model is reduced to 0 wounds, roll a D6. On a 4+ it explodes, and each unit within D6" suffers D3 mortal wounds.

FACTION KEYWORDS ORK, <CLAN>

KEYWORDS VEHICLE, SPEED FREEKS, BOOMDAKKA SNAZZWAGONS

5 POWER

MEGATRAKK SCRAPJETS

NAME	M	WS	BS	S	T	W	A	Ld	Sv
Megatrakk Scrapjet	10"	4+	5+	6	6	9	4	6	4+

This unit contains 1 Megatrakk Scrapjet. It can include 1 additional Megatrakk Scrapjet (**Power Rating +5**) or 2 additional Megatrakk Scrapjets (**Power Rating +11**). Each model is equipped with a rokkit kannon, two twin big shootas, wing missiles and a nose drill.

WEAPON	RANGE	TYPE	S	AP	D	ABILITIES
Rokkit kannon	24"	Assault 2D3	8	-2	3	-
Twin big shoota	36"	Assault 6	5	0	1	-
Wing missiles	24"	Assault 1	8	-2	3	Add 1 to hit rolls for attacks made with this weapon against VEHICLE units. Subtract 1 from hit rolls for attacks made with this weapon against all other targets.
Nose drill	Melee	Melee	+2	-2	D3	-

ABILITIES

'Ere We Go, Mob Rule, Dakka! Dakka! Dakka!, Speed Mob (pg 82)

Spiked Ram: Each time this model finishes a charge move, select an enemy unit within 1" of it and roll a D6; on a 4+ that unit suffers D3 mortal wounds.

Explodes: If this model is reduced to 0 wounds, roll a D6. On a 6 it explodes, and each unit within 3" suffers D3 mortal wounds.

FACTION KEYWORDS ORK, <CLAN>

KEYWORDS VEHICLE, SPEED FREEKS, MEGATRAKK SCRAPJETS

7 POWER

RUKKATRUKK SQUIGBUGGIES

NAME	M	WS	BS	S	T	W	A	Ld	Sv
Rukkatrukk Squigbuggy	10"	4+	5+	5	6	9	4	6	4+

This unit contains 1 Rukkatrukk Squigbuggy. It can include 1 additional Rukkatrukk Squigbuggy (**Power Rating +7**) or 2 additional Rukkatrukk Squigbuggies (**Power Rating +14**). Each model is equipped with a heavy squig launcha and saw blades, and each model's crew is armed with a squig launcher, shotgun and stikksquigs.

WEAPON	RANGE	TYPE	S	AP	D	ABILITIES
Heavy squig launcha	When attacking with this weapon, choose one of the profiles below.					
- Bile squig	36"	Assault 2D6	*	0	1	This weapon always wounds on a 4+ unless it is targeting a VEHICLE or TITANIC unit, in which case it wounds on a 6+.
- Bitey squig	36"	Assault 2	5	-3	2	-
- Boom squig	36"	Assault 2D3	6	-1	D3	-
Shotgun	12"	Assault 2	3	0	1	If the target is within half range, add 1 to this weapon's Strength.
Squig launcha	When attacking with this weapon, choose one of the profiles below.					
- Bile squig	36"	Assault D6	*	0	1	This weapon always wounds on a 4+ unless it is targeting a VEHICLE or TITANIC unit, in which case it wounds on a 6+.
- Bitey squig	36"	Assault 1	5	-3	2	-
- Boom squig	36"	Assault D3	6	-1	D3	-
Stikksquig	6"	Grenade D6	3	0	1	-
Saw blades	Melee	Melee	+1	-1	1	-

ABILITIES

'Ere We Go, Mob Rule, Dakka! Dakka! Dakka!, Speed Mob (pg 82)

Grot Gunner: Add 1 to hit rolls for attacks made with this model's heavy squig launcha.

Riding Shotgun: When this model shoots, it can throw a Grenade and shoot with its Pistol(s) in addition to any other weapons.

Explodes: If this model is reduced to 0 wounds, roll a D6. On a 6 it explodes, and each unit within 3" suffers D3 mortal wounds.

Squig Mine: Once per battle, in the Movement phase, this model can deploy a squig mine. At any point during this model's move, place the squig mine within 1" of it and more than 3" from any enemy models. The squig mine is represented by the squig mine model, but does not count as a model for any rules purposes. From the start of the next phase, that squig mine is detonated if any unit (friend or foe) moves within 3" of it. Resolve the detonation after the unit that detonated it has ended its move. When a squig mine is detonated, roll a D6: on a 2-3 it inflicts 1 mortal wound on the unit that detonated it; on a 4-5 it inflicts D3 mortal wounds on the unit that detonated it; and on a 6 it inflicts 3 mortal wounds on the unit that detonated it. The squig mine is then removed from the battlefield.

FACTION KEYWORDS: ORK, <CLAN>

KEYWORDS: VEHICLE, SPEED FREEKS, RUKKATRUKK SQUIGBUGGIES

3 POWER — STORMBOYZ

NAME	M	WS	BS	S	T	W	A	Ld	Sv
Stormboy	12"	3+	5+	4	4	1	2	6	6+
Boss Nob	12"	3+	5+	5	4	2	3	7	6+

This unit contains 5 Stormboyz. It can include up to 5 additional Stormboyz (**Power Rating +2**), up to 15 additional Stormboyz (**Power Rating +6**), or up to 25 additional Stormboyz (**Power Rating +11**). A Boss Nob can take the place of one Stormboy. Each model is armed with a slugga, choppa and stikkbombs.

WEAPON	RANGE	TYPE	S	AP	D	ABILITIES
Slugga	12"	Pistol 1	4	0	1	-
Choppa	Melee	Melee	User	0	1	Each time the bearer fights, it can make 1 additional attack with this weapon.
Stikkbomb	6"	Grenade D6	3	0	1	-

WARGEAR OPTIONS
- The Boss Nob may replace his slugga and choppa with items from the *Nob Weapons* list.

ABILITIES

'Ere We Go, Mob Rule, Dakka! Dakka! Dakka! (pg 82)

Full Throttle: When this unit Advances, you can add 6" to its Move characteristic instead of rolling a dice, but if you do, roll a D6 for each model in this unit at the end of the phase; for each roll of 1, the unit suffers 1 mortal wound.

Stormboyz Strike: During deployment, you can set up this unit flying high in the skies instead of placing it on the battlefield. At the end of any of your Movement phases this unit can plummet onto the battlefield – set them up anywhere on the battlefield, more than 9" away from any enemy models.

FACTION KEYWORDS ORK, <CLAN>

KEYWORDS INFANTRY, JUMP PACK, FLY, STORMBOYZ

2 POWER — DEFFKOPTAS

NAME	M	WS	BS	S	T	W	A	Ld	Sv
Deffkopta	14"	3+	5+	4	5	4	2	6	4+

This unit contains 1 Deffkopta. It can include up to 2 additional Deffkoptas (**Power Rating +3**) or up to 4 additional Deffkoptas (**Power Rating +6**). Each model is equipped with a twin big shoota, slugga and spinnin' blades.

WEAPON	RANGE	TYPE	S	AP	D	ABILITIES
Kopta rokkits	24"	Assault 2	8	-2	3	-
Slugga	12"	Pistol 1	4	0	1	-
Twin big shoota	36"	Assault 6	5	0	1	-
Spinnin' blades	Melee	Melee	+1	0	1	Make D3 hit rolls for each attack made with this weapon.

WARGEAR OPTIONS
- Any model may replace its twin big shoota with kopta rokkits.

ABILITIES

'Ere We Go, Mob Rule, Dakka! Dakka! Dakka! (pg 82)

Turbo-boost: When this unit Advances, add 6" to its Move characteristic for that Movement phase instead of rolling a dice.

Scoutin' Ahead: During deployment, you can set up this unit behind enemy lines instead of placing it on the battlefield. At the end of any of your Movement phases, they can swoop around to ambush the foe – set them up anywhere on the battlefield that is more than 9" away from any enemy models and within 14" of a battlefield edge.

FACTION KEYWORDS ORK, <CLAN>

KEYWORDS VEHICLE, FLY, SPEED FREEKS, DEFFKOPTAS

2 POWER

MEK GUNZ

NAME	M	WS	BS	S	T	W	A	Ld	Sv
Mek Gun	3"	5+	4+	2	5	6	6	4	5+

This unit contains 1 Mek Gun and 6 grot krew, one manning the weapon and five standing alongside it. It can include up to 5 additional Mek Gunz and their krew (**Power Rating +2 per Mek Gun**). Each Mek Gun is equipped with either a bubblechukka, kustom mega-kannon, smasha gun or traktor kannon.

WEAPON	RANGE	TYPE	S	AP	D	ABILITIES
Bubblechukka	48"	Heavy D6	D6	-D6	D6	-
Kustom mega-kannon	36"	Heavy D6	8	-3	D6	If you roll one or more unmodified hit rolls of 1, the bearer suffers 1 mortal wound after all of this weapon's attacks have been resolved.
Smasha gun	48"	Heavy D3	*	-4	D6	Instead of making a wound roll for this weapon, roll 2D6. If the result is equal to or greater than the target's Toughness, the attack successfully wounds.
Traktor kannon	48"	Heavy 1	8	-2	D6	This weapon automatically hits its target. If the target is an enemy VEHICLE unit that can FLY, roll two dice when inflicting damage with this weapon and discard the lowest result. If a VEHICLE unit that can FLY is destroyed by this weapon, the model automatically crashes and burns (or its equivalent) – do not roll a dice.

ABILITIES

Dakka! Dakka! Dakka! (pg 82)

Mek Gunz: The first time this unit is set up on the battlefield, all of its Mek Gunz must be placed within 6" of at least one other Mek Gun, and with each grot krew within 1" of their Mek Gun. From that point onwards, each Mek Gun operates independently and is treated as a separate unit for all rules purposes.

Grot Krew: Each Mek Gun and its grot krew are treated as a single model for all rules purposes. The krew must remain within 1" of their Mek Gun and cannot be targeted or attacked separately. The range and visibility of all attacks made by a Mek Gun are measured from the Mek Gun, not the krew.

FACTION KEYWORDS ORK, <CLAN>

KEYWORDS VEHICLE, ARTILLERY, GRETCHIN, MEK GUNZ

Grot krew scurry around their bubblechukka, preparing their weird weapon to unleash force field-based carnage on the enemy.

BATTLEWAGON

8 POWER

NAME	M	WS	BS	S	T	W	A	Ld	Sv
Battlewagon	*	5+	5+	*	7	16	*	7	4+

A Battlewagon is a single model.

DAMAGE
Some of this model's characteristics change as it suffers damage, as shown below:

REMAINING W	M	S	A
8-16+	12"	8	6
4-7	9"	6	D6
1-3	6"	4	D3

WEAPON	RANGE	TYPE	S	AP	D	ABILITIES
Big shoota	36"	Assault 3	5	0	1	-
Kannon	When attacking with this weapon, choose one of the profiles below.					
- Frag	36"	Heavy D6	4	0	1	-
- Shell	36"	Heavy 1	8	-2	D6	-
Killkannon	24"	Heavy D6	8	-2	2	-
Zzap gun	36"	Heavy 1	2D6	-3	3	Before firing this weapon, roll to determine the Strength of the shot. If the result is 11+ do not make a wound roll – instead, if the attack hits it causes 3 mortal wounds. The bearer then suffers 1 mortal wound.
Deff rolla	Melee	Melee	+1	-2	2	Add 3 to hit rolls for attacks made with this weapon.

WARGEAR OPTIONS

- This model may take either a kannon, killkannon or zzap gun.
- This model may take up to four big shootas.
- This model may take an 'ard case and/or deff rolla.
- This model may take items from the *Battlewagon Equipment* list.

ABILITIES

Dakka! Dakka! Dakka! (pg 82)

Open-topped: Models embarked on this model can attack in their Shooting phase. Measure the range and draw line of sight from any point on this model. When they do so, any restrictions or modifiers that apply to this model also apply to its passengers; for example, the passengers cannot shoot if this model Fell Back in the same turn, cannot shoot (except with Pistols) if this model is within 1" of an enemy unit, and so on.

'Ard Case: If this model is equipped with an 'ard case, its Toughness characteristic is increased by 1 and it loses the Open-topped ability.

Explodes: If this model is reduced to 0 wounds, roll a D6 before removing it from the battlefield and before any embarked models disembark. On a 6 it explodes, and each unit within 6" suffers D6 mortal wounds.

Mobile Fortress: This model ignores the penalty for moving and firing Heavy weapons.

TRANSPORT

This model can transport 20 FLASH GITZ or <CLAN> INFANTRY models. Each MEGA ARMOUR or JUMP PACK model takes the space of two other models. If this model is equipped with a killkannon, it can only transport 12 models.

FACTION KEYWORDS: ORK, <CLAN>

KEYWORDS: VEHICLE, TRANSPORT, BATTLEWAGON

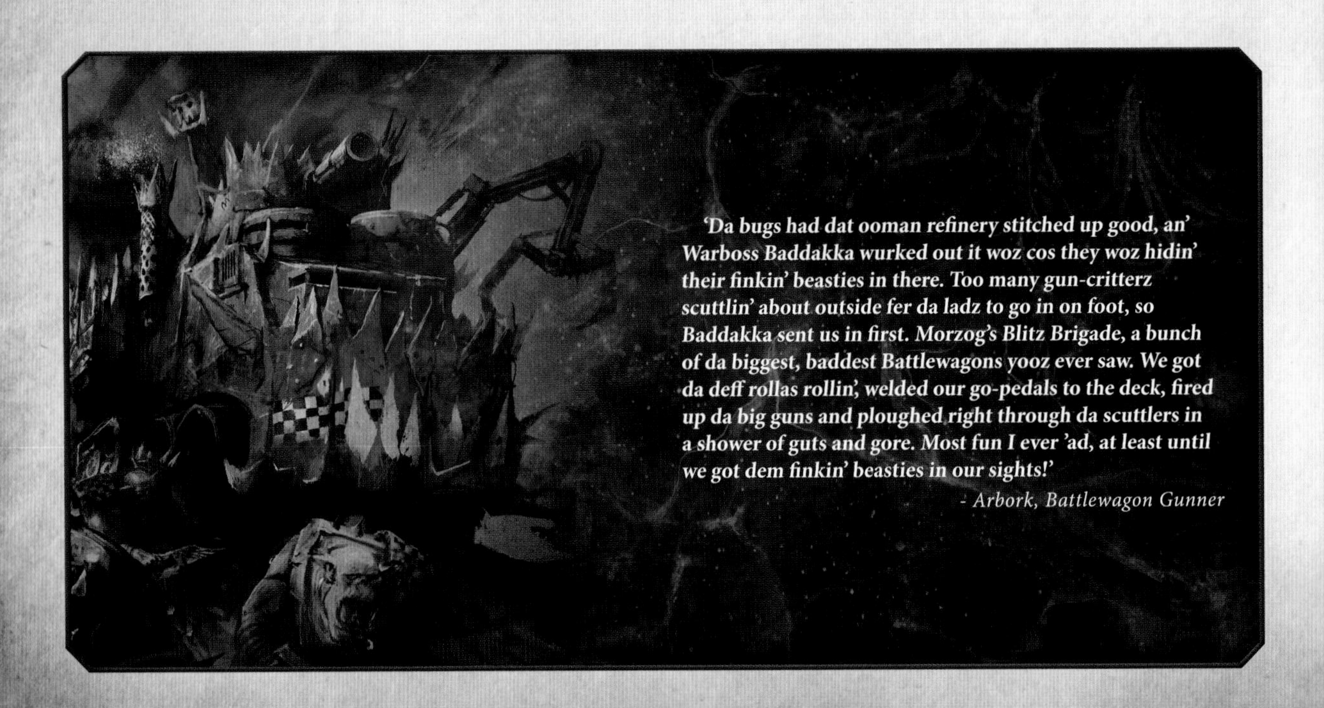

'Da bugs had dat ooman refinery stitched up good, an' Warboss Baddakka wurked out it woz cos they woz hidin' their finkin' beasties in there. Too many gun-critterz scuttlin' about outside fer da ladz to go in on foot, so Baddakka sent us in first. Morzog's Blitz Brigade, a bunch of da biggest, baddest Battlewagons yooz ever saw. We got da deff rollas rollin', welded our go-pedals to the deck, fired up da big guns and ploughed right through da scuttlers in a shower of guts and gore. Most fun I ever 'ad, at least until we got dem finkin' beasties in our sights!'

- Arbork, Battlewagon Gunner

9 POWER

GUNWAGON

NAME	M	WS	BS	S	T	W	A	Ld	Sv
Gunwagon	*	5+	5+	*	8	16	*	7	4+

DAMAGE
Some of this model's characteristics change as it suffers damage, as shown below:

REMAINING W	M	S	A
8-16+	12"	8	6
4-7	9"	6	D6
1-3	6"	4	D3

A Gunwagon is a single model equipped with a kannon and periscope.

WEAPON	RANGE	TYPE	S	AP	D	ABILITIES
Big shoota	36"	Assault 3	5	0	1	-
Kannon	When attacking with this weapon, choose one of the profiles below.					
- Frag	36"	Heavy D6	4	0	1	-
- Shell	36"	Heavy 1	8	-2	D6	-
Killkannon	24"	Heavy D6	8	-2	2	-
Zzap gun	36"	Heavy 1	2D6	-3	3	Before firing this weapon, roll to determine the Strength of the shot. If the result is 11+ do not make a wound roll – instead, if the attack hits it causes 3 mortal wounds. The bearer then suffers 1 mortal wound.

WARGEAR OPTIONS

- This model may replace its kannon with a killkannon or zzap gun.
- This model may take up to four big shootas.
- This model may take items from the *Battlewagon Equipment* list.

ABILITIES

Dakka! Dakka! Dakka! (pg 82)

Periscope: If this model remains stationary or moves under half speed in its Movement phase (i.e. it moves a distance in inches less than half of its current Move characteristic) it can shoot twice in the following Shooting phase with its kannon, killkannon or zzap gun (the weapon must target the same unit both times).

Mobile Fortress: This model ignores the penalty for moving and firing Heavy weapons.

Explodes: If this model is reduced to 0 wounds, roll a D6 before removing it from the battlefield and before any embarked models disembark. On a 4+ it explodes, and each unit within 6" suffers D6 mortal wounds.

TRANSPORT

This model can transport 12 FLASH GITZ or <CLAN> INFANTRY models. Each MEGA ARMOUR or JUMP PACK model takes the space of two other models.

FACTION KEYWORDS: ORK, <CLAN>

KEYWORDS: VEHICLE, TRANSPORT, GUNWAGON

A Goff Gunwagon rumbles forwards amidst the Ork advance, spitting fury into the enemy lines.

9 POWER

BONEBREAKA

NAME	M	WS	BS	S	T	W	A	Ld	Sv
Bonebreaka	*	5+	5+	*	8	16	*	7	4+

A Bonebreaka is a single model equipped with a deff rolla.

DAMAGE
Some of this model's characteristics change as it suffers damage, as shown below:

REMAINING W	M	S	A
8-16+	12"	8	6
4-7	9"	6	D6
1-3	6"	4	D3

WEAPON	RANGE	TYPE	S	AP	D	ABILITIES
Big shoota	36"	Assault 3	5	0	1	-
Kannon	When attacking with this weapon, choose one of the profiles below.					
- Frag	36"	Heavy D6	4	0	1	-
- Shell	36"	Heavy 1	8	-2	D6	-
Killkannon	24"	Heavy D6	8	-2	2	-
Zzap gun	36"	Heavy 1	2D6	-3	3	Before firing this weapon, roll to determine the Strength of the shot. If the result is 11+ do not make a wound roll – instead, if the attack hits it causes 3 mortal wounds. The bearer then suffers 1 mortal wound.
Deff rolla	Melee	Melee	+1	-2	2	Add 3 to hit rolls for attacks made with this weapon.

WARGEAR OPTIONS
- This model may take a kannon, killkannon or zzap gun.
- This model may take up to four big shootas.
- This model may take items from the *Battlewagon Equipment* list.

ABILITIES

Dakka! Dakka! Dakka! (pg 82)

Explodes: If this model is reduced to 0 wounds, roll a D6 before removing it from the battlefield and before any embarked models disembark. On a 6 it explodes, and each unit within 6" suffers D6 mortal wounds.

Bonebreaka Ram: Add D6 to the Attacks characteristic of this model in the Fight phase until the end of that phase if it made a charge move this turn.

Mobile Fortress: This model ignores the penalty for moving and firing Heavy weapons.

TRANSPORT
A Bonebreaka can transport 12 Flash Gitz or <Clan> Infantry models. Each Mega Armour or Jump Pack model takes the space of two other models.

FACTION KEYWORDS
Ork, <Clan>

KEYWORDS
Vehicle, Transport, Bonebreaka

A Bonebreaka rumbles unstoppably towards the foe, guns roaring even as its deff rolla grinds ominously up to speed.

KILLA KANS

2 Power

NAME	M	WS	BS	S	T	W	A	Ld	Sv
Killa Kan	6"	5+	4+	5	5	5	3	6	3+

This unit contains 1 Killa Kan. It can include up to 2 additional Killa Kans (**Power Rating +5**), or up to 5 additional Killa Kans (**Power Rating +12**). Each Killa Kan is equipped with either a big shoota, rokkit launcha, grotzooka or skorcha, and either a buzz saw, Kan klaw or drilla.

WEAPON	RANGE	TYPE	S	AP	D	ABILITIES
Big shoota	36"	Assault 3	5	0	1	-
Grotzooka	18"	Heavy 2D3	6	0	1	-
Rokkit launcha	24"	Assault 1	8	-2	3	-
Skorcha	8"	Assault D6	5	-1	1	This weapon automatically hits its target.
Buzz saw	Melee	Melee	+2	-2	2	Each time the bearer fights it can make 1 additional attack with this weapon.
Drilla	Melee	Melee	+1	-4	2	Each time you roll an unmodified wound roll of 6 for an attack with this weapon, the target suffers 1 mortal wound in addition to any other damage.
Kan klaw	Melee	Melee	+3	-3	3	-

ABILITIES

Dakka! Dakka! Dakka! (pg 82)

Scrag 'Em: Add 1 to the Attacks characteristic of models in this unit while it contains 3 or more models.

Explodes: If a model in this unit is reduced to 0 wounds, roll a D6 before removing the model from the battlefield. On a 6 it explodes, and each unit within 3" suffers 1 mortal wound.

FACTION KEYWORDS: Ork, <Clan>

KEYWORDS: Vehicle, Gretchin, Killa Kans

DEFF DREADS

5 Power

NAME	M	WS	BS	S	T	W	A	Ld	Sv
Deff Dread	6"	3+	5+	5	7	8	2	7	3+

This unit contains 1 Deff Dread. It can include 1 additional Deff Dread (**Power Rating +5**), or 2 additional Deff Dreads (**Power Rating +11**). Each Deff Dread is equipped with two big shootas and two Dread klaws.

WEAPON	RANGE	TYPE	S	AP	D	ABILITIES
Big shoota	36"	Assault 3	5	0	1	-
Kustom mega-blasta	24"	Assault 1	8	-3	D6	If you roll one or more unmodified hit rolls of 1, the bearer suffers 1 mortal wound after all of this weapon's attacks have been resolved.
Rokkit launcha	24"	Assault 1	8	-2	3	-
Skorcha	8"	Assault D6	5	-1	1	This weapon automatically hits its target.
Dread klaw	Melee	Melee	x2	-3	3	Each time the bearer fights, it can make 1 additional attack with each dread klaw it is equipped with.
Dread saw	Melee	Melee	+4	-2	2	Each time the bearer fights, it can make 1 additional attack with each dread saw it is equipped with.

WARGEAR OPTIONS

- Any model may replace any of its big shootas and/or Dread klaws with a rokkit launcha, kustom mega-blasta, skorcha or Dread saw.

ABILITIES

'Ere We Go, Dakka! Dakka! Dakka! (pg 82)

Explodes: If a model in this unit is reduced to 0 wounds, roll a D6 before removing the model from the battlefield. On a 6 it explodes, and each unit within 3" suffers D3 mortal wounds.

Dread Mob: The first time this unit is set up on the battlefield, all of its models must be placed within 6" of at least one other model from the unit. From that point onwards, each operates independently and is treated as a separate unit for all rules purposes.

FACTION KEYWORDS: Ork, <Clan>

KEYWORDS: Vehicle, Deff Dreads

15 POWER

MORKANAUT

NAME	M	WS	BS	S	T	W	A	Ld	Sv
Morkanaut	*	*	5+	8	8	18	*	7	3+

A Morkanaut is a single model equipped with a kustom mega-blasta, two twin big shootas, two rokkit launchas, a kustom mega-zappa and a klaw of Gork (or possibly Mork).

DAMAGE
Some of this model's characteristics change as it suffers damage, as shown below:

REMAINING W	M	WS	A
10-18+	8"	3+	4
5-9	6"	4+	3
1-4	4"	5+	2

WEAPON	RANGE	TYPE	S	AP	D	ABILITIES
Kustom mega-blasta	24"	Assault 1	8	-3	D6	If you roll one or more unmodified hit rolls of 1, the bearer suffers 1 mortal wound after all of this weapon's attacks have been resolved.
Kustom mega-zappa	36"	Heavy 3D3	8	-3	D6	If you roll one or more unmodified hit rolls of 1, the bearer suffers 1 mortal wound after all of this weapon's attacks have been resolved.
Rokkit launcha	24"	Assault 1	8	-2	3	-
Twin big shoota	36"	Assault 6	5	0	1	-
Klaw of Gork (or possibly Mork)	When attacking with this weapon, choose one of the profiles below.					
- Crush	Melee	Melee	x2	-4	D6	-
- Smash	Melee	Melee	User	-2	2	Make 3 hit rolls for each attack made with this weapon.

WARGEAR OPTIONS
- This model may take a kustom force field.

ABILITIES

'Ere We Go, Dakka! Dakka! Dakka! (pg 82)

Big 'n' Stompy: This model can Fall Back in the Movement phase and still shoot and/or charge in the same turn. In addition, this model can move and fire Heavy weapons without suffering the penalty to its hit rolls. Finally, this model only gains a bonus to its save for being in cover if at least half of the model is obscured from the firer.

Kustom Force Field: If this model is equipped with a kustom force field, friendly **ORK** units have a 5+ invulnerable save against attacks made with ranged weapons while they are wholly within 9" of it.

Explodes: If this model is reduced to 0 wounds, roll a D6 before removing it from the battlefield and before any embarked models disembark. On a 6 it explodes, and each unit within 9" suffers D6 mortal wounds.

TRANSPORT
This model can transport 6 **FLASH GITZ** or **<CLAN> INFANTRY** models. Each **MEGA ARMOUR** or **JUMP PACK** model takes the space of two other models.

FACTION KEYWORDS
ORK, <CLAN>

KEYWORDS
VEHICLE, TRANSPORT, MORKANAUT

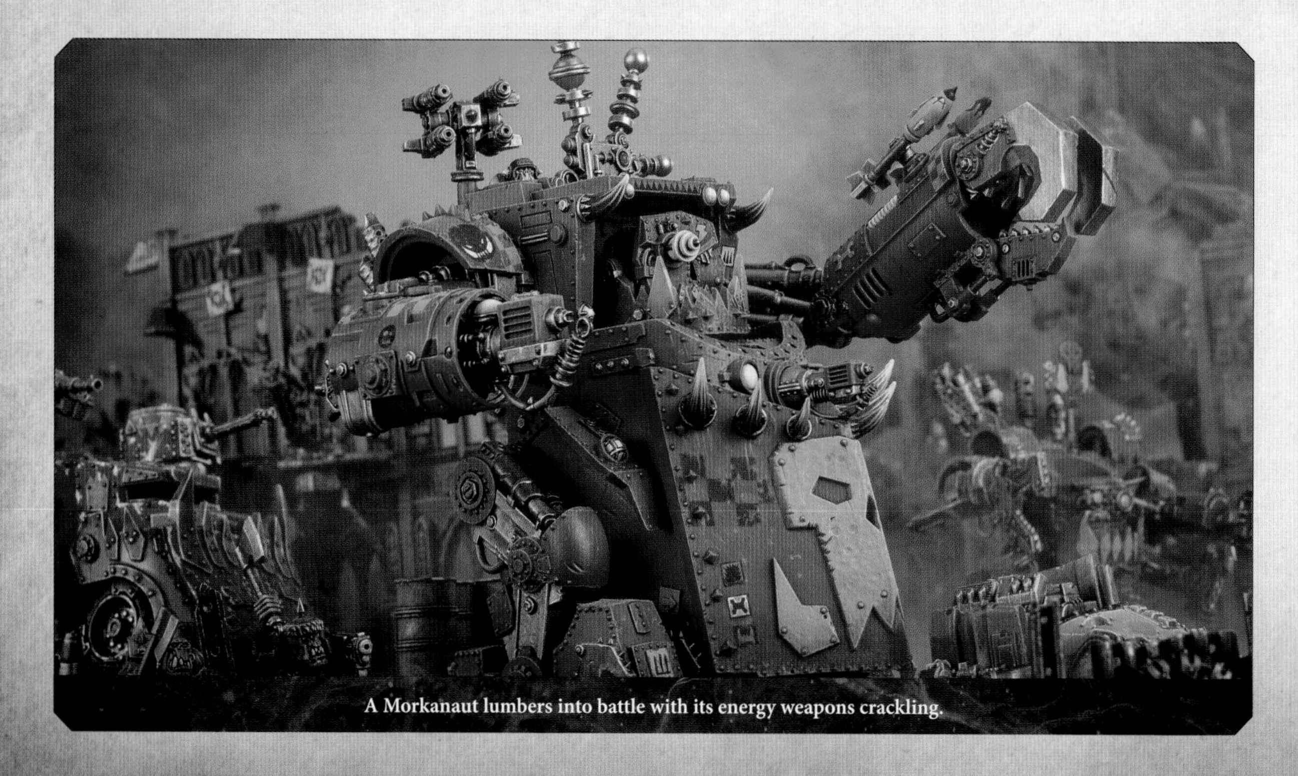

A Morkanaut lumbers into battle with its energy weapons crackling.

15 POWER

GORKANAUT

NAME	M	WS	BS	S	T	W	A	Ld	Sv
Gorkanaut	*	*	5+	8	8	18	*	7	3+

A Gorkanaut is a single model equipped with a deffstorm mega-shoota, two twin big shootas, two rokkit launchas, a skorcha and a klaw of Gork (or possibly Mork).

DAMAGE
Some of this model's characteristics change as it suffers damage, as shown below:

REMAINING W	M	WS	A
10-18+	8"	3+	6
5-9	6"	4+	5
1-4	4"	5+	4

WEAPON	RANGE	TYPE	S	AP	D	ABILITIES
Deffstorm mega-shoota	36"	Heavy 18	6	-1	1	-
Rokkit launcha	24"	Assault 1	8	-2	3	-
Skorcha	8"	Assault D6	5	-1	1	This weapon automatically hits its target.
Twin big shoota	36"	Assault 6	5	0	1	-
Klaw of Gork (or possibly Mork)	When attacking with this weapon, choose one of the profiles below.					
- Crush	Melee	Melee	x2	-4	D6	-
- Smash	Melee	Melee	User	-2	2	Make 3 hit rolls for each attack made with this weapon.

ABILITIES

'Ere We Go, Dakka! Dakka! Dakka! (pg 82)

Explodes: If this model is reduced to 0 wounds, roll a D6 before removing it from the battlefield and before any embarked models disembark. On a 6 it explodes, and each unit within 9" suffers D6 mortal wounds.

Big 'n' Stompy: This model can Fall Back in the Movement phase and still shoot and/or charge in the same turn. In addition, this model can move and fire Heavy weapons without suffering the penalty to its hit rolls. Finally, this model only gains a bonus to its save for being in cover if at least half of the model is obscured from the firer.

TRANSPORT

This model can transport 6 **FLASH GITZ** or **<CLAN> INFANTRY** models. Each **MEGA ARMOUR** or **JUMP PACK** model takes the space of two other models.

FACTION KEYWORDS: ORK, <CLAN>

KEYWORDS: VEHICLE, TRANSPORT, GORKANAUT

4 POWER

LOOTAS

NAME	M	WS	BS	S	T	W	A	Ld	Sv
Loota	5"	3+	5+	4	4	1	2	6	6+
Spanner	5"	3+	5+	4	4	1	2	6	6+

This unit contains 5 Lootas. It can include up to 5 additional Lootas **(Power Rating +4)** or up to 10 additional Lootas **(Power Rating +9)**. For every 5 models in the unit, a Spanner can take the place of one Loota. Each Loota is armed with a deffgun and stikkbombs. Each Spanner is armed with stikkbombs and either a kustom mega-blasta, big shoota or rokkit launcha.

WEAPON	RANGE	TYPE	S	AP	D	ABILITIES
Big shoota	36"	Assault 3	5	0	1	-
Deffgun	48"	Heavy D3	7	-1	2	Before a unit fires this weapon, roll once for the number of attacks and use this for all deffguns fired by the unit until the end of the phase.
Kustom mega-blasta	24"	Assault 1	8	-3	D3	If you roll one or more unmodified hit rolls of 1, the bearer suffers 1 mortal wound after all of this weapon's attacks have been resolved.
Rokkit launcha	24"	Assault 1	8	-2	3	-
Stikkbomb	6"	Grenade D6	3	0	1	-

ABILITIES

'Ere We Go, Mob Rule, Dakka! Dakka! Dakka! (pg 82)

Mekaniak: At the end of your Movement phase, a Spanner can repair a single friendly **<CLAN> VEHICLE** model within 1". That model regains 1 lost wound. A model can only be repaired once per turn.

FACTION KEYWORDS: ORK, <CLAN>

KEYWORDS: INFANTRY, LOOTAS

7 POWER

FLASH GITZ

NAME	M	WS	BS	S	T	W	A	Ld	Sv
Flash Git	5"	3+	4+	5	4	2	3	6	4+
Kaptin	5"	3+	4+	5	4	2	3	6	4+
Ammo Runt	5"	5+	4+	2	2	1	1	4	6+

This unit contains 4 Flash Gitz and 1 Kaptin. It can include up to 5 additional Flash Gitz (**Power Rating +7**). For every 5 Flash Gitz and/or Kaptins in the unit, it may be accompanied by an Ammo Runt. Each Flash Git and Kaptin is armed with a snazzgun and stikkbombs.

WEAPON	RANGE	TYPE	S	AP	D	ABILITIES
Slugga	12"	Pistol 1	4	0	1	-
Snazzgun	24"	Heavy 3	6	-2	2	-
Choppa	Melee	Melee	User	0	1	Each time the bearer fights, it can make 1 additional attack with this weapon.
Stikkbomb	6"	Grenade D3	3	0	1	-

WARGEAR OPTIONS

- The Kaptin may take a choppa or slugga.
- The Kaptin may take a gitfinda squig.

ABILITIES

'Ere We Go, Mob Rule, Dakka! Dakka! Dakka! (pg 82)

Gun-crazy Show-offs: After this unit has shot in the Shooting phase, roll a D6. On a 6 the unit can immediately shoot again, but can only target the nearest enemy unit.

Gitfinda Squig: Add 1 to hit rolls for shooting attacks made by a Kaptin with a gitfinda squig.

Ammo Runt: Each time this unit shoots, you can re-roll one hit roll for each Ammo Runt accompanying it.

When rolling to wound this unit, use the Flash Gitz' or Kaptin's Toughness while they are on the battlefield. The death of an Ammo Runt is ignored for the purposes of Morale tests.

FACTION KEYWORDS: Ork, Freebooterz

KEYWORDS (FLASH GITZ): Infantry, Flash Gitz

KEYWORDS (AMMO RUNTS): Infantry, Gretchin, Ammo Runts

3 POWER

TRUKK

NAME	M	WS	BS	S	T	W	A	Ld	Sv
Trukk	*	5+	5+	*	6	10	*	6	4+

A Trukk is a single model equipped with a big shoota.

DAMAGE
Some of this model's characteristics change as it suffers damage, as shown below:

REMAINING W	M	S	A
6-10+	12"	6	3
3-5	8"	5	D3
1-2	6"	4	1

WEAPON	RANGE	TYPE	S	AP	D	ABILITIES
Big shoota	36"	Assault 3	5	0	1	-
Stikkbomb chukka	12"	Assault D6	3	0	1	This weapon can only be fired if a unit is embarked within the vehicle equipped with it.
Grabbin' klaw	Melee	Melee	User	-3	D3	Each time the bearer fights, it can only make a single attack with this weapon.
Wreckin' ball	Melee	Melee	+2	-1	2	Each time the bearer fights, it can make no more than 3 attacks with this weapon.

WARGEAR OPTIONS
- This model may take a wreckin' ball or grabbin' klaw.
- This model may take a stikkbomb chukka.

ABILITIES

Dakka! Dakka! Dakka! (pg 82)

Open-topped: Models embarked on this model can attack in their Shooting phase. Measure the range and draw line of sight from any point on this model. When they do so, any restrictions or modifiers that apply to this model also apply to its passengers; for example, the passengers cannot shoot if this model has Fallen Back in the same turn, cannot shoot (except with Pistols) if this model is within 1" of an enemy unit, and so on.

Ramshackle: Roll a D6 each time this model suffers damage from an attack that has a Damage characteristic of more than 1. On a 6 reduce the damage caused by the attack to 1.

Explodes: If this model is reduced to 0 wounds, roll a D6 before removing it from the battlefield and before any embarked models disembark. On a 6 it explodes, and each unit within 6" suffers D3 mortal wounds.

TRANSPORT
This model can transport 12 FLASH GITZ or <CLAN> INFANTRY models. Each MEGA ARMOUR or JUMP PACK model takes the space of two other models.

FACTION KEYWORDS
ORK, <CLAN>

KEYWORDS
VEHICLE, TRANSPORT, TRUKK

A Trukk speeds through the ruins of the battlefield with its big shoota at the ready.

7 POWER

DAKKAJET

NAME	M	WS	BS	S	T	W	A	Ld	Sv
Dakkajet	*	5+	*	6	6	12	*	6	4+

A Dakkajet is a single model equipped with four supa-shootas.

WEAPON	RANGE	TYPE	S	AP	D	ABILITIES
Supa-shoota	36"	Assault 3	6	-1	1	-

WARGEAR OPTIONS
- This model may take two additional supa-shootas.

ABILITIES

Dakka! Dakka! Dakka! (pg 82)

Airborne: This model cannot charge, can only be charged by units that can FLY, and can only attack or be attacked in the Fight phase by units that can FLY.

Hard to Hit: Subtract 1 from hit rolls for attacks that target this model in the Shooting phase.

All da Dakka: Add 1 to hit rolls for this model's attacks in the Shooting phase if all of those attacks target the same unit that phase.

Supersonic: Each time this model moves, first pivot it on the spot up to 90° (this does not contribute to how far the model moves), and then move the model straight forwards. Note that it cannot pivot again after the initial pivot. When this model Advances, increase its Move characteristic by 20" until the end of the phase – do not roll a dice.

Crash and Burn: If this model is reduced to 0 wounds, roll a D6 before removing it from the battlefield. On a 6 it crashes in a fiery explosion, and each unit within 6" suffers D3 mortal wounds.

FACTION KEYWORDS ORK, <CLAN>

KEYWORDS VEHICLE, FLY, DAKKAJET

DAMAGE
Some of this model's characteristics change as it suffers damage, as shown below:

REMAINING W	M	BS	A
7-12+	20-60"	5+	3
4-6	20-40"	6+	D3
1-3	20-25"	6+	1

7 POWER

BURNA-BOMMER

NAME	M	WS	BS	S	T	W	A	Ld	Sv
Burna-bommer	*	5+	*	6	6	12	*	6	4+

A Burna-bommer is a single model equipped with a twin big shoota and two supa-shootas.

WEAPON	RANGE	TYPE	S	AP	D	ABILITIES
Skorcha missiles	24"	Assault D6	5	-1	1	Units do not receive the benefit of cover to their saving throws for attacks made with this weapon.
Supa-shoota	36"	Assault 3	6	-1	1	-
Twin big shoota	36"	Assault 6	5	0	1	-

WARGEAR OPTIONS
- This model may take skorcha missiles.

ABILITIES

Dakka! Dakka! Dakka! (pg 82)

Airborne: This model cannot charge, can only be charged by units that can FLY, and can only attack or be attacked in the Fight phase by units that can FLY.

Hard to Hit: Subtract 1 from hit rolls for attacks that target this model in the Shooting phase.

Supersonic: Each time this model moves, first pivot it on the spot up to 90° (this does not contribute to how far the model moves), and then move the model straight forwards. Note that it cannot pivot again after the initial pivot. When this model Advances, increase its Move characteristic by 20" until the end of the phase – do not roll a dice.

Burna Bombs: Up to twice per battle, this model can drop a burna bomb as it flies over enemy units in its Movement phase. After the model has moved, select an enemy unit that it moved over and roll a D6 for each model in that unit, up to a maximum of 10 dice. Add 1 to the roll for a model if it is INFANTRY. For each roll of 5+ the enemy unit suffers 1 mortal wound.

Grot Gunner: Add 1 to hit rolls for attacks made with this model's twin big shoota.

Crash and Burn: If this model is reduced to 0 wounds, roll a D6 before removing it from the battlefield. On a 4+ it crashes in a fiery explosion, and each unit within 6" suffers 3 mortal wounds.

FACTION KEYWORDS ORK, <CLAN>

KEYWORDS VEHICLE, FLY, BURNA-BOMMER

DAMAGE
Some of this model's characteristics change as it suffers damage, as shown below:

REMAINING W	M	BS	A
7-12+	20-50"	5+	3
4-6	20-30"	6+	D3
1-3	20-25"	6+	1

BLITZA-BOMMER

6 POWER

NAME	M	WS	BS	S	T	W	A	Ld	Sv
Blitza-bommer	*	5+	*	6	6	12	*	6	4+

A Blitza-bommer is a single model equipped with a big shoota and two supa-shootas.

DAMAGE
Some of this model's characteristics change as it suffers damage, as shown below:

REMAINING W	M	BS	A
7-12+	20-50"	5+	3
4-6	20-30"	6+	D3
1-3	20-25"	6+	1

WEAPON	RANGE	TYPE	S	AP	D	ABILITIES
Big shoota	36"	Assault 3	5	0	1	-
Supa-shoota	36"	Assault 3	6	-1	1	-

ABILITIES

Dakka! Dakka! Dakka! (pg 82)

Airborne: This model cannot charge, can only be charged by units that can FLY, and can only attack or be attacked in the Fight phase by units that can FLY.

Hard to Hit: Subtract 1 from hit rolls for attacks that target this model in the Shooting phase.

Supersonic: Each time this model moves, first pivot it on the spot up to 90° (this does not contribute to how far the model moves), and then move the model straight forwards. Note that it cannot pivot again after the initial pivot. When this model Advances, increase its Move characteristic by 20" until the end of the phase – do not roll a dice.

Boom Bomb: Up to twice per battle, this model can drop a boom bomb as it flies over enemy units in your Movement phase. After the model has moved, select an enemy unit that it moved over. Roll a D6 for each model in that unit, rolling three dice instead if the model is a VEHICLE or MONSTER, up to a maximum of 12 dice. For each roll of 4+ the enemy unit suffers 1 mortal wound.

Grot Gunner: Add 1 to hit rolls for attacks made with this model's big shoota.

Crash and Burn: If this model is reduced to 0 wounds, roll a D6 before removing it from the battlefield. On a 6 it crashes in a fiery explosion, and each unit within 6" suffers D3 mortal wounds.

FACTION KEYWORDS: ORK, <CLAN>

KEYWORDS: VEHICLE, FLY, BLITZA-BOMMER

Flying perilously low over the battlefield, a Blitza-bommer prepares to dump its lethal payload.

8 POWER

WAZBOM BLASTAJET

NAME	M	WS	BS	S	T	W	A	Ld	Sv
Wazbom Blastajet	*	5+	*	6	6	12	*	6	4+

A Wazbom Blastajet is a single model equipped with two wazbom mega-kannons, a smasha gun and a stikkbomb flinga.

DAMAGE
Some of this model's characteristics change as it suffers damage, as shown below:

REMAINING W	M	BS	A
7-12+	20-60"	5+	3
4-6	20-40"	6+	D3
1-3	20-25"	6+	1

WEAPON	RANGE	TYPE	S	AP	D	ABILITIES
Smasha gun	48"	Heavy D3	*	-4	D6	Instead of making a wound roll for this weapon, roll 2D6. If the result is equal to or greater than the target's Toughness characteristic, the attack successfully wounds.
Stikkbomb flinga	12"	Assault 2D6	3	0	1	-
Supa-shoota	36"	Assault 3	6	-1	1	-
Tellyport mega-blasta	24"	Assault 3	8	-2	D3	If a model suffers any unsaved wounds from this weapon and is not slain, roll a D6 at the end of the phase. If the result is greater than that model's Wounds characteristic, it is slain.
Wazbom mega-kannon	36"	Heavy D3	8	-3	D6	If you roll one or more unmodified hit rolls of 1 for this weapon, the bearer suffers 1 mortal wound after all of this weapon's attacks have been resolved.

WARGEAR OPTIONS

- This model may replace both wazbom mega-kannons with two tellyport mega-blastas.
- This model may take two supa-shootas.
- This model may replace its stikkbomb flinga with a kustom force field.

ABILITIES

Dakka! Dakka! Dakka! (pg 82)

Airborne: This model cannot charge, can only be charged by units that can **FLY**, and can only attack or be attacked in the Fight phase by units that can **FLY**.

Hard to Hit: Subtract 1 from hit rolls for attacks that target this model in the Shooting phase.

Supersonic: Each time this model moves, first pivot it on the spot up to 90° (this does not contribute to how far the model moves), and then move the model straight forwards. Note that it cannot pivot again after the initial pivot. When this model Advances, increase its Move characteristic by 20" until the end of the phase – do not roll a dice.

Mekbrain-enhanced Weapon-sights: This model ignores the penalty for moving and firing Heavy weapons. In addition, at the beginning of your Shooting phase, you can choose an enemy unit; until the end of the phase, add 1 to hit rolls for attacks made against that unit with this model's smasha gun.

Kustom Force Field: If this model is equipped with a kustom force field, friendly **ORK** units have a 5+ invulnerable save against attacks made with ranged weapons while they are wholly within 9" of it.

Crash and Burn: If this model is reduced to 0 wounds, roll a D6 before removing it from the battlefield. On a 6 it crashes in a fiery explosion, and each unit within 6" suffers D3 mortal wounds.

FACTION KEYWORDS: ORK, <CLAN>

KEYWORDS: VEHICLE, FLY, WAZBOM BLASTAJET

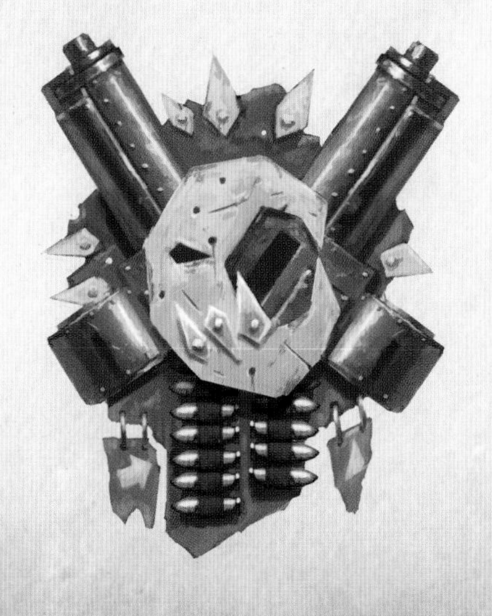

STOMPA

46 POWER

DAMAGE
Some of this model's characteristics change as it suffers damage, as shown below:

REMAINING W	M	WS	A
31-40+	12"	3+	6
21-30	9"	4+	5
11-20	6"	5+	4
1-10	4"	6+	3

NAME	M	WS	BS	S	T	W	A	Ld	Sv
Stompa	*	*	5+	10	8	40	*	8	3+

A Stompa is a single model equipped with a deffkannon, supa-gatler, three big shootas, a twin big shoota, three supa-rokkits, a skorcha and a mega-choppa.

WEAPON	RANGE	TYPE	S	AP	D	ABILITIES
Big shoota	36"	Assault 3	5	0	1	-
Deffkannon	72"	Heavy 3D6	10	-4	D6	-
Skorcha	8"	Assault D6	5	-1	1	This weapon automatically hits its target.
Supa-gatler	48"	Heavy 3D6	7	-2	1	See Psycho-Dakka-Blasta!, below
Supa-rokkit	100"	Heavy D6	8	-3	D6	Only one supa-rokkit can be fired by the bearer per turn, and each can only be fired once per battle.
Twin big shoota	36"	Assault 6	5	0	1	-
Mega-choppa	When attacking with this weapon, choose one of the profiles below.					
- Smash	Melee	Melee	x2	-5	6	-
- Slash	Melee	Melee	User	-2	D3	Make 3 hit rolls for each attack made with this weapon.

WARGEAR OPTIONS
- This model may take up to two additional supa-rokkits.

ABILITIES

'Ere We Go, Dakka! Dakka! Dakka! (pg 82)

Psycho-Dakka-Blasta!: In your Shooting phase, after firing this model's supa-gatler for the first time that phase, you can attempt to fire it a second time by rolling a D6; on a 1 the weapon's ammo has been expended, and it cannot be used for the rest of the battle. On a 2+ you can fire the supa-gatler a second time that phase, and after resolving those attacks, you can then attempt to fire the weapon a third time by rolling a D6; on a 4 or less the weapon's ammo has been expended, and it cannot be used for the rest of the battle. On a 5+ you can fire the supa-gatler a third time that phase.

Explodes: If this model is reduced to 0 wounds, roll a D6 before removing it from the battlefield and before any embarked models disembark. On a 6 it explodes, and each unit within 2D6" suffers D6 mortal wounds.

Bigger 'n' Stompier: This model can Fall Back in the Movement phase and still shoot and/or charge in the same turn. When this model Falls Back, it can move over enemy INFANTRY and SWARM models, though it must end its move more than 1" from any enemy units. In addition, this model can move and fire Heavy weapons without suffering the penalty to its hit rolls. Finally, this model only gains a bonus to its saving throws for being in cover if at least half of the model is obscured from the firer.

Stompa Rigger Crew: This model's grot riggers can attempt repairs at the end of your Movement phase. If they do so, roll a D6; on a 2+ this model regains D3 lost wounds. A model can only be repaired once each turn.

Effigy: You can re-roll Morale tests for friendly ORK units while they are within 6" of this model.

TRANSPORT
This model can transport 20 FLASH GITZ or <CLAN> INFANTRY models. Each MEGA ARMOUR or JUMP PACK model takes the space of two other models.

FACTION KEYWORDS
ORK, <CLAN>

KEYWORDS
VEHICLE, TRANSPORT, TITANIC, STOMPA

Mekboy Workshop

A Mekboy Workshop is a single model.

ABILITIES	**Ork Structure:** After it is set up, a Mekboy Workshop is treated as a terrain feature. It cannot move for any reason, is not treated as a friendly or enemy model, and cannot be targeted or affected by any attacks or abilities. **Mek's Grabbin' Klaw:** At the start of the Fight phase, before any units have been chosen to fight, one ORK INFANTRY unit from your army that is within 1" of this model can operate the Mekboy Workshop's grabbin' klaw. If it does so, select an enemy unit within 1" of this model and roll a D6; on a 4+ that enemy unit suffers D3 mortal wounds. **Kustom Job:** At the end of your Movement phase, one ORK VEHICLE unit from your army that is within 1" of this model can receive a kustom job. If it does so, then until the end of the turn, that unit cannot shoot or charge and the Attacks characteristic of models in that unit is reduced to 1, but you can choose and resolve one of the following effects: • **More Speed:** Until the end of your next Movement phase, increase the Move characteristic of models in that unit by 6". In addition, roll a D6 to see if the unit receives something 'extra speshul'; on a 6 add 1 to charge rolls for that unit for the rest of the battle. • **More Rivets:** That unit regains D3 lost wounds. If there is a BIG MEK or MEK from your army within 1" of this model, and it has not used its Big Mekaniak or Mekaniak ability to repair a vehicle this turn, it can oversee the kustom job; if it does so, the unit regains 3 lost wounds instead of D3, and the model that oversaw the kustom job cannot use its Big Mekaniak or Mekaniak ability this turn. In addition, roll a D6 to see if the unit receives something 'extra speshul'; on a 6 add 1 to the Toughness characteristic of models in that unit for the rest of the battle. • **More Dakka:** Choose one weapon (excluding a bubblechukka) that a model in that unit is equipped with. The next time any models in the unit fire that weapon, the weapon makes the maximum number of attacks (e.g. a weapon with the Heavy 2D6 Type will fire 12 shots). In addition, roll a D6 to see if the unit receives something 'extra speshul'; on a 6 add 1 to the chosen weapon's Damage characteristic for the rest of the battle. A unit can only receive a kustom job once per turn.
FACTION KEYWORDS	ORK, <CLAN>
KEYWORDS	MEKBOY WORKSHOP

As one Speed Freek guns his engine and roars away, the next 'kustomer' pulls up into the Mekboy Workshop.

GUNZ AND GUBBINZ

Ork weaponry and wargear ranges from the crude and brutal to the bewilderingly high-tech and dangerously unstable. Often their wielders have as little an idea of what will happen when they pull the trigger as their enemies do, but the results are invariably spectacularly violent! The profiles for all of their wargear are listed below.

RANGED WEAPONS						
WEAPON	**RANGE**	**TYPE**	**S**	**AP**	**D**	**ABILITIES**
Big shoota	36"	Assault 3	5	0	1	-
Blitz missiles	18"	Assault 1	6	-1	D3	-
Bubblechukka	48"	Heavy D6	D6	-D6	D6	-
Burna (shooting)	8"	Assault D3	4	0	1	Before a unit fires this weapon, roll once for the number of attacks and use this for all burnas fired by the unit until the end of the phase. This weapon automatically hits its target.
Burna bottles	6"	Grenade 2D6	4	0	1	Units do not receive the benefit of cover to their saving throws for attacks made with this weapon.
Burna exhaust	8"	Assault D3	4	0	1	This weapon automatically hits its target.
Da Rippa	When attacking with this weapon, choose one of the profiles below.					
- Standard	24"	Heavy 3	7	-3	2	-
- Supercharge	24"	Heavy 3	8	-3	3	If you roll one or more unmodified hit rolls of 1, the bearer suffers 1 mortal wound after all of this weapon's attacks have been resolved.
Dakkagun	18"	Assault 3	5	0	1	-
Deffgun	48"	Heavy D3	7	-1	2	Before a unit fires this weapon, roll once for the number of attacks and use this for all deffguns fired by the unit until the end of the phase.
Deffkannon	72"	Heavy 3D6	10	-4	D6	-
Deffstorm mega-shoota	36"	Heavy 18	6	-1	1	-
Grot blasta	12"	Pistol 1	3	0	1	-
Grotzooka	18"	Heavy 2D3	6	0	1	-
Heavy squig launcha	When attacking with this weapon, choose one of the profiles below.					
- Bile squig	36"	Assault 2D6	*	0	1	This weapon always wounds on a 4+ unless it is targeting a **VEHICLE** or **TITANIC** unit, in which case it wounds on a 6+.
- Bitey squig	36"	Assault 2	5	-3	2	-
- Boom squig	36"	Assault 2D3	6	-1	D3	-
Kannon	When attacking with this weapon, choose one of the profiles below.					
- Frag	36"	Heavy D6	4	0	1	-
- Shell	36"	Heavy 1	8	-2	D6	-
Killa jet	When attacking with this weapon, choose one of the profiles below.					
- Burna	8"	Assault D6	5	-1	1	This weapon automatically hits its target.
- Cutta	8"	Assault 2	8	-4	D6	If the target is within half range of this weapon, roll two dice when inflicting damage with it and discard the lowest result.
Killkannon	24"	Heavy D6	8	-2	2	-
Kombi-weapon with rokkit launcha	When attacking with this weapon, choose one or both of the profiles below. If you choose both, subtract 1 from all hit rolls.					
- Rokkit launcha	24"	Assault 1	8	-2	3	-
- Shoota	18"	Assault 2	4	0	1	-
Kombi-weapon with skorcha	When attacking with this weapon, choose one or both of the profiles below. If you choose both, subtract 1 from all hit rolls.					
- Shoota	18"	Assault 2	4	0	1	-
- Skorcha	8"	Assault D6	5	-1	1	This weapon automatically hits its target.
Kopta rokkits	24"	Assault 2	8	-2	3	-
Kustom mega-blasta	24"	Assault 1	8	-3	D6	If you roll one or more unmodified hit rolls of 1, the bearer suffers 1 mortal wound after all of this weapon's attacks have been resolved.
Kustom mega-kannon	36"	Heavy D6	8	-3	D6	
Kustom mega-slugga	12"	Pistol 1	8	-3	D6	
Kustom mega-zappa	36"	Heavy 3D3	8	-3	D6	
Kustom shokk rifle	24"	Assault 2	8	-3	D6	If you roll one or more unmodified hit rolls of 1 for this weapon, the bearer suffers 1 mortal wound after all of this weapon's attacks have been resolved. Each time you make a wound roll of 6+ for this weapon, the target suffers 1 mortal wound in addition to any other damage.

RANGED WEAPONS						
WEAPON	**RANGE**	**TYPE**	**S**	**AP**	**D**	**ABILITIES**
Kustom shoota	18"	Assault 4	4	0	1	-
Lobba	48"	Heavy D6	5	0	1	This weapon can target units that are not visible to the bearer.
Mek speshul	24"	Assault 9	5	-2	1	-
Rivet kannon	36"	Assault 6	7	-2	2	-
Rokkit kannon	24"	Assault 2D3	8	-2	3	-
Rokkit launcha	24"	Assault 1	8	-2	3	-
Pair of rokkit pistols	12"	Pistol 2	7	-2	D3	-
Shokk attack gun	60"	Heavy D6	2D6	-5	D6	Before firing this weapon, roll once to determine the Strength of all its shots. If the result is 11+ each successful hit inflicts D3 mortal wounds on the target in addition to any normal damage.
Shoota	18"	Assault 2	4	0	1	-
Shotgun	12"	Assault 2	3	0	1	If the target is within half range, add 1 to this weapon's Strength.
Skorcha	8"	Assault D6	5	-1	1	This weapon automatically hits its target.
Skorcha missiles	24"	Assault D6	5	-1	1	Units do not receive the benefit of cover to their saving throws for attacks made with this weapon.
Slugga	12"	Pistol 1	4	0	1	-
Smasha gun	48"	Heavy D3	*	-4	D6	Instead of making a wound roll for this weapon, roll 2D6. If the result is equal to or greater than the target's Toughness characteristic, the attack successfully wounds.
Snagga klaw (shooting)	8"	Assault 1	4	0	1	You can re-roll wound rolls for attacks made with this weapon.
Snazzgun	24"	Heavy 3	6	-2	2	-
Squig bomb	18"	Assault 1	8	-2	D6	This weapon cannot target units that can **Fly**. After making an attack with this weapon, the bearer is slain.
Squig launcha	When attacking with this weapon, choose one of the profiles below.					
- Bile squig	36"	Assault D6	*	0	1	This weapon always wounds on a 4+ unless it is targeting a **Vehicle** or **Titanic** unit, in which case it wounds on a 6+.
- Bitey squig	36"	Assault 1	5	3	2	-
- Boom squig	36"	Assault D3	6	-1	D3	-
Stikkbomb	6"	Grenade D6	3	0	1	-
Stikkbomb chukka	12"	Assault D6	3	0	1	This weapon can only be fired if a unit is embarked within the vehicle equipped with it.
Stikkbomb flinga	12"	Assault 2D6	3	0	1	-
Stikksquig	6"	Grenade D6	3	0	1	-
Supa-shoota	36"	Assault 3	6	-1	1	-
Supa-gatler	48"	Heavy 3D6	7	-2	1	See Stompa datasheet (pg 117)
Supa-rokkit	100"	Heavy D6	8	-3	D6	Only one supa-rokkit can be fired by the bearer per turn, and each can only be fired once per battle.
Tankbusta bomb	6"	Grenade D3	8	-2	D6	-
Tellyport blasta	12"	Assault 3	8	-2	1	If a model suffers any unsaved wounds from this weapon and is not slain, roll a D6 at the end of the phase. If the result is greater than that model's Wounds characteristic, it is slain.
Tellyport mega-blasta	24"	Assault 3	8	-2	D3	
Traktor kannon	48"	Heavy 1	8	-2	D6	This weapon automatically hits its target. If the target is an enemy **Vehicle** unit that can **Fly**, roll two dice when inflicting damage with this weapon and discard the lowest result. If a **Vehicle** unit that can **Fly** is destroyed by this weapon, the model automatically crashes and burns (or its equivalent) – do not roll a dice.
Twin big shoota	36"	Assault 6	5	0	1	-
Twin boomstikk	12"	Assault 2	5	0	1	If the target is within half range, add 1 to hit rolls for this weapon.
Wazbom mega-kannon	36"	Heavy D3	8	-3	D6	If you roll one or more unmodified hit rolls of 1 for this weapon, the bearer suffers 1 mortal wound after all of this weapon's attacks have been resolved.
Wing missiles	24"	Assault 1	8	-2	3	Add 1 to hit rolls for attacks made with this weapon against **Vehicle** units. Subtract 1 from hit rolls for attacks made with this weapon against all other targets.
Zzap gun	36"	Heavy 1	2D6	-3	3	Before firing this weapon, roll to determine the Strength of the shot. If the result is 11+ do not make a wound roll – instead, if the attack hits it causes 3 mortal wounds. The bearer then suffers 1 mortal wound.

MELEE WEAPONS

WEAPON	RANGE	TYPE	S	AP	D	ABILITIES
Attack squig	Melee	Melee	4	-1	1	Each time a model with an attack squig fights, it can make 2 additional attacks with this weapon.
Big choppa	Melee	Melee	+2	-1	2	-
Burna (melee)	Melee	Melee	User	-2	1	-
Buzz saw	Melee	Melee	+2	-2	2	Each time the bearer fights, it can make 1 additional attack with this weapon.
Choppa	Melee	Melee	User	0	1	Each time the bearer fights, it can make 1 additional attack with this weapon.
Da Vulcha's Klaws	Melee	Melee	+2	-3	D3	Each time the bearer fights, it can make no more than 3 attacks with this weapon.
Deff rolla	Melee	Melee	+1	-2	2	Add 3 to hit rolls for attacks made with this weapon.
Dread klaw	Melee	Melee	x2	-3	3	Each time the bearer fights, it can make 1 additional attack with each dread klaw it is equipped with.
Dread saw	Melee	Melee	+4	-2	2	Each time the bearer fights, it can make 1 additional attack with each dread saw it is equipped with.
Drilla	Melee	Melee	+1	-4	2	Each time you roll an unmodified wound roll of 6 for an attack with this weapon, the target suffers 1 mortal wound in addition to any other damage.
Grabba stikk	Melee	Melee	+1	0	1	Each time the bearer fights, it can make 1 additional attack with this weapon.
Grabbin' klaw	Melee	Melee	User	-3	D3	Each time the bearer fights, it can only make a single attack with this weapon.
Grot-prod	Melee	Melee	+2	-1	1	-
Kan klaw	Melee	Melee	+3	-3	3	-
Killsaw	Melee	Melee	x2	-4	2	When attacking with this weapon, you must subtract 1 from the hit roll. If a model is armed with two killsaws, add 1 to its Attacks characteristic.
Klaw of Gork (or possibly Mork)	When attacking with this weapon, choose one of the profiles below.					
- Crush	Melee	Melee	x2	-4	D6	-
- Smash	Melee	Melee	User	-2	2	Make 3 hit rolls for each attack made with this weapon.
Kustom klaw	Melee	Melee	x2	-3	3	-
Mega-choppa	When attacking with this weapon, choose one of the profiles below.					
- Smash	Melee	Melee	x2	-5	6	-
- Slash	Melee	Melee	User	-2	D3	Make 3 hit rolls for each attack made with this weapon.
Mork's Teeth	Melee	Melee	User	-1	2	-
Nose drill	Melee	Melee	+2	-2	D3	-
Power klaw	Melee	Melee	x2	-3	D3	When attacking with this weapon, you must subtract 1 from the hit roll.
Power stabba	Melee	Melee	User	-2	1	-
Saw blades	Melee	Melee	+1	-1	1	-
Snagga klaw (melee)	Melee	Melee	+2	-2	D3	You can re-roll wound rolls for attacks made with this weapon.
Spinnin' blades	Melee	Melee	+1	0	1	Make D3 hit rolls for each attack made with this weapon.
Tankhammer	Melee	Melee	-	-	-	Each time the bearer fights, it can only make a single attack with this weapon. If the attack hits, the target suffers D3 mortal wounds and the bearer is slain.
'Urty syringe	Melee	Melee	User	0	1	Each time the bearer fights, it can make 1 additional attack with this weapon. This weapon always wounds on a 4+ unless it is targeting a **VEHICLE** or **TITANIC** unit, in which case it wounds on a 6+.
Waaagh! banner	Melee	Melee	+2	0	2	-
Weirdboy staff	Melee	Melee	+2	-1	D3	-
Wreckin' ball	Melee	Melee	+2	-1	2	Each time the bearer fights, it can make no more than 3 attacks with this weapon.

OTHER WARGEAR

WARGEAR	EFFECT
'Ard case	If a model is equipped with an 'ard case, its Toughness characteristic is increased by 1 and it loses the Open-topped ability.
Cybork body	Each time a model with a Cybork body loses a wound, roll a D6; on a 6 that wound is not lost. You cannot make a Dok's Tools roll for this model if you do so.
Gitfinda squig	Add 1 to hit rolls for shooting attacks made by a Kaptin with a gitfinda squig.
Grot lash	Re-roll hit rolls of 1 in the Fight phase for attacks made by units comprised entirely of **GRETCHIN INFANTRY** while they are within 3" of any friendly **RUNTHERD** models with a grot lash.
Grot rigger	If a model has a grot rigger, the grot can attempt repairs at the end of your Movement phase. If they do so, roll a D6; on a 2+ this model regains 1 lost wound. A vehicle can only be repaired once each turn.
Kustom force field	If a model is equipped with a kustom force field, friendly **ORK** units have a 5+ invulnerable save against attacks made with ranged weapons while they are wholly within 9" of it. If a model equipped with a kustom force field is embarked, the vehicle transporting it has a 5+ invulnerable save against attacks made with ranged weapons instead.
Squig hound	If a unit comprised entirely of **GRETCHIN INFANTRY** fails a Morale test while it is within 3" of any friendly **RUNTHERD** models with a squig hound, ignore the result. D3 models from the unit are slain instead.

Upon the war-torn world of Falsehope, the full and terrifying might of an Ork Waaagh! thunders down upon the massed ranks of the Crimson Slaughter Chaos Space Marines. The air fills with a deafening cry of 'Waaagh!' as the greenskin charge slams home.

WAYS OF THE WARBANDS

In this section you'll find rules for Battle-forged armies that include ORK Detachments – that is, any Detachment that includes only ORK units. These rules include the abilities below and a series of Stratagems that can only be used by the Orks. This section also includes the Orks' unique Warlord Traits, psychic discipline, relics and Tactical Objectives. Together, these rules reflect the character and fighting style of the Orks in your games of Warhammer 40,000.

ABILITIES

All ORK Detachments (excluding Super-heavy Auxiliary Detachments) gain the following abilities:

DIS IS OURS! ZOG OFF!

Once the greenskins have claimed a big pile of loot, a scrappable wreck, an important technological whatnot or indeed anything else that the boss orders them to retrieve or protect, greenskins rabidly guard their prize. Quickly covering the site in trophy poles, clan banners and hastily daubed glyphs, they will commit grievous violence against anyone foolish enough to try to shift them.

If your army is Battle-forged, all Troops units in ORK Detachments gain this ability. Such a unit that is within range of an objective marker (as specified in the mission) controls the objective marker even if there are more enemy models within range of that objective marker. If an enemy unit within range of the same objective marker has a similar ability, then the objective marker is controlled by the player who has the most models within range of it as normal.

CLAN KULTURS

Each Ork clan has developed its own instinctive customs, known as its 'kultur', the societal and military leanings of which influence everything from their style of dress and chosen colours, to the ways in which they prefer to engage the foe. Though this may sound like quite a highbrow concept for greenskins to engage with, the truth is that most of it comes down to the Orks' preferred methods of kicking people's teeth in.

If your army is Battle-forged, all <CLAN> units in ORK Detachments (excluding those in Super-heavy Auxiliary Detachments) gain a Clan Kultur, so long as every unit in that Detachment is from the same clan. The Clan Kultur gained depends upon the clan they are drawn from, as shown on the table on the right. For example, all units in an EVIL SUNZ Detachment gain the 'Red Ones Go Fasta' Clan Kultur. If you have chosen a clan that does not have an associated Clan Kultur, you can choose the kultur that best suits the fighting style and strategies of the greenskins that hail from it.

GUNZ FOR HIRE

Whether voluntarily or by force, Flash Gitz have left their tribes and clan affiliations behind them. They will gladly fight as mercenaries for any Warboss with the spare teef to pay their exorbitant fees, but they have no interest in aping the kultur of the Orks they fight alongside.

FLASH GITZ units (including Kaptin Badrukk) can be included in an ORK Detachment without preventing other units in that Detachment from gaining a Clan Kultur. Note, however, that the FLASH GITZ units do not themselves benefit from any Clan Kultur unless the Clan Kultur selected for the Detachment is the FREEBOOTERZ Clan Kultur.

GROTS

Grots always try to get in on the action, and do everything in their power to wear the right colours – or rags of an approximate hue, at least – and copy the kultur of their hulking Ork cousins. No matter how hard they try, however, they will never really be more than servile hangers-on.

Units comprised entirely of GRETCHIN cannot benefit from any Clan Kultur. In addition, Ork Stratagems can only be used on these units if the Stratagem explicitly states so (e.g. the 'Grot Shields' Stratagem).

'Lissen up, ya humie gitz, cos I ain't gonna say dis twice. We krumped dem marine boyz on da Big Red Wurld. We skragged yer spaceships when dey popped outta the asteroids, and we did fer yer big church-world an' all. Now we'z comin' fer ya, so yooz better get ready cos we want a proppa scrap before we burn yer world down around ya!'

- The Arch-Arsonist of Charadon, before the invasion of Esmadoria hive world

CLAN KULTURS

GOFFS: NO MUKKIN' ABOUT

Goff Orks are the biggest, meanest and most ferocious of their kind. They put little stock in cunning or strategy, preferring instead to simply surge across the battlefield in a roaring green tide. Once they get stuck into hand-to-hand combat, the Goffs quickly overwhelm their enemies by dint of sheer violent ferocity.

Each time you roll an unmodified hit roll of 6 for an attack with a melee weapon made by a model with this kultur, immediately make an additional hit roll against the same target using the same weapon. These additional hit rolls cannot themselves generate any further hit rolls.

BAD MOONS: ARMED TO DA TEEF

Bad Moons are ostentatious show-offs, whose predilection for toting about the biggest, loudest and shiniest shootas is facilitated by the fact their teef grow with such remarkable speed. With all manner of targeting arrays, underslung bomb launchas, extra ammo feeds and bandoliers of additional munitions to call their own, Bad Moons can typically lay down a storm of dakka that eclipses the firepower of any other clan.

Re-roll hit rolls of 1 for attacks made by models with this kultur in the Shooting phase.

EVIL SUNZ: RED ONES GO FASTA

The Evil Sunz are firm believers in the old Ork adage 'red ones go fasta'. Many claim that the need for speed is in their blood, and so the Orks of this clan make sure to daub their vehicles, themselves, and – in especially ambitious cases – even their bullets bright red. Bizarrely, the practice actually seems to work.

Add 1 to the Move characteristic of models with this kultur (adding 2 instead if that model is a **SPEED FREEK**), and add 1 to Advance and charge rolls made for them. In addition, models with this kultur do not suffer the penalty to their hit rolls for Advancing and firing Assault weapons.

DEATHSKULLS: LUCKY BLUE GITZ

All Orks believe blue to be a lucky colour, but the notoriously superstitious Deathskulls are fervent in that belief. The clan's members are in the habit of daubing themselves liberally with blue warpaint before every battle, making sure to mark their vehicles with the colour, too. Of course, this habit doubles as a great way of rapidly covering up any marks of previous ownership on wagons, wargear and other loot the light-fingered Deathskulls have 'acquired' from their fellow Orks.

Models with this kultur have a 6+ invulnerable save. In addition, you can re-roll a single hit roll, a single wound roll and a single damage roll for each unit with this kultur each time it shoots or fights. In addition, **INFANTRY** units with this kultur gain the 'Dis is Ours! Zogg Off!' ability (pg 124), even if they do not have the Troops battlefield role.

SNAKEBITES: DA OLD WAYS

There is no doubting that Snakebites appear somewhat backwards to the other Ork clans. Their technology base and traditional mindsets rarely advance far past the level of Wildboyz, and if a Snakebite can fix a problem with a big stick, a handy squig and a length of old rope, he will gladly do so. However, between their refusal to rely upon 'newfangled rubbish' and their bizarre habit of actually allowing themselves to be bitten by venomous serpents to prove their toughness, the clan's ways breed remarkably resilient warriors.

Roll a dice each time a model with this kultur loses a wound. On a 6 the wound is not lost. If a model has a similar ability (e.g. the Supa-Cybork Shiny Gubbinz or Ramshackle ability) you can choose which ability to use when a model loses a wound, but you cannot use both.

BLOOD AXES: TAKTIKS

The Blood Axes are viewed by all other Ork clans as being duplicitous, untrustworthy gits who wouldn't know a proper scrap if it came out of the drops and bit off their backsides. The Blood Axes, for their part, couldn't care less; they possess an instinctive grasp of battlefield strategy that – while still undeniably Orky in its application – allows them to surprise even the most seasoned enemy commanders with their manoeuvres, feints and ambushes.

A unit with this kultur gains the benefit of cover, even while they are not entirely on or in a terrain feature, if the enemy model making the attack is at least 18" away. In addition, units with this kultur can shoot or charge (but not both) even if they Fell Back in the same turn.

FREEBOOTERZ: COMPETITIVE STREAK

There's something a little off about most Freebooterz, and all the other Orks know it. These mercenary loot-hounds are just that bit more mean-spirited, vicious and sneaky, and certainly substantially more egocentric, self-centred and competitive than their fellow greenskins. It is no wonder, then, that most become outcasts, for they struggle to fit into the rough and ready hierarchy of Ork society and operate best when knocking around the galaxy with others of their dubious kind. In battle, the Freebooterz' desire to 'be da best' and nab the shiniest loot for themselves sees them strive to outdo their fellow greenskins; if one mob of Freebooterz starts doing well, their comrades will strive all the harder to show them up and grab the glory for themselves.

Add 1 to hit rolls for attacks made by models with this kultur if any other friendly unit with this kultur within 24" has destroyed an enemy unit this phase.

STRATAGEMS

If your army is Battle-forged and includes any ORK Detachments (excluding Auxiliary Support Detachments), you have access to the Stratagems shown below, meaning you can spend Command Points to activate them. These help to reflect the unique tactics and strategies used by the forces of the Orks on the battlefield.

1CP

MOB UP

Orks Stratagem

Smaller Ork mobs tend to be caught up and swept along when a large enough horde of greenskins stampedes across the battlefield.

Use this Stratagem at the end of your Movement phase. Select two <CLAN> INFANTRY units from your army that are within 2" of each other and have the same datasheet (e.g. select two Boyz units, or two Stormboyz units). If one of the units has 10 or more models, and the other has 10 or fewer, the two units merge and, for the rest of the battle, they are counted as a single unit for all rules purposes.

1CP

MEDI-SQUIG

Orks Stratagem

From syringe squigs to vaccine squigs, Painboyz make use of all kinds of medical beasties.

Use this Stratagem at the end of your Movement phase. Select a <CLAN> CHARACTER from your army that is within 3" of a friendly <CLAN> PAINBOY. The selected model immediately regains D3 lost wounds.

1CP

SNAGGA GRAPPLE

Orks Stratagem

The Speedboss fires his snagga claw into a luckless victim as his Wartrike races past, pulling his target bloodily along behind him – or at least, a meaty chunk of them.

Use this Stratagem when a DEFFKILLA WARTRIKE model from your army Falls Back in the Movement phase. Before the model moves, select an enemy unit within 1" and roll a D6; on a 2+ that enemy unit suffers D3 mortal wounds.

1CP

WARPHEAD

Orks Stratagem

Some Weirdboyz become addicted to the thrill of soaking up and unleashing Waaagh! energy. These lunatics actively seek out battle with reckless abandon.

Use this Stratagem before the battle begins. Select a WEIRDBOY model from your army to become a Warphead. This model knows 1 additional psychic power from the Power of the Waaagh! discipline (pg 129) and can attempt to manifest 1 additional psychic power in each of your Psychic phases.

2CP

RAMMING SPEED

Orks Stratagem

Ork drivers are infamous for using their vehicles as huge blunt instruments with which to clobber the foe.

Use this Stratagem in your Charge phase. Select an ORK VEHICLE unit from your army. You can roll 3D6 when making a charge move with that unit this phase. In addition, if the unit finishes a charge move this phase, select an enemy unit within 1" of it and roll a D6; on a 2+ that enemy unit suffers D3 mortal wounds.

1CP

BOARDING ACTION

Orks Stratagem

Using a boarding plank built onto their wagon, the Orks launch a daring high-speed attack upon an enemy vehicle.

Use this Stratagem at the end of the Fight phase. Select an enemy VEHICLE unit that cannot FLY and is within 1" of a TRUKK or BATTLEWAGON model from your army. Any models embarked within that TRUKK or BATTLEWAGON can make a single attack with one of their melee weapons against that enemy unit.

1CP/3CP

EXTRA GUBBINZ

Orks Stratagem

Some lucky gits get more than their fair share of shiny gubbinz.

Use this Stratagem before the battle. Your army can have one extra Shiny Gubbinz for 1 CP, or two extra Shiny Gubbinz for 3 CPs. All of the Shiny Gubbinz that you include must be different and be given to different ORK CHARACTERS. You can only use this Stratagem once per battle.

3CP

GET STUCK IN, LADZ!

Orks Stratagem

Laying about himself with ferocious blows and bellowing loud enough to burst eardrums, the biggest Ork present 'persuades' his ladz to fight even harder.

Use this Stratagem in the Fight phase when it is your turn to select a unit to fight, or at the end of the Fight phase. Select an ORK INFANTRY unit from your army that has already fought once this Fight phase to fight a second time.

2CP

ORKS IS NEVER BEATEN

Orks Stratagem

So resilient is Ork physiology – and so slow are Orks on the uptake – that even killing wounds can take a while to register.

Use this Stratagem when an **Ork Character** model from your army is slain. That model is not removed from the battlefield as normal, and can immediately either shoot as if it were your Shooting phase, or fight as if it were the Fight phase. The slain model is then removed from the battlefield.

3CP

FORCE-FIELD PROJEKTA

Orks Stratagem

While the effects are sometimes unstable and always short-lived, Big Meks are able to briefly supercharge their kustom force fields.

Use this Stratagem at the start of a battle round. Select a **Big Mek** model from your army. Until the start of the next battle round, increase the range of that model's Kustom Force Field ability to 18". You can only use this Stratagem once per battle.

1CP

BILLOWING EXHAUST CLOUDS

Orks Stratagem

These impetuous Orks create massive clouds of dust and exhaust fumes that cloak their advance.

Use this Stratagem at the start of your Movement phase. Select a **Speed Freeks** unit from your army. Until the start of your next turn, subtract 1 from hit rolls for attacks made by ranged weapons that target that unit.

2CP

MORE DAKKA!

Orks Stratagem

There is no such thing as too much dakka.

Use this Stratagem before an **Ork** unit from your army shoots in your Shooting phase. Until the end of the phase, that unit's Dakka! Dakka! Dakka! ability triggers on unmodified hit rolls of 5 or 6, instead of 6.

2CP

'ARD BOYZ

Orks Stratagem

Clad from head-to-toe in bits of scrap metal, 'Ard Boyz weather the enemy's fire amidst a cacophony of discordant clanging.

Use this Stratagem before the battle begins. Select a **Boyz** unit (excluding **Skarboyz**) from your army; that unit gains the **'Ard Boyz** keyword, and the Save characteristic of models in that unit is changed to 5+. That unit can only use the Mob Up Stratagem to merge with other units of **'Ard Boyz**.

2CP

TELLYPORTA

Orks Stratagem

Nothing shocks the enemy like an angry mob of Boyz or looming war effigy suddenly appearing in a blast of green lightning!

Use this Stratagem during deployment. You can set up an **Ork** unit from your army with a Power Rating of 20 or less on a tellyporta pad instead of placing it on the battlefield. Units on a tellyporta pad can teleport down at the end of any of your Movement phases – set them up anywhere on the battlefield that is more than 9" from any enemy models. If you use this Stratagem on a **Transport**, all units embarked inside it remain so when it is set up on a tellyporta.

1CP

EXTRA STIKKBOMBS

Orks Stratagem

Orks are not subtle creatures, and if they get their hands on a surplus of explosives, they are less likely to stockpile them than they are to simply pull out all the pins at once and get lobbing.

Use this Stratagem at the start of your Shooting phase. Select an **Ork Infantry** unit from your army. Up to 10 models in that unit can fire a Grenade weapon in that phase, instead of only 1.

1CP

GROT SHIELDS

Orks Stratagem

Orks often use nearby grot mobs as bullet shields.

Use this Stratagem after a **<Clan> Infantry** unit from your army (excluding units comprised entirely of **Gretchin** models) has been hit by a ranged weapon. Until the end of the phase, you can roll a D6 each time a model from that unit loses a wound if there is a friendly unit comprised entirely of **<Clan> Gretchin Infantry** models within 6" of it, and the **Gretchin** unit is closer to the attacking model than the target. On a 2+ the original model does not lose that wound but one model in that **Gretchin** unit (your choice) is slain. Otherwise, the model loses the wound as normal.

1CP

LOOT IT!

Orks Stratagem

After a spot of mid-battle larceny, these Orks have become so laden down with loot that it actually acts as ablative armour!

Use this Stratagem when a **Vehicle** unit is destroyed within 3" of an **Ork Infantry** unit from your army. Improve the Save characteristic of that infantry unit by 1. A unit can only be affected by this Stratagem once per battle, and once affected, cannot be selected for the Mob Up Stratagem. If this Stratagem is used on a **Lootas** unit from your army, roll a D6; on a 4+ the CP spent to use this Stratagem is immediately refunded.

1CP LONG, UNCONTROLLED BURSTS

Orks Stratagem

Ork Flyboyz will fill the skies with lead in an attempt to bring down enemy aircraft.

Use this Stratagem at the start of your Shooting phase. Select an **Ork Vehicle** unit from your army that can **Fly**. Until the end of the phase, add 1 to hit rolls for shooting attacks made by that unit that target enemy units that can **Fly**.

3CP UNSTOPPABLE GREEN TIDE

Orks Stratagem

Wave after wave of Orks overwhelm the enemy's defence lines.

Use this Stratagem at the end of your Movement phase. Select a unit of **Boyz** from your army that has less than half its starting number of models and remove it from the battlefield. You can then set it up again wholly within 6" of the edge of the battlefield and more than 9" from any enemy models, at its full starting strength. You cannot select a unit for this Stratagem that has been merged via the Mob Up Stratagem. You can only use this Stratagem once per battle.

3CP MONSTER HUNTERS

Snakebite Stratagem

Snakebites are old hands at hunting large, foul-tempered beasts.

Use this Stratagem at the start of any phase. Select an enemy model with a Wounds characteristic of 10 or more. Add 1 to wound rolls for attacks made by **Snakebite** units from your army that target that model until the end of that phase.

1CP DRIVE-BY KRUMPIN'

Evil Sunz Stratagem

Evil Sunz Speed Freeks are notorious for their deadly hit-and-run attacks.

Use this Stratagem at the end of the Shooting phase. Select an **Evil Sunz Speed Freeks** unit from your army. That unit can immediately make a move as if it were the Movement phase, but cannot charge this turn.

2CP WRECKERS

Deathskulls Stratagem

Deathskulls can take apart an enemy vehicle ready for looting before its bewildered crew have even stopped fighting back.

Use this Stratagem at the start of any phase. Select a **Deathskulls** unit from your army. You can re-roll wound rolls for attacks made by that unit that target enemy **Vehicle** units until the end of the phase.

2CP SHOWIN' OFF

Bad Moons Stratagem

Bad Moons Orks love nothing better than flaunting their wealth through demonstrations of ballistic largesse that leave other greenskins' jaws agape and the enemy reduced to flaming ruin.

Use this Stratagem immediately after resolving a shooting attack with a **Bad Moons Infantry** unit from your army. That unit can shoot all of its weapons a second time. This Stratagem can only be used once per phase.

1CP/2CP DEAD SNEAKY

Blood Axe Stratagem

These sneaky gits never appear where you expect them to.

Use this Stratagem during deployment. If you spent 1 CP, select a **Blood Axe Infantry** unit from your army that has a Power Rating of 8 or less and set it up in hiding instead of placing it on the battlefield. If you spent 2 CPs, select a **Blood Axe Infantry** unit that has a Power Rating of 9 or more instead. At the end of any of your Movement phases that unit can emerge from hiding - set it up anywhere on the battlefield that is more than 9" away from any enemy models.

3CP KILL-KROOZER BROADSIDE

Freebooterz Stratagem

Freebooterz will often call upon orbiting kill kroozers to shell the battlefield from space, causing utter devastation.

Use this Stratagem at the start of your Shooting phase. Select up to D3 points on the battlefield, each more than 6" away from the others and visible to a **Freebooterz** unit from your army. Roll a D6 for each unit (friend or foe) within 3" of any of those points. Subtract 1 from the result if the unit being rolled for is a **Character**. On a 5+ that unit suffers D3 mortal wounds. You can only use this Stratagem once per battle.

1CP SKARBOYZ

Goff Stratagem

The biggest and meanest Goff Boyz are known as Skarboyz, and are rumoured to be able to cave in a Space Marine helmet with their bare knuckles.

Use this Stratagem before the battle. Select a **Goff Boyz** unit (excluding **'Ard Boyz**) from your army; that unit gains the **Skarboyz** keyword, and the Strength characteristic of models in that unit is changed to 5. That unit can only use the Mob Up Stratagem to merge with other units of **Skarboyz**.

POWER OF THE WAAAGH! DISCIPLINE

Weirdboyz channel the power of the Waaagh! into glowing green blasts of psychic destruction, or else yoke those roiling energies to create crude but spectacular results – if, that is, the attempt doesn't cause their heads to explode like they swallowed a stikkbomb.

Before the battle, generate the psychic powers for PSYKERS that can use powers from the Power of the Waaagh! discipline using the table below. You can either roll a D6 to generate their powers randomly (re-roll any duplicate results), or you can select the psychic powers you wish the psyker to have.

D6 RESULT

1 'EADBANGER

A bolt of raw power erupts from the Weirdboy's sloping forehead and rockets across the battlefield, causing the head of the first unfortunate victim caught in its path to explode in a shower of brains and gore.

'Eadbanger has a warp charge value of 8. If manifested, roll a D6 and compare it to the Toughness characteristic of the closest enemy model that is visible to and within 18" of the psyker. If the result is higher than the model's Toughness, it is slain.

2 WARPATH

The Weirdboy disperses the Waaagh! energy coursing through his frame into the Ork warriors around him, stoking their already bellicose nature to a roaring fever pitch.

Warpath has a warp charge value of 7. If manifested, select a friendly ORK unit within 18" of the psyker. Increase that unit's Attacks characteristic by 1 until your next Psychic phase.

3 DA JUMP

The Weirdboy closes his eyes tight and, in a storm of flashing green light, teleports a mass of confused greenskins to another part of the battlefield.

Da Jump has a warp charge value of 7. If manifested, select a friendly ORK INFANTRY unit within 12" of the psyker. Remove that unit from the battlefield, and then set it up anywhere on the battlefield more than 9" away from any enemy units. That unit counts as having moved for any rules purposes, such as firing Heavy weapons.

4 FISTS OF GORK

The Weirdboy channels Waaagh! energy into his own fists or those of a nearby Ork, providing strength enough to punch through tank hulls.

Fists of Gork has a warp charge value of 6. If manifested, select a friendly ORK CHARACTER model that is visible to and within 12" of the psyker. Add 2 to that model's Strength and Attacks characteristics until the start of your next Psychic phase.

5 DA KRUNCH

Green energies erupt from the Weirdboy's eyes and coalesce in a roiling cloud above the enemy. That cloud then solidifies into the vast green foot of Gork (or Mork) himself, which commences to repeatedly stamp down on the foe.

Da Krunch has a warp charge value of 8. If manifested, select an enemy unit within 18" of the psyker. Roll a D6 for each model in that unit. For each roll of 6, that unit suffers 1 mortal wound. Then roll 2D6; on a 10+ roll a D6 once more for each model in that unit. For each roll of 6, that unit suffers 1 mortal wound.

6 ROAR OF MORK

The Weirdboy opens his gob impossibly wide and gives vent to a bellowing roar that reverberates through his enemies' minds. Coherent thought becomes nigh-impossible, and as the roar thunders on, panic begins to spread.

Roar of Mork has a warp charge value of 8. If manifested, subtract 1 from the Leadership characteristic of enemy units while they are within 18" of the psyker until your next Psychic phase.

'These pointy-eared gitz fink they'z so clever wiv all their jumpin' about and their flyin' tanks and fancy swords. I've 'ad just about enough of it. Tell ya wot ladz, bring up da Weirdboyz and get 'em good and riled. Let's see how clever dem pointy-earz are when they'z dissolvin' into puddles of glowin' green puke!'

- Goffboss Drogg, shortly before the hideous massacre of the Masque of Dawning Hope

SHINY GUBBINZ

Certain remarkable examples of the Mekboyz' craft are so potent that they have developed reputations amongst the Ork tribes, and accrued legends of their own. Such renowned implements of mayhem pass from one greenskin leader to another by right of conquest. Tribes have fought battles over them, and Waaaghs! have gathered around those who wield them.

If your army is led by an ORK Warlord, then before the battle you may give one of the following Shiny Gubbinz to an ORK CHARACTER. Named characters such as Ghazghkull Thraka cannot be given any of the following Shiny Gubbinz – they have their own unique wargear.

Note that some weapons replace one of the character's existing weapons. Where this is the case, you must, if you are playing a matched play game or are otherwise using points values, still pay the cost of the weapon that is being replaced. Write down any Shiny Gubbinz your characters may have on your army roster.

DA DEAD SHINY SHOOTA

Rumoured to have been made by Big Mek Buzzgob, da Dead Shiny Shoota is a double-barrelled brute packed full of dakka. The gun kicks out a deafening storm of hot lead, much to the enjoyment of the Ork pulling the trigger, and its volume of fire is so great that even the most inaccurate greenskin can land a respectable number of hits.

Model with kustom shoota only. Da Dead Shiny Shoota replaces the bearer's kustom shoota and has the following profile:

WEAPON	RANGE	TYPE	S	AP	D
Da Dead Shiny Shoota	18"	Assault 12	4	-1	1

HEADWOPPA'S KILLCHOPPA

Grand Warboss Headwoppa had a real thing for decapitating his enemies, and whenever he did so his ladz would raise a raucous cheer. Headwoppa and his tribe were last seen charging headlong into a horde of Khornate Daemons, but legend speaks of a blood-slick big choppa that still turns up occasionally. Though this weapon looks normal, a dark voice is said to growl in the mind of its wielder, driving them on to ever-greater excesses of violence.

Model with a big choppa only. Headwoppa's Killchoppa replaces the bearer's big choppa and has the following profile:

WEAPON	RANGE	TYPE	S	AP	D
Headwoppa's Killchoppa	Melee	Melee	+2	-2	2
Abilities: Wound rolls of 6+ made for attacks with this weapon inflict 2 mortal wounds instead of any normal damage.					

SUPA-CYBORK BODY

In the only recorded collaboration between Mad Dok Grotsnik and the renowned Mekaniak Orkimedes, a nameless greenskin was upgraded with a preposterous yet powerful full-body bionik. The original owner of this one-of-a-kind endoskeleton became the envy of every Warboss around, and was soon gutted and stripped for parts by a stronger rival. The Supa-Cybork Body has been re-transplanted several times since then, filling its new owner with confidence, resilience, and a belated hope that the Painboyz gave it a quick clean before shoving it back in place…

Each time the bearer loses a wound, roll a D6; on a roll of 5+ that wound is not lost. You cannot make a Dok's Tools roll for this model if you do so.

DA KILLA KLAW

Orkimedes himself fashioned this fearsome weapon from the blades of a Soul Grinder of Khorne. Thanks to its reputation for being dead killy, the baleful crimson glow emitted by da Killa Klaw has yet to discourage any Orks from donning the fabled gauntlet.

Model with power klaw only. Da Killa Klaw replaces the bearer's power klaw and has the following profile:

WEAPON	RANGE	TYPE	S	AP	D
Da Killa Klaw	Melee	Melee	x2	-3	3
Abilities: You can re-roll wound rolls for attacks made with this weapon.					

SCORCHED GITBONEZ

During the Second War for Armageddon, the name of Oddgit the Weirdboy garnered fame amongst the Ork race after he vomited a tide of psycho-plasma across the renowned Blood Angels Captain Tycho. Oddgit was swiftly incinerated by retaliatory fire, and at battle's end, his bones were collected by a mob of Madboyz. They have been carried, worn and chewed on by various Weirdboyz since then, their latent power seeping into the half-sane brain of their owner.

PSYKER only. You can add 1 to Psychic tests taken by the bearer when manifesting a psychic power from the Power of the Waaagh! discipline.

GITSTOPPA SHELLS

When Warboss Skarkrusha first encountered Primaris Space Marines, he was impressed by their incredible resilience. While he relished the chance to fight decent enemies, Skarkrusha couldn't have these 'big beekies' making his shoota look rubbish, and so he ordered his Mekboyz to cook up something special. The result was a self-loading ammunition microfactory (quite possibly cobbled together from looted T'au weaponry) that plugged into Skarkrusha's shoota and allowed it to fire armour-piercing high-explosive thermobaric shells, or, as Skarkrusha preferred to call them, Gitstoppaz.

Model with kustom shoota, kombi-weapon with skorcha or kombi-weapon with rokkit launcha only. Add 1 to the Strength and Damage characteristic of that weapon's shoota or kustom shoota profile. In addition, improve the AP of that weapon's shoota or kustom shoota profile by 1 (e.g. AP -1 becomes AP -2).

DA LUCKY STIKK

Makari was an exceptionally lucky grot banner-bearer of the Goff Clan who survived to the ripe old age of nine before finally meeting his end under the posterior of his hulking master, the mighty Ghazghkull Thraka. When the grot's remains were peeled off his boss' rear end, Makari's wavin' stikk was reclaimed, hosed down, and used as an impressive bosspole.

GOFF model only. Add 1 to hit rolls for attacks made by friendly **GOFF CHARACTER** models while they are within 6" of the bearer in the Fight phase. In addition, you can re-roll hit and wound rolls for attacks made by the bearer in the Fight phase.

MORGOG'S FINKIN' KAP

Looted from a Schola Progenium training facility, this tangle of electrodes was incorporated into a helmet on the orders of Blood Axe Warboss Morgog. Upon donning the headgear, Morgog was bombarded by fragments of what he realised were strategies and tactics; though the crackling humie voices and flashes of imagery were confusing, the Warboss was able to make use of the concepts his new Finkin' Kap imparted. Soon his foes would learn that the only thing more dangerous than a savage three-hundred-pound brute is a savage three-hundred-pound brute with a plan.

BLOOD AXE model only. If the bearer is your Warlord, you can generate a second Warlord Trait for them. If the bearer is not your Warlord, generate a Warlord Trait for them (note that the bearer is only regarded as your Warlord for the purposes of that Warlord Trait). The same Warlord Trait cannot be generated for both the bearer and your Warlord.

REZMEKKA'S REDDER ARMOUR

Badmek Rezmekka formulated a type of paint so red that staring directly at it for too long caused actual retinal damage. So red was Rezmekka's new colour – which, in a moment of inspiration, he named Redder – that he immediately daubed it over his best suit of 'eavy armour. In order to cement the reputation of his Redder Armour, the wily Mek built in a massive set of cable-plug capacitors that could be attached by squig-jaw clips to the engine of any vehicle he hopped aboard. This not only ensured that Rezmekka's armour really did make his ride go faster, but also had the amusing side effect of electrocuting nearby enemies with an extremely satisfying 'fzzap!'.

EVIL SUNZ model only. Add 1 to the Move characteristic of a **TRANSPORT** while the bearer is embarked within it. In addition, if the bearer is embarked, then at the start of your Movement phase roll a D6 for each enemy unit within 1" of the **TRANSPORT** the bearer is embarked within. On a 4+ that unit suffers D3 mortal wounds.

DA GOBSHOT THUNDERBUSS

Requiring an entire chest of teef to be loaded into its breach before each shot, the Gobshot Thunderbuss' worky gubbinz plates its unconventional ammunition in gold before firing it in an inescapable cone of fanged death. Not only can this madcap weapon sweep away swathes of enemies with every shot, it also fires a literal fortune in teef every time, proclaiming its owner's obscene wealth in the process.

BAD MOONS model with kustom shoota, kombi-weapon with skorcha or kombi-weapon with rokkit launcha only. Da Gobshot Thunderbuss replaces the bearer's kustom shoota or shoota profile with the following profile:

WEAPON	RANGE	TYPE	S	AP	D
Da Gobshot Thunderbuss	12"	Heavy 2D6	5	-1	1
Abilities: This weapon automatically hits its target.					

DA FIXER UPPERZ

Originally the tools of Deathskull Mekaniak Frazdak, it is claimed that da Fixer Upperz can repair any wagon, no matter how badly junked it might appear. In typically Orky fashion, the sheer belief that these tools can work wonders often seems to mean they do just that!

DEATHSKULLS model only. The bearer gains the Big Mekaniak ability (pg 86). If the bearer already has the Big Mekaniak ability, the target of the ability regains 3 lost wounds instead of D3 each time it is used.

BROGG'S BUZZBOMB

Runtboss Brogg was the 'genius' behind the now infamous Buzzbomb. By building an oversized stikkbomb around an entire buzzer-squig hive, he created an unstable device that could be flung at the enemy to send enraged buzzer squigs all through their lines. Only once the squigs have settled down post-battle and returned to their stikkbomb home can the weapon be carefully gathered up – usually by unfortunate grot 'volunteers' – and pumped full of fungus-smoke, putting the buzzer squigs to sleep until their fury is needed again.

SNAKEBITE model only. Brogg's Buzzbomb has the following profile:

WEAPON	RANGE	TYPE	S	AP	D
Brogg's Buzzbomb	6"	Grenade 3D6	5	-1	1
Abilities: This weapon can only be used once per battle, and automatically hits its target. After all of its attacks have been resolved, you can immediately select another enemy unit within 6" of the target and resolve 2D6 attacks against it with the same weapon.					

DA BADSKULL BANNER

Every Freebooter Warboss has their own Jolly Ork, a glyph-banner that proclaims their dread reputation. Yet there is one ancient Jolly Ork so saturated with Waaagh! energy that it has become infamous. Known as da Badskull Banner, this totemic flag is said by many to be the original Jolly Ork, the first of its kind, and the ultimate proclamation of a Freebooter leader's might.

FREEBOOTERZ model only. Once per battle, at the start of the Morale phase, the bearer of Da Badskull Banner can choose to fly the flag on its bosspole. If they do so, friendly **FREEBOOTERZ** units automatically pass Morale tests until the end of the phase.

WARLORD TRAITS

If an **Ork Character** is your Warlord, they can generate a Warlord Trait from the table below instead of the one in the *Warhammer 40,000* rulebook. You can either roll on the table to randomly generate a Warlord Trait, or you can select the one that best suits their temperament and preferred style of waging war.

'You buncha worthless grot-lovers wanna know why I'm da boss, do ya? I'm da boss cos I'm da biggest! I'm da boss cos I'm da meanest, and da loudest, and da 'ardest! I'm killier than any of yooz lot and I could kick all of yer teef in at once in a fight, then rip yer faces off fer good measure! So unless any of ya wanna 'av a go right now, den I'm da boss! No? Didn't fink so...'

- Warboss Grukk Face-rippa

D6 RESULT

1 FOLLOW ME, LADZ!

Always found at the forefront of an assault, this Ork likes to be the first into the fray, leading a tide of bellowing greenskins crashing into the enemy lines.

Your Warlord gains the Waaagh! and Breakin' Heads abilities (pg 85). If your Warlord already has the Waaagh! and Breakin' Heads abilities, the range of each ability is increased by 3". In addition, if your army is Battle-forged, you receive an additional 1 Command Point.

2 BIGKILLA BOSS

Nothing is more satisfying to this boss than matching his might against the biggest and meanest enemies on the battlefield and coming out on top. One savage engagement after another has made him an expert giant-slayer.

Add 1 to wound rolls for your Warlord's attacks that target a **Vehicle** or **Monster** unit.

3 'ARD AS NAILS

This greenskin has a hide as thick as a Squiggoth's. It takes a blow of truly phenomenal strength to even give him pause.

Add 1 to your Warlord's Toughness characteristic.

4 BRUTAL BUT KUNNIN'

This Ork has a particular talent for close-quarters choppa-work, even amongst his brutal kin.

You can re-roll hit rolls in the Fight phase for attacks made by your Warlord. In addition, add 1 to the Damage characteristic of your Warlord's melee weapons if, in the same turn, they finished a charge move, were charged, or performed a Heroic Intervention.

5 KUNNIN' BUT BRUTAL

This leader has a knack for flanking and surprising his enemies.

At the start of the first battle round but before the first turn begins, you can remove your Warlord and up to D3 friendly **<Clan>** units from the battlefield and set them up again as described in the Deployment section of the mission you are playing (if you pick a **Transport**, units embarked inside it remain so when it is removed and set up again).

6 MIGHT IS RIGHT

A solid slab of muscle and aggression, this Ork's strength is unsurpassed.

Add 1 to your Warlord's Strength and Attacks characteristics.

NAMED CHARACTERS AND WARLORD TRAITS

If a named character with a specific clan keyword is your Warlord, they must be given the associated Warlord Trait. For example, Ghazghkull Thraka must take the Goff 'Proper Killy' Warlord Trait (see opposite) as he has the **Goff** keyword.

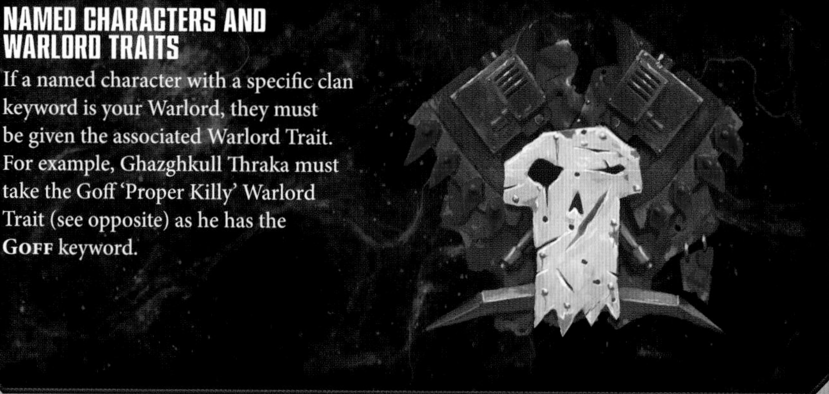

CLAN WARLORD TRAITS

If you wish, you can pick a Clan Warlord Trait from the list below instead of from the Ork Warlord Traits table on the previous page, but only if your Warlord is from the relevant clan.

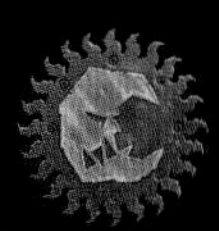

BAD MOONS: DA BEST ARMOUR TEEF CAN BUY

Bad Moons leaders spare no expense on their gear, and their armour is no exception. In the process of adorning themselves in the biggest, most gilded and ostentatious suits of plate they can get, they often end up inadvertently providing themselves with substantial protection against the foe.

Your Warlord has a 4+ invulnerable save.

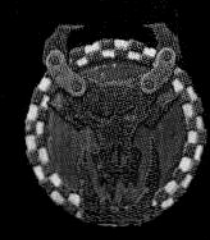

BLOOD AXES: I'VE GOT A PLAN, LADZ!

Blood Axe bosses are never short of a kunnin' plan featuring actual tactics, and sometimes even have a grasp of grand strategy that goes beyond simply kicking the enemies' teeth down their throats.

If your Warlord is on the battlefield, roll a dice for each Command Point you spend when using Stratagems. On a 6+ that Command Point is immediately refunded.

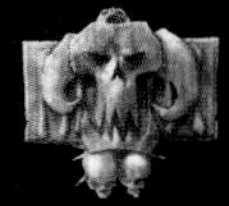

DEATHSKULLS: OPPORTUNIST

This Warlord is always on the lookout for gubbinz to scavenge, and is wily enough to know that the best loot can be bashed, blasted and ripped from the mangled remains of the enemy's biggest wagons and bosses.

Re-roll wound rolls of 1 for attacks made by your Warlord that target enemy VEHICLE units. In addition, in the Shooting phase, this Warlord can target enemy CHARACTER units within 18" even if they are not the closest enemy unit.

EVIL SUNZ: SPEED FREEK

The thrill-seeking greenskins at the head of Evil Sunz warbands will lead their Kult of Speed brethren in multiple high-velocity passes, bellowing with glee each time they hurtle at, and then straight through, the enemy lines.

Your Warlord and friendly EVIL SUNZ units within 6" of them can charge even if they Fell Back earlier in the turn.

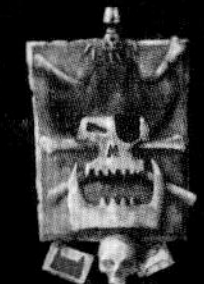

FREEBOOTERZ: KILLA REPUTATION

This Freebooter leader has a fearsome – and well deserved – reputation for being a stone-cold killer. It is enough to make even the fractious and self-serving Freebooterz fight harder beneath his glowering gaze.

Re-roll hit rolls of 1 for attacks made by friendly FREEBOOTERZ units in the Fight phase while they are within 6" of your Warlord.

GOFFS: PROPER KILLY

Goff bosses are the most brutal of an already brutal breed. They are unstoppable engines of destruction who rampage through the enemy ranks and leave mounds of crushed and brutalised corpses in their wake.

Add 1 to your Warlord's Attacks characteristic.

SNAKEBITES: SURLY AS A SQUIGGOTH

Infamously foul-tempered, entirely lacking in any kind of sense of humour, and with an evil eye and a bodily stench that could drop a Nob at thirty paces, this Snakebite is the terror of his underlings, and few prospects are more terrifying than failing him in battle.

You can re-roll Morale tests for friendly SNAKEBITE units while they are within 6" of your Warlord. In addition, friendly SNAKEBITE GRETCHIN units automatically pass Morale tests while they are within 12" of your Warlord.

'Ya got da Bad Moons, wiv all dem teef and flashy guns. Then ya got da sneaky Blood Axes and da thievin' Deathskulls. Dem Evil Sunz go fasta than anyone else, and da Goffs will clobber anyfing up close. Da Snakebites is as tough as dey come, and as fer dem Freebooterz, murderin' gitz da lot of 'em. Dat's why Gork and Mork made da clans how dey is, cos dis way us Orks is good at everyfing!'

- Runtherd Narglug

POINTS VALUES

If you are playing a matched play game, or a game that uses a points limit, you can use the following lists to determine the total points cost of your army. Simply add together the points costs of all your models and the wargear they are equipped with to determine your army's total points value.

HQ

UNIT	MODELS PER UNIT	POINTS PER MODEL (Does not include wargear)
Big Mek in Mega Armour	1	77
- Grot Oiler	0-1	4
Big Mek with Shokk Attack Gun	1	55
- Grot Oiler	0-1	4
Deffkilla Wartrike	1	120
Warboss	1	65
Weirdboy	1	62

TROOPS

UNIT	MODELS PER UNIT	POINTS PER MODEL (Does not include wargear)
Boyz	10-30	7
Gretchin	10-30	3

ELITES

UNIT	MODELS PER UNIT	POINTS PER MODEL (Does not include wargear)
Burna Boyz	5-15	12
Kommandos	5-15	8
Meganobz	3-10	20
Mek	1	22
- Grot Oiler	0-1	4
Nob with Waaagh! Banner	1	75
Nobz	5-10	14
- Ammo Runts	0-2	4
Nobz on Warbikes	3-9	38
Painboy	1	52
Runtherd	1	35
Tankbustas	5-15	5
- Bomb Squigs	0-6	10

FAST ATTACK

UNIT	MODELS PER UNIT	POINTS PER MODEL (Does not include wargear)
Boomdakka Snazzwagons	1-3	95
Deffkoptas	1-5	30
Kustom Boosta-blastas	1-3	100
Megatrakk Scrapjets	1-3	90
Rukkatrukk Squigbuggies	1-3	140
Shokkjump Dragstas	1-3	108
Stormboyz	5-30	9
Warbikers	3-12	23

HEAVY SUPPORT

UNIT	MODELS PER UNIT	POINTS PER MODEL (Does not include wargear)
Battlewagon	1	120
Bonebreaka	1	140
Deff Dreads	1-3	55
Flash Gitz	5-10	30
- Ammo Runts	0-2	4
Gorkanaut	1	250
Gunwagon	1	140
Killa Kans	1-6	40
Lootas	5-15	17
Mek Gunz (including krew)	1-6	15
Morkanaut	1	220

DEDICATED TRANSPORTS

UNIT	MODELS PER UNIT	POINTS PER MODEL (Does not include wargear)
Trukk	1	59

FLYERS

UNIT	MODELS PER UNIT	POINTS PER MODEL (Does not include wargear)
Blitza-bommer	1	108
Burna-bommer	1	102
Dakkajet	1	88
Wazbom Blastajet	1	99

LORDS OF WAR

UNIT	MODELS PER UNIT	POINTS PER MODEL (Does not include wargear)
Stompa	1	850

FORTIFICATIONS

UNIT	MODELS PER UNIT	POINTS PER MODEL
Mekboy Workshop	1	80

NAMED CHARACTERS

UNIT	MODELS PER UNIT	POINTS PER MODEL (Including wargear)
Boss Snikrot	1	70
Boss Zagstruk	1	88
Ghazghkull Thraka	1	235
Kaptin Badrukk	1	84
- Ammo Runt	0-1	4
Mad Dok Grotsnik	1	86

RANGED WEAPONS

WEAPON	POINTS PER WEAPON
Big shoota	5
Bubblechukka	30
Burna	0
Burna bottles	0
Burna exhaust	0
Dakkagun	0
Deffgun	0
Deffkannon	0
Deffstorm mega-shoota	0
Grot blasta	0
Grotzooka	10
Heavy squig launcha	0
Kannon	15
Killa jet	0
Killkannon	15
Kombi-weapon with rokkit launcha	12
Kombi-weapon with skorcha	17
Kopta rokkits	24
Kustom mega-blasta	9
Kustom mega-kannon	45
Kustom mega-slugga	7
Kustom mega-zappa	17
Kustom shokk rifle	0
Kustom shoota	2
Lobba	18
Mek speshul	0
Rivet kannon	0
Rokkit kannon	0
Rokkit launcha	12
Pair of rokkit pistols	12
Shokk attack gun	25
Shoota	0
Shotgun	0
Skorcha	17
Skorcha missiles	20
Slugga	0
Smasha gun	16
Snagga klaw	0
Snazzgun	0
Squig bomb	0
Squig launcha	0
Stikkbomb chukka	5
Stikkbomb flinga	4
Stikkbombs	0
Stikksquigs	0
Supa-shoota	10
Supa-gatler	28
Supa-rokkit	0
Tankbusta bombs	0

RANGED WEAPONS

WEAPON	POINTS PER WEAPON
Tellyport blasta	11
Tellyport mega-blasta	18
Traktor kannon	30
Twin big shoota	10
Twin boomstikk	0
Wazbom mega-kannon	12
Wing missiles	0
Zzap gun	18

MELEE WEAPONS

WEAPON	POINTS PER WEAPON
Attack squig	0
Big choppa	5
Buzz saw	0
Choppa	0
Deff rolla	19
Dread klaw	15
Dread saw	10
Drilla	0
Grabba stikk	0
Grabbin' klaw	5
Grot-prod	0
Kan klaw	0
Killsaw/two killsaws	15/23
Klaw of Gork (or possibly Mork)	0
Mega-choppa	0
Nose drill	0
Power klaw	13
Power stabba	3
Saw blades	0
Spinnin' blades	0
Tankhammer	10
'Urty syringe	0
Waaagh! banner	0
Weirdboy staff	0
Wreckin' ball	3

OTHER WARGEAR

WARGEAR	POINTS PER ITEM
'Ard case	0
Cybork body	5
Gitfinda squig	0
Grot lash	0
Grot rigger	5
Kustom force field	20
Squig hound	0

TACTICAL OBJECTIVES

Orks live for a good fight, and so long as they're wreaking havoc, getting stuck in, and laying down as much deafening dakka as they can then as far as they're concerned, they've already won!

If your army is led by an **Ork** Warlord, these Tactical Objectives replace the Capture and Control Tactical Objectives (numbers 11-16) in the *Warhammer 40,000* rulebook. If a mission uses Tactical Objectives, players use the normal rules for using Tactical Objectives with the following exception: when an Ork player generates a Capture and Control objective (numbers 11-16), they instead generate the corresponding Orks Tactical Objective, as shown below. Other Tactical Objectives (numbers 21-66) are generated normally.

D66	TACTICAL OBJECTIVE
11	Give 'em some Dakka!
12	Get 'em, Boss!
13	Stomp 'em, Boyz!
14	More Speed, Go Fasta!
15	Grab Da Loot!
16	'Ere We Go! Waaagh!

11 GIVE 'EM SOME DAKKA! — Orks

Prove yooz got the best dakka around by blowin' yer enemies to bits with it. Feel free to keep shootin' after they'z dead, too – always gives da ladz a laugh watchin' da corpses dance.

Score 1 victory point if an enemy unit was destroyed during the Shooting phase this turn.

12 GET 'EM, BOSS! — Orks

Time to show 'em all how its done by gettin' stuck in and claimin' a shiny new skull for yer bosspole!

Score 1 victory point if an enemy model was slain by your Warlord in the Fight phase this turn. Score D3 victory points instead if that model was the enemy Warlord.

13 STOMP 'EM, BOYZ! — Orks

Wot are you lot waitin' for? Get in there an' bash some 'eads!

Score 1 victory point if an enemy unit was destroyed during the Fight phase this turn. Score D3 victory points instead if 3-5 enemy units were destroyed in the Fight phase this turn. Score D3+3 victory points instead if 6 or more enemy units were destroyed in the Fight phase this turn.

14 MORE SPEED, GO FASTA! — Orks

Nothing beats leggin' it into battle as quick as you can go. Even better, dis way ya get to da fight even fasta!

Score 1 victory point if 3 or more **Ork** units from your army Advanced in your Movement phase this turn.

15 GRAB DA LOOT! — Orks

There's loadsa gubbinz to loot, but if you don't get it soon some other thievin' git will nick it.

Roll a D6 when this Tactical Objective is generated. Score 1 victory point if you control the objective marker corresponding to the D6 result at the end of this turn.

16 'ERE WE GO! WAAAGH! — Orks

Time to show this cowardly buncha wimps that Orks is da best. Waaagh!

Score 1 victory point if 3 or more **Ork** units from your army made a charge move this turn. Score D3 victory points instead if 5 or more **Ork** units from your army made a charge move this turn.

'The Orks plague the galaxy from end to end with their ceaseless warring and strife. They are a race rooted so deeply in violence that peace is utterly incomprehensible to them. They cannot be bargained with or bought, save with weapons that they will inevitably turn against those who tried to bribe them. I pray with all my faith that some great catastrophe will annihilate them, but I fear that ultimately it is they, not we, who shall rule the galaxy.'

- Xanthius, High Lord of Terra